SPORTS PARKS

Directions in Design
for Recreational Zones

Edited by Jim Barnum

SPORTS PARKS

Directions in Design for Recreational Zones

Publishing

Contents

7   Preface

8   Introduction

10   **Sports Parks Design Guidelines**
10   1 Site planning
13   2 Grading and drainage
13   3 Standard field and court layouts
14   4 Paving, walkways and mow curbs
15   5 Fences and walls
15   6 Site furniture
16   7 Multipurpose courts (basketball and volleyball courts)
18   8 Tennis courts
19   9 Swimming pools
19   10 Multipurpose fields (softball and soccer fields/turf areas)
21   11 Playgrounds and equipment
26   12 Parking areas
27   13 Irrigation
30   14 Planting
31   15 Lighting
33   16 User facility
34   17 Concessionary areas
34   18 Skate parks

35   **References**

36	St Kilda	162	Sportpark Meerpark
40	Blandan Park	166	Lippepark Schacht Franz
48	Chinguacousy Sports Park Redevelopment	172	Moabiter Stadtgarten—Park on the former freight station Moabit
54	Bijlmerpark	178	Schmul Park
62	Freestyle Park	182	Lemvig Skatepark
68	Heerenschürli Sport Complex	188	Zhangmiao Exercise Park
72	Aqua Soccer	194	Belconnen Skate Park
76	Dymaxion Golf	198	Wylde Mountain Bike Trail
80	Kavel K	202	Venecia Recreational Park
86	Nieuwegein	206	Culture and activity space in Hedehusene
92	Spectrum	212	Rocket Park Mini-Golf Course
96	Collie	218	Nordic Ski Centre Planica
102	Bahndeckel Theresienhöhe	226	Sportpark Gaarden
108	3D Athletics Track	232	Multifunctional sports facility in Ratingen
114	The Lawn on D	238	Children's Bicentennial Park
118	The Esplanade Youth Plaza—Fremantle	244	Philadelphia Navy Yard Corporate Center
126	Israel's Square		
132	Leyton Open Spaces	252	Index
140	Purple Pleasure		
144	Smile Playground		
148	Van Beuningenplein Sportsfield		
154	Argenteuil Skatepark		
158	Elmira Skatepark		

Foreword

Jim Barnum

Sports parks and their associated landscape design grow more and more important as the world's population continues to move from rural areas to urban and city environments. Scientific studies continue to reinforce what common sense and personal experience tell us, namely that exercise, recreation and spending time in naturalized settings are not simply superfluous self-indulgent activities serving no practical function. Rather they are vital to the greater health and welfare of human beings. It has become too readily accepted that an average level of mental, physical and spiritual wellbeing is acceptable, being just fit enough to perform one's basic social functions and to survive. Designing and building spaces that facilitate and encourage people to be healthy and happy, so they can reach their full potential, is a powerful way to improve our human experience.

A holistic perspective reveals the importance of all three key aspects of the human experience to our full development. Studies in exercise and muscle building provide an analogy, demonstrating that if one body part is neglected, the others will only grow so much to maintain equilibrium. The same is true for our overall wellbeing, made up of mental, physical and spiritual components. Science shows that mental faculties improve with increases in physical health and muscle mass, and spiritual adepts report that capacity for mystical experience grows with improvements to mental cognition, and vice versa. Each part affects the whole. In more detail, studies demonstrate increased cognition, improved neuroplasticity, and even an increase in neuroreceptors in those who exercise regularly. Smarter, more capable people are just one of the social benefits to the creation of sports parks and landscape design. The release of endorphins and other chemicals that induce positive moods from exercise and immersion in nature is also well documented. This stress reduction reduces health-care costs and improves relations between people. In the workplace, happy, healthy staff are more productive, taking fewer sick days. Psychologists report better mental resilience among those who are physically active.

In regards to creating naturalized, landscaped park environments, a telling study demonstrated notable improvements on test scores of university students after spending time walking in a greened park area. Interestingly, simply looking at the colour green also improved scores, but not as much as actually being immersed in a natural setting. Richard Louv's Nature Deficit Disorder hypothesis is a bit of a summation of the body of research showing that contact with nature has many positive social and developmental benefits. Exposure to nature helps children to develop cognitive, emotional, and behavioral connections to their nearby social and biophysical environments. Nature experiences are important for encouraging imagination and creativity, cognitive and intellectual development, and social relationships. The experience of nature helps to restore the mind from the mental fatigue of work or studies, contributing to improved work performance and satisfaction. Urban nature, when provided as parks and walkways and incorporated into building design, provides calming and inspiring environments and encourages learning, inquisitiveness, and alertness. Outdoor activities can help alleviate symptoms of Alzheimers disease, dementia, stress, and depression, and improve cognitive function in those recently diagnosed with breast cancer. Symptoms of ADHD in children can be reduced through activity in green settings, thus 'green time' can act as an effective supplement to traditional medicinal and behavioral treatments. The benefits to individuals and society as a whole from creating places to recreate, relax, and experience natural landscape are too many to list here.

Play (specifically separated from exercise) also serves a function. It's said that nature doesn't create anything without a utilitarian purpose. Play is an important, hands-on way of learning. Just as animals learn through play, so do we. As young animals are playing, they're most often learning the vital life skills of hunting and fighting. As we play team sports like soccer and football, we're learning core life skills including communication, strategy, teamwork, reading body language, learning to win and lose with grace, and conflict resolution. As we practice individual sports we learn other lessons. Whether it's a competitive individual sport such as tennis and cycle racing, or an individual sport where we most typically compete only with ourselves such as skateboarding and freestyle BMX riding, we learn self-reliance, self-motivation and self-discipline. There is usually no coach or trainer to push us, to force us to rise again after each fall or failure. Finally, nearly all sports foster courage as we push ourselves beyond our limitations as the baseball player dives harder to catch a line drive and the skateboarder launches higher into the air than ever before. All of the traits learned at play transmit directly into the rest of our lives, making us better at everything we do. As John Locke suggested, many people learn better by doing rather than reading from a book.

Beyond all of the studies and quantifiable benefits, recreation and play are simply fun! Since the dawn of civilization, human beings have created games and places to play them. This book celebrates this important work and the passion of those who do it.

Introduction

1. Definition

Sports parks are provided at local and citywide levels. They have a primary purpose to provide spaces for organized sport and physical activity, and as such have a high degree of organization and are required to cater for a wide variety of sporting events from junior team training to major competitions.

In this book, we provide two types of recreational and sports parks: resource-based sports parks (citywide sports parks) and population-based sports parks (local sports parks). Resource-based sports parks serve users from the entire city and elsewhere, and are located at or centered around natural or constructed features. Beaches (such as Mission Bay Park), historical sites (such as Balboa Park), and natural canyons and water courses (such as Mission Trails Regional Park) are examples of this type of sports parks. Population-based sports parks are intended to serve local daily needs in residential areas. Where possible, they adjoin schools in order to share facilities, and ideally are within walking distance of the residences within their service area.

Resource-based sports parks (citywide sports parks)

Resource-based sports parks are intended to preserve, and make available to the public, areas of outstanding scenic, natural, or cultural interest. They are meant to supplement the neighborhood and citywide sports parks, and they serve the entire city and its visitors rather than any one community. However, they can also function to fulfill local neighborhood and community sports parks needs of surrounding residents.

Population-based sports parks (local sports parks)

Population-based sports parks are typically of two categories: community sports parks and neighborhood sports parks.

Community sports parks typically serve 18,000 to 25,000 residents within approximately a half- to 1-mile (0.8- to 1.6-kilometer) radius. Ideally they should have at least 13 useable acres (5.3 hectares) if they are adjacent to a school, or 20 useable acres (8.1 hectares) if not adjacent to a school ('useable acres' is defined as being 2 percent or less in grade). They should provide a wide range of facilities that supplement those of the local sports parks and which are determined by the needs and preferences of the community. Recreation centers, athletic fields, multipurpose courts, picnic facilities, play areas, parking areas, comfort stations, landscaping and lawn areas are standard amenities. When possible and desirable, swimming pools and tennis courts may be provided.

Neighborhood sports parks serve resident populations of 3500 to 5000 people within approximately a half-mile (0.8-kilometer) radius. Ideally, they should have a minimum useable area of 5 acres (2.0 hectares) when located adjacent to a school or 10 useable acres (4.0 hectares) when not adjacent to a school. The design and type of facilities should be determined by the population and use characteristics of the neighborhood. Play areas, multipurpose fields and courts, comfort stations, picnic facilities, landscaping and lawn areas are typical amenities in local sports parks.

2. Design objectives and principles

Aesthetics

Sports parks should project a positive image and establish a permanent character for the community and city. Sports park designs should provide a sense of arrival with reference points to promote circulation. They should provide places for groups and individuals for both formal and impromptu events. They should indicate nature through seasonal changes and provide something unique, obvious, complex, and simple. They should be designed to demonstrate both a human and a monumental scale and should be visible from a distance. Overall, a sense of place and community should be created through the design of each sports park.

Function

Sports parks should be designed for all community members to use and enjoy. They must also be functionally designed for ease of maintenance. The most current products and industry standards should be applied to the park's design.

Economics

Sports parks should be designed while taking into consideration the allocated budget for the initial build and ongoing maintenance.

Parkland groupings

Parkland grouping allows for a number of sports parks to be provided in certain circumstances, instead of one single sports park, for example, where topography and available land size do not allow for a sport park to be provided in a single location or where accessibility to a single sport park from its catchment (e.g. a local recreation park) is restricted by features such as a major road, railway line, or creek. It must be demonstrated that accessibility by residents in the catchment is not reduced, and facilities provided are shared across the grouping to provide the overall level of service in aggregate, not duplicate embellishments. The calculation of the offset for embellishment and land dedication for a parkland grouping will be on the basis of the grouping in aggregate, as if it were a single park.

Amenity impacts

The potential amenity impacts of certain sports parks on both nearby residents and other park users is an important consideration in determining the overall suitability, design, and location of sports parks embellishments. These embellishments may involve installations that are likely to generate noise or after-hours activities, and may include off-leash dog areas, rebound walls or courts, skate bowls, or jump parks. Therefore adjoining uses, location, and design factors are important considerations in determining whether such embellishments are appropriate for individual parks, and access to some of these facilities may need to be restricted after hours.

Cost of embellishment and offsets

Sports parks should be designed within the allocated budget, and provide economical means of maintaining the sports parks. The cost of embellishment is a set amount and forms the basis of the calculation of the infrastructure charge and the maximum offset value for embellishment of a park. The adoption of an alternative approach to park embellishments does not entitle a developer to any additional credits for their contributed infrastructure.

Sports Parks Design Guidelines

1. Site planning

Sports parks design and site planning shall include analysis and integration of on-site and off-site features such as bicycle and pedestrian trails, open space areas, topography, views, existing vegetation and joint-use needs of adjacent schools. Community plans, master or precise plans, general development plans and other local city-planning documents should be referenced when analyzing and evaluating the project during site planning.

1.1 Sloping land and smaller sites

In some cases, sports parks designers may consider the use of sloping blocks or smaller sites, such as sites smaller than 12.4 acres (5 hectares), for local sports parks in existing urban areas. The development of such land for local sports parks will only be acceptable where it is demonstrated that no other suitable land is available under the following conditions.

Solutions that use these less than optimal sites will also only be considered if a minimum of at least one full-size field complemented by hard court space and smaller 'field space' for training use is provided; amenities and parking can be easily accessed from the main use area; grassed batters are less than 16 slope and can be maintained by machinery, or retaining walls are provided with adequate user-safety considerations; and mulched vegetated embankments are no greater than 13 slope.[1]

1.2 Site access and paths

All parks have requirements in regard to boundary treatments, provision of car parking and elements such as pathways, bikeways, and drinking water. While the standard requirements differ for different types of parks, there is a range of alternatives that may be considered. The following section provides some alternative solutions for some elements common to all park types or alternatives that may be applicable to specific park types. Where there are no alternatives discussed for specific elements, it may be assumed that the standard requirements must be adhered to.

Site access

Access to parks should be managed carefully to ensure that all users have safe access to the facilities within the park. However the boundary of the site needs to be managed to

Figure 1: Examples of approaches to local sports park developed on a sloping block

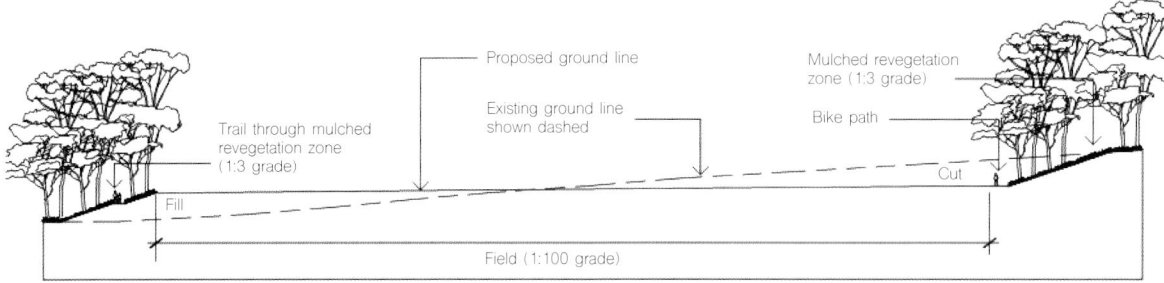
Section though sports field on sloping site

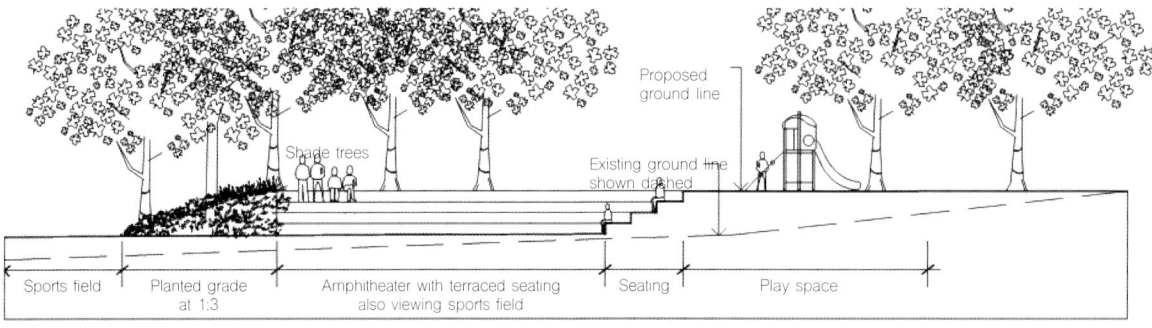
Section through local sports park on sloping site

ensure that vehicles are restricted to purpose-designed areas only. Entry to and exit from the park also needs to consider the surrounding residents and maximize opportunities for users to easily and safely access the park. In some cases, this will mean restricting pedestrians or other traffic at certain points.

Standard requirements for site access

For citywide and local sports parks, sealed internal road networks provide access to clubhouse and parking areas; and an 'access control' barrier to all accessible park boundaries/frontages should be installed, for example, bollards spaced at 4.9 feet (1.5 meters). Local recreation parks should also have this type of 'access control' barrier.

Possible alternative solutions

- Any boundary treatment that meets local city's landscape guidelines and restricts vehicle access without reducing casual surveillance of the park.
- Use of post and top rail fencing or open pool-style fencing.
- Dense plantings of low shrubs that will not grow above 2 feet (0.6 meters) or trees with a 6.6-foot (2-meter) clear understory to the base of canopy.
- Alternative treatments using bollard materials such as square timber, stone, recycled plastic or a combination of materials and planted features.

Other requirements for alternative solutions

- Use of topography features, such as embankments or drainage depressions.
- Alternative boundary treatments must provide for people with mobility challenges.
- Materials and construction used must not increase maintenance costs beyond that expected for the standard bollard treatment.[1]

Pedestrian pathways, bikeways and trails

Pedestrian pathways and bikeways are integral to parks as they provide access to facilities and interest points within the park as well as facilitating access to the park itself. Pathways have also become significant recreation facilities in their own right, and provide for walking, running, cycling, and a range of other informal recreation activities. Therefore, the recreational value of pathways needs be considered in the design of parks, as well as their service in providing access to internal park features.

Standard requirements for pathways

- Constructed concrete pathway (7.2 feet [2.2 meters] wide) circuit to park perimeter integrated with bikeway/pathway network.
- Internal concrete pathway (7.2 feet [2.2 meters] wide) connection providing access (120 maximum grade) to major activity areas.
- For all types of parks, an internal path network that facilitates access, provides recreation opportunity and meets the minimum width of 7.2 feet (2.2 meters) may be considered.
- The path provided should be a network appropriate to the type of park. For citywide recreation parks this should include a network that covers a significant proportion of the perimeter and offers linear distance of at least 1.7 miles (2.7 kilometers), preferably with distance markers.
- Pathways forming part of a regional bikeway network need to comply with the width standard for that network.

Figure 2: Alternative boundary treatments

Bollards combined with boulders and planting

Post and top rail barriers

Hard sculpted elements with dense low planting

Figure 3: Alternative path solution, showing perimeter contact and circuit opportunities

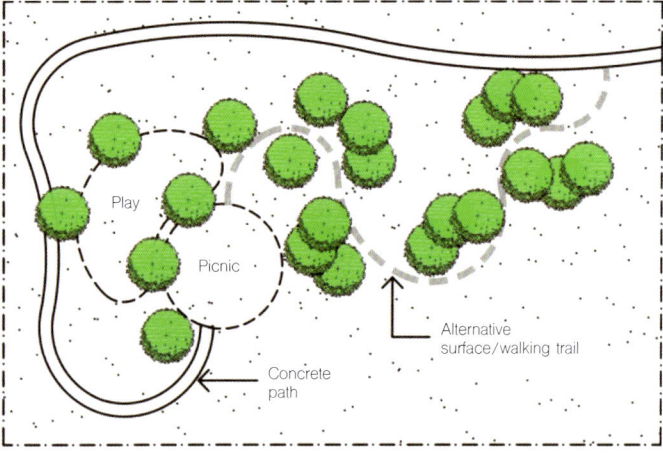

Figure 4: Alternative path layout for district parks, showing recreational trail treatment

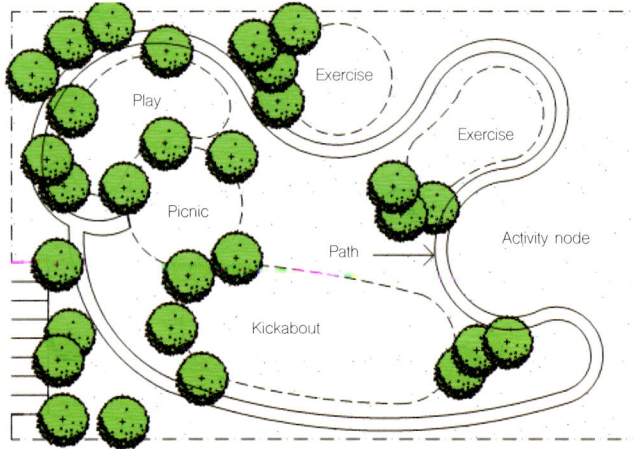

- Path networks must provide sufficient access to key facilities within the park and connect the main elements of the park.
- Variation in path widths may be considered where paths wider than 7.2 feet (2.2 meters) are provided as 'main' paths, shared paths or connecting paths, are 9.8 feet (3 meters) or wider, and are complemented with narrower paths for less traffic and recreational walking use, providing no paths are less than 4.9 feet (1.5 meters) wide.
- Concrete paths combined with alternative path surfaces may be considered. Asphalt compounds, textured concrete, paving and other hardscaping may be considered, provided the sports park design team approves the surface as appropriate for the intended use and location. Gravel or decomposed rock surfaces are not to be used owing to drainage and erosion concerns. The following examples illustrate some alternative approaches.

For citywide and district waterside parks

- Constructed concrete pathway (7.2 feet [2.2 meters] wide) for the length of the park (preferably adjacent to the water body, river or creek) integrated with cycle/pedestrian network.
- Internal concrete pathway (7.2 feet [2.2 meters] wide) connection providing access to major activity areas (to follow contours if possible or minimum 120 grade).

For citywide and local sports linear parks

- Constructed concrete pathway (7.2 feet [2.2 meters] wide) for the length of the park (preferably adjacent to the water body, river or creek) integrated with cycle/pedestrian network.

For local recreation parks

- Constructed concrete pathway (7.2 feet [2.2 meters] wide) circuit to park perimeter integrated with bikeway/pathway network.[1]

Trails

Trails provide for the use of alternative modes of transportation, as well as recreational activities. The various trail components within normal cities include pedestrian, cycling, and equestrian trails. Trail design shall be included where possible to provide connections to other parks, schools, and public facilities, in addition to accessing local city open space areas and regional trails. User safety is of the utmost concern when locating and designing trails. Trails shall intersect each other at 90 degrees if possible, with clear site distances. The design of trails shall include the trail width and a clear zone on either side of the trail. The trail width shall be free and clear of any horizontal or vertical obstructions (do not locate any valve boxes, vaults, or drain inlets in the trail). Trails shall have a minimum overhead clearance of 12 feet (3.7 meters) for both built and natural features.

Motorized vehicles, except for emergency vehicles, shall not be permitted on trails and shall be prevented through proper design and detailing. Preferred surfacing is stabilized decomposed granite on compacted stabilized subgrade with a cross slope for drainage. Native soil/surfacing shall be compacted. For the width, position and clear zone of specific trails, table 1 gives proposed data.

2. Grading and drainage

All sports parks projects shall have positive drainage (drainage is to be directed away from buildings, electrical enclosures, backstops, and irrigation controllers) and provide the necessary components for drainage.

2.1 Site grading and drainage

Site grading and drainage designing shall conform to the following requirements. (Refer to table 2.)

2.2 Drainage systems

Area drainage systems shall be designed and sized per flow requirements and engineered accordingly. For drainage that exceeds the capacity of a 6-inch (15.2-centimeter) PVC pipe, the drainage system will have to conform to the local city's grading development regulations.

Table 1

	Maximum width	Clear zone	Position
Pedestrian trails	2 feet (0.6 meters); minimum 6 feet (1.8 meters)	0.6 meters (2 feet)	each side of the trail
Equestrian trails	4 feet (1.2 meters); minimum 6 feet (1.8 meters)	2 feet (0.6 meters)	on each side
Multipurpose trails	6 feet (1.8 meters); minimum 8 feet (2.4 meters)	2 feet (0.6 meters)	on each side

Notes a post and rail fence shall be provided along the side of the trail when a slope condition within 5 feet (1.5 meters) of either side of the trail is steeper than 21 or more than 5 feet (1.5 meters) in height. All trails shall be sufficiently signed for type of use and users.

Table 2

Use	Grade
Paving (pedestrian walkways and monolithic surfaces of concrete, asphalt or unit pavers)	1.5% min. – 4.5% max. 1.5% max. cross slope, no exceptions
Basketball and volleyball courts (multipurpose paved courts)	Drain end to end at 1%
Tennis courts	Drain side to side or end to end at 1%, never allow high point at net
Multipurpose fields	1.5% min. – 2% max.
Softball fields	1.5% for skinned and turf infields, outfield turf, provide positive drainage away from home plate in all cases
Parking areas (asphalt)	1% min. – 4% max. with a 4.5% cross slope or 1.5% where disabled access is provided, no exceptions
Lawn areas (passive recreation)	2% min. – 20% max.(51)
Shrub and groundcover areas	2% min. – 50% max (21)
Mulch areas	2% min. – 33% max. (31)

2.3 Stormwater runoff and best management practices

All sports parks projects shall be designed to meet the local water department's regulations about water pollution prevention. A best management practices (BMP) plan shall be prepared for all sports parks projects in order to control the long-term erosion and reduce the amount of pollutants and other sediments discharged from the project site into the stormwater system. In addition, a stormwater pollution prevention plan (SWPPP) shall be prepared for the construction activity of the sports parks when the sports park site is more than 1 acre (4046.9 square kilometers).

2.4 Finished grade

Finish grade for lawn areas shall be 1 inch (2.5 centimeters) below walks, mow curbs, or other paving, and finish grade for shrub, groundcover, or mulch areas shall be 2 inches (5.1 centimeters) below.

Grading and planting should be such that a police officer seated in a vehicle may observe the entire sports park while driving through or around it. Avoid mounds or berms that provide hiding places.

3. Standard field and court layouts

For citywide sports parks standard field and court layouts: four rectangular fields of 459.3 by 229.6 feet (140 by 70 meters) capable of providing an overlay for two cricket ovals of 225 feet (68.6 meters) radius center of pitch (lit to 250 lux) or 1 premier field or oval (size 567.5 by 469.2 feet [173 by 143 meters]) including training field (lit to 250 lux); at least one citywide facility in each district to incorporate an athletics track around the perimeter of field or oval; eight multipurpose courts (concrete with sports surfacing over); associated infrastructure including perimeter or inter-court fencing, nets or goal posts, line marking, lighting to 250 lux.

For local sports parks standard field and court layout: two rectangular fields of 459.3 by 229.6 feet (140 by 70 meters) capable of providing one cricket oval overlay of 225.1 feet (68.6 meters) radius center of pitch (lit to 250 lux); four multipurpose courts (concrete with sports surfacing over); associated infrastructure such as perimeter or inter-court fencing, nets or goal posts, line marking, lighting to 250 lux).[1]

Example alternative solutions for citywide sports parks

- A single area developed with a combination of senior fields and ovals to provide a minimum area of 19.8 acres (8 hectares) formal playing surface, and a combination of netball, tennis and basketball (or other outdoor court sports) courts provided to ensure a minimum of eight courts.
- Council may allow all fields to be rectangular or oval if the proposed citywide sports parks is providing a headquarters/regional facility for a particular code and will accommodate both winter and summer use.
- Development of a 'precinct' of grouped smaller sports parks/fields in close proximity, which provide the same field and court outcomes, may be considered where land availability or topography make provision of a single area very difficult or impossible. This approach will only be considered if the 'precinct' or group has all elements within easy walking distance (generally up to approximately 656 feet [200 meters]), is planned in an integrated way that keeps similar codes (e.g. rectangular field users) together and minimizes any repetition of ancillary infrastructure (e.g. clubhouse, toilets, canteens).
- Alternative playing surfaces (such as synthetic materials) for both field sport and court sports may be considered where availability of suitable land is very limited and use of artificial/alternative playing surfaces will provide for high-intensity multiuse in highly accessible locations.
- Practice facilities may include a range of elements and are not restricted to cricket practice nets. For example, rebound walls for tennis or football (soccer), half courts or other features such as outdoor exercise equipment may all be acceptable provided they are appropriate to the sport provided on the site.[1]

Example alternative solutions for local sports parks

- A combination of senior fields and ovals to provide a minimum of two fields catering to at least two codes, plus the provision of sports courts as described below.
- Provision of a combination of synthetic and turf fields (e.g. to service hockey or soccer), plus the provision of sports courts as described below.
- One small oval and one large oval field with a rectangular field internal, plus the provision of sports courts as described below.
- One senior rectangular field inside a grass running track of 1312 feet (400 meters), plus the provision of sports courts as described below.
- The combination of courts can include four or more single-purpose courts if the park is to provide a 'home' for a particular sport.
- Alternative playing surfaces for both field sport and court sports may be considered where availability of suitable land is limited and use of artificial/alternative playing surfaces can deliver good multiuse and highly accessible opportunities.
- Local sports parks may be delivered using a 'precinct' approach, which groups two sites in close proximity with one providing for field sports and the other providing for court sports. This will be considered where land availability or topography makes provision of a single area very difficult or impossible. The two sites must be within easy walking distance (generally up to approximately 656 feet [200 meters]) and ideally would share a common street. The precinct should be planned in an integrated way.[1]

4. Paving, walkways and mow curbs
4.1 Designs

Walkways are provided in all sports parks for functional and aesthetic purposes. Functionally, walkways should provide a connection to different parts of the sports parks and lead to special landmarks. Walkways that provide a loop system are preferred. Primary walkways in the sports parks shall be concrete paving without color. At sports parks perimeter(s) and sports park lots, walkways should be located to provide a logical, convenient, and aesthetic means of accessing the sports parks. Walkways should be accessible to all users and in some areas they must be designed for emergency and maintenance vehicles. Aesthetically, walkways should be designed for the user to enjoy on- and off-site views and the different amenities of the sports parks.

Decomposed granite walkways or trails may be proposed as a secondary component of a sports park's circulation system. These walkways shall be stabilized decomposed granite, pre-mixed by the plant at the rate recommended by the manufacturer, prior to delivery. Walkway depth and sub-base shall be based on the soils report. A weed barrier is recommended below all decomposed granite paving. Walkway edging is preferred to be concrete or non-corrosive metal.

Concrete mow curbs shall be provided to separate all lawn areas from shrub or groundcover areas; to contain decomposed granite paving; under fencing, where fencing is adjacent to turf or groundcover that requires edging or mowing; and as an integral component of any wall (both at the top and bottom where lawn is proposed or where it exists). Mow curbs width to be 8 inches (20.3 centimeters) minimum.

4.2 Walkway locations and construction

Where possible, provide walkways to separate lawn areas from shrub and groundcover areas to reduce edging costs. Detailed information refers to table 3.

5. Fences and walls

Sports parks should be designed functionally and be visually as open as possible with minimal fencing. Fencing should only be provided for multipurpose fields or where there is a safety issue that cannot be addressed by some other means.

Tubular steel fencing used is to maintain views or to be consistent with the project's design theme. All components shall be tubular steel and galvanized (free of burrs and sharp edges). Fence color is to be a powder-coated paint applied electrostatically.

Chain-link fencing may vary in height and detailing as per the specific site use(s) and requirements. If the fence exceeds 8 feet (2.4 meters) in height, a mid-rail will be required. Specify a top and bottom rail for all chain-link fences, and 9-gauge fabrics before thermal coating, knuckled on top and bottom. All materials shall be free of burrs and sharp edges. Fence posts, chain link, rails and all hardware are to be coated in thermally infused polyvinyl chloride. Chain-link fabric shall be located on the side adjacent to play or use areas.

Table 3

Walkway construction	Width
Primary pedestrian/maintenance access walkways and security lighting	9 feet (2.7 meters) min.
Walkways adjacent to ball field lights	12 feet (3.7 meters) min.
Walkways adjacent to parking stalls without wheel stops	9 feet (2.7 meters) min.
Secondary pedestrian walkways without maintenance access or security lighting	6 feet (1.8 meters) min.

Walkway construction and reinforcement shall be based on the soil report. Soil testing shall be provided during the design phase and recommendations shall be included in the bid documents. Concrete walkways shall have expansion joints and score lines.

Gate openings for pedestrians shall be a minimum of 4 feet (1.2 meters) wide. Gate openings for maintenance vehicles shall be a minimum of 14 feet (4.2 meters) wide.

Walls shall be designed and located to discourage skateboarding and graffiti vandalism. All concrete block walls shall be finished with a wall cap made of precast units that are sized for the block, or a custom cap. Retaining walls shall be installed with wall drains. Safety railings shall be provided when walls are taller than 30 inches (76.2 centimeters) and adjacent to walkways, as necessary or required by local municipal code.

6. Site furniture

All sports parks shall have picnic tables, benches, drinking fountains, barbecues, bicycle racks, trash receptacles, and other site furnishings as necessary. Types of site furniture selected shall be based on the type of sports parks, design character, durability, and maintenance. The site furnishings should compliment each other in color, materials, and form. Site furniture shall be permanently secured to the concrete with dowels and epoxy or within decomposed granite paving per manufacturers recommendations.

6.1 Locations

Site furniture in lawn areas shall be spaced a minimum of 12 feet (3.6 meters) from other site furniture, fencing/walls, and trees/shrubs to accommodate local lawnmowers. Site furniture shall be located to avoid conflicts with irrigation systems and other park improvements.

6.2 Picnic tables

Picnic tables shall be placed on concrete pads with a 1 percent cross slope for drainage. Pads shall extend 4 feet (1.2 meters) beyond the table/bench dimensions on all sides. Some of the picnic tables should be contiguous to walkways or have walkways leading to them for disabled access. Orientation of the picnic tables adjacent to walkways shall be perpendicular to walkways to discourage skateboard activity. One-piece tables with benches are preferred.

6.3 Sports park benches

Sports parks benches shall be placed on a concrete pad when located in lawn areas and designed and located to discourage skateboard activity. Some of the benches should provide an area for companion seating.

6.4 Drinking fountains

Each sports park shall have at least one high/low drinking fountain for disabled access. Fence-hung fountains may be used if a disabled-access fountain has been provided elsewhere in the sports park. Provide a stainless-steel high/low fixture wall hung at the comfort station or a stainless-steel high/low pedestal fixture behind the backstop.

6.5 Barbecues and hot-coal receptacles

Metal barbecues shall be located outside the circulation routes and installed with a concrete hot-coal receptacle in a visible location. If located in lawn areas, provide a concrete pad as a mow curb.

6.6 Bicycle racks

These shall be located on concrete paving and outside the major circulation routes.

6.7 Trash receptacles

Concrete trash receptacles shall be square and provided with side openings or top openings per the direction of the sports park manager. All trash receptacles shall have a protective hood cover.

6.8 Trash enclosures

Concrete block trash receptacle enclosures shall be located within parking lot areas. A heavy-vehicle paving section for the drive lane and the concrete apron shall be provided at the head of the enclosure. Minimum size of the concrete apron shall be sufficient to allow refuse vehicle access to the trash receptacles. The enclosures shall have solid steel doors or chain-link doors with screening slats with locking ability.

6.9 Signs

All sports parks shall have at least one permanently installed sports park identification sign. The sign should harmonize with the sports park's theme or natural character. Signs are typically one sided and parallel to the most prominent public street, or angled if located at the intersection of two streets. The sports park's identification sign shall have vandal-resistant light fixtures.

7. Multipurpose courts (basketball and volleyball courts)

When possible and space permitting, basketball and volleyball courts shall be separate. When site constraints dictate, courts can be combined into multipurpose courts.

7.1 Basketball courts

Basketball courts shall be a poured concrete surface of 104 by 70 feet (31.6 by 21.3 meters) in dimension, with a playing area of 84 by 50 feet (25.6 by 15.2 meters). Court construction and reinforcing shall be based on the soil report. Rebar dowels and sleeves to be provided at all cold joints and all sleeves shall be greased. Court surface shall be a non-skid surface or

Figure 5: Multipurpose court design

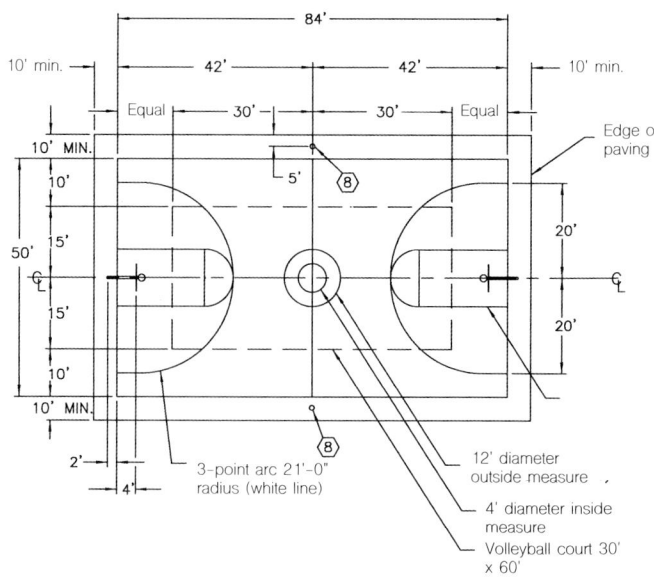

Notes:
1) Basketball court striping shall be 2 inches (5.1 centimeters) volleyball wide and colored white.
2) Volleyball court striping shall be 1.5 inches (3.8 centimeters) wide and colored yellow (court lines are shown dashed for clarity only).
3) Dimensions are to the outside edge of the lines unless indicated otherwise.
4) The white line shall dominate where white and other colored lines intersect.
5) Contractor shall be responsible for court layouts.
6) Basketball goal posts shall be set 2 feet (45.7 centimeters) beyond baseline with 6-foot (1.8-meter) extensions. Rim height shall be 10 feet (3.0 meters) above finish surface of court.

Figure 6: Multipurpose court design

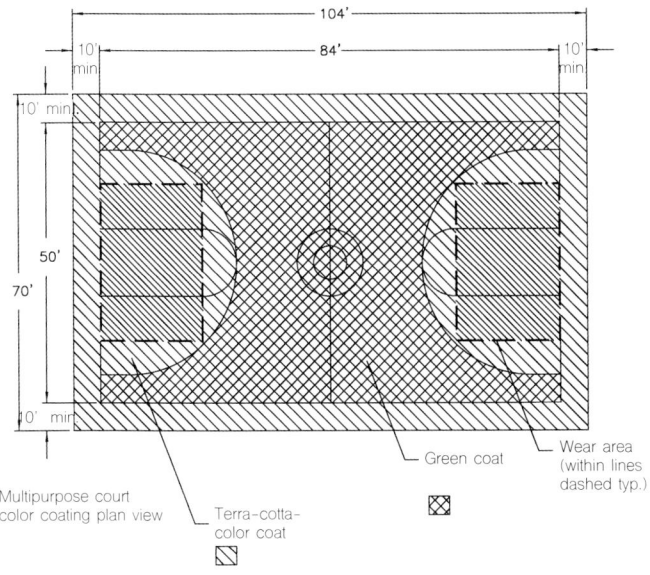

Multipurpose court color coating plan view

Notes:
1) Wear area to receive additional coat of court surfacing.
2) Terra-cotta-color coat to extend to edges of paving unless otherwise noted.

Figure 7: Basketball court

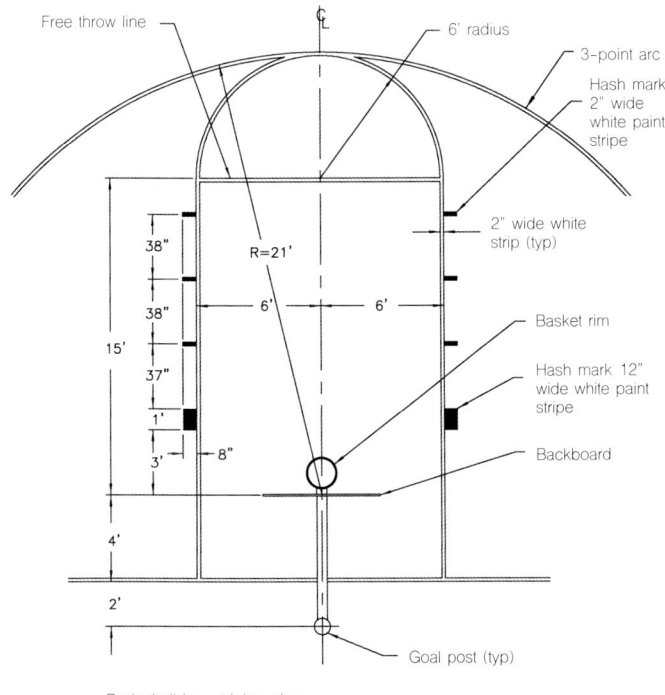

Basketball key striping plan

Notes:
Dimensions are to the outside edge of the lines unless indicated otherwise.

a medium broom finish. All striping on the playing surface shall be applied using a wear-resistant substance.

Preferred court orientation should be along the north–south axis. The minimum distance between courts when two or more courts are side by side or end to end is 10 feet (3 meters). Backboards shall be all steel with emulsion-type undercoat, fan-shaped, with 6 feet (1.8 meters) extensions. Rims shall be double rimmed with nylon netting nets. Pole shall be galvanized steel.

7.2 Volleyball courts

Paved volleyball courts

Paved volleyball courts shall be a poured concrete surfaces of 50 by 80 feet (15 by 24 meters) in dimension, with a playing area of 30 by 60 feet (9.1 by 18.3 meters). Court construction and reinforcing shall be based on the soil report. Rebar dowels and sleeves to be provided at all cold joints and all sleeves shall be greased. Court surface should be a non-skid surface or a medium broom finish. When two courts are side by side, there should be a minimum of 10 feet (3 meters) between them. Courts placed end to end shall have a minimum distance of 15 feet (4.6 meters) between them. (See figure 5.)

Sand volleyball courts

Sand volleyball courts shall have a playing area of 30 by 60 feet (9.1 by 18.2 meters) with a 10-foot (3-meter) safety zone on the sides and a 15-foot (4.6-meter) safety zone on the ends, total area to be 50 by 90 feet (15.2 by 27.4 meters) in dimension. The sand shall be contained by a concrete curb, 8 inches (20.3 centimeters) minimum width, which is the same elevation around the perimeter of the court. The sand surfacing shall be a minimum of 12 inches (30.5 centimeters) deep. Sand shall be clean, doubled washed, manufactured #20 silica sand, and free of deleterious organic materials. A subsurface drainage system shall be provided that connects to the site drainage system.

Volleyball nets and poles

All volleyball standards shall be galvanized. The net post shall be 8 feet (2.4 meters) above the finished playing surface. The net shall have the cable along the top and rope along the bottom. The pole spacing shall accommodate a 32 by 3 foot (9.8 by 0.9 meter) net.

8. Tennis courts

8.1 General design requirement

Tennis court shall be a poured concrete surface of 36 by 78 feet (11 by 23.8 meters), with 12 feet (3.7 meters) side clearance on each side, and 21 feet (6.4 meters) between each baseline and the fence. Court construction and reinforcing shall be based on the soil report. Score lines (saw cut) per the soil report shall be provided to eliminate stress cracking in monolithic pours. Rebar dowels and sleeves to be provided at all cold joints and all sleeves shall be greased. Court surface shall be a non-skid surface. The courts will have markings for both singles and doubles play. Lines shall be painted 2 inches (5.1 centimeters) wide, except for the baseline which shall be painted 4 inches (10.2 centimeters) wide.

8.2 Orientation and placement

Preferred orientation should be along the north–south axis (recommended 22 degrees west of north). The minimum distance between courts when two or more courts are side by side or end to end should be 12 feet (3.7 meters) between adjacent side lines. When two or more courts are placed side by side, a 12-foot-high (3.7-meter-high) fence shall separate the courts by extending 24 feet (7.3 meters) in from the rear of the courts. Minimum distance between each end of the court and the fence shall be 21 feet (6.4 meters).

8.3 Tennis court fencing

Fencing shall be 12 feet (3.7 meters) high with chain-link fabric installed on the inside of the court. Fence posts, chain

Figure 8: Tennis court design

Figure 9: Tennis court design

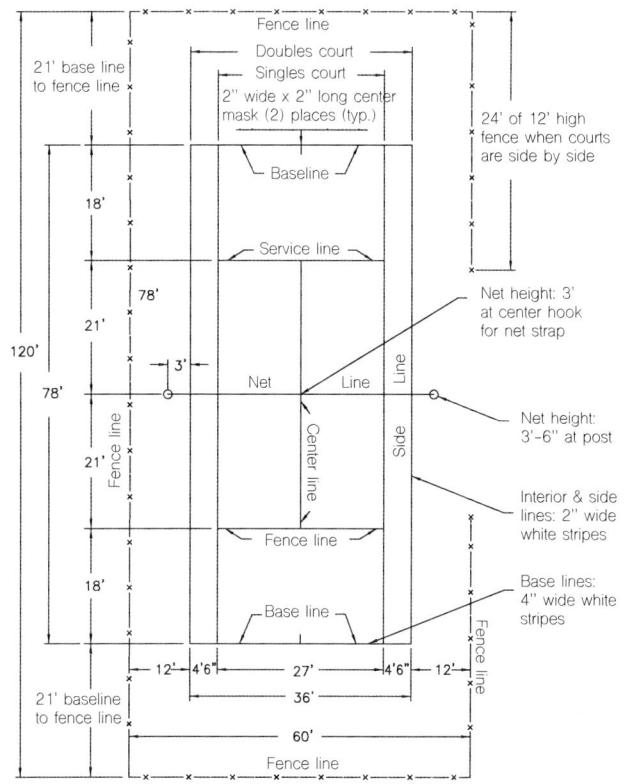

Tennis court striping plan

Notes:
1) Tennis court striping shall be colored white. Dimensions are to outside edge of the lines unless indicated otherwise.
2) Contractor shall be responsible for court layout.

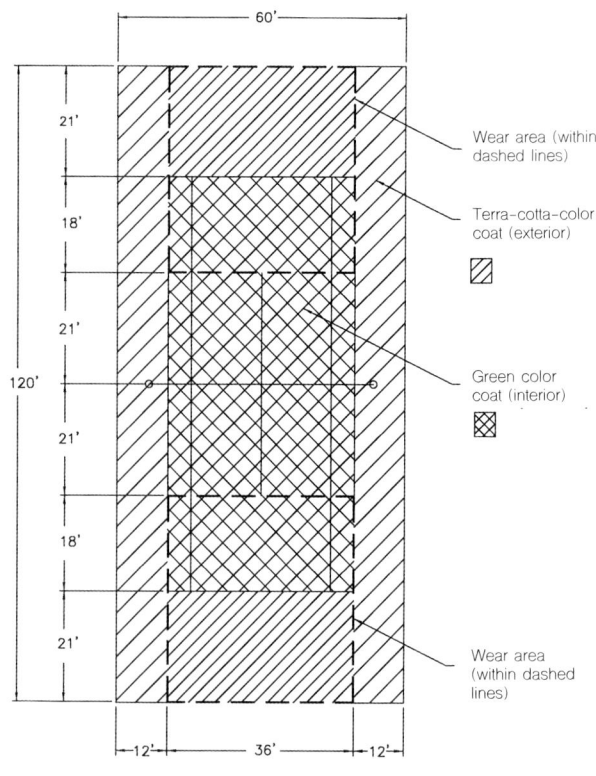

Tennis court color coating

Notes:
Wear area to receive additional color coat of court surfacing per specifications.

link, rails, and hardware should be black, thermally fused polyvinyl chloride. Fine mesh wind screening shall be attached to the inside of the fence. Gates shall be located within the fence so as to disrupt play as little as possible.

9. Swimming pools

9.1 Swimming pool requirements and standards

The deep area of the pool shall be designed to accommodate competitive swimming, water polo, and synchronized swimming, measuring 75.5 feet (23 meters) by either 82 feet (25 meters) or 164 feet (50 meters) with a minimum of six lanes at a minimum depth of 9 feet (2.7 meters). Deep water is also required for high-level instruction (lifeguard training and diving). Orientation for lap lanes should be north–south, however, anchor sockets should be installed so that lane directions can be changed to allow for multiple programs in the pool at one time.

The shallow area of the pool shall be designed to best serve the instructional needs of participants. Shallow areas shall be up to 5 feet (1.5 meters) with the majority of the shallow water being in the 18 inches (46 centimeters) to 4 feet (1.2 meters) range.

- There should be a separate room for first-aid facilities.
- The pool manager's office must connect to main front office area (where guests pay to enter the facility) and have a view of the pool area.
- The pool deck shall be provided with sufficient lighting so that persons walking on the deck can identify hazards.
- A ramp or zero depth entry shall be provided into the pool.
- A spectator seating area that is physically separated from the pool deck shall be provided.
- If the pool is a separate, stand-alone facility, a large meeting room shall be provided for special events, meetings, community aquatic safety training courses, and staff training.
- A storage area (with shelving) for pool equipment and instructional items shall be provided.
- Shade structure shall be provided on the deck area.
- Emergency/repair vehicle access provide a 14-foot (4.3-meter) wide, double gate at the deck area for emergency and repair vehicles.

10. Multipurpose fields (softball and soccer fields/turf areas)

Multipurpose fields shall be free of all half-inch (1.3-centimeter) diameter or larger rocks to a depth of 15 inches (38.1 centimeters), or the field shall be provided with a 15-inch (38.1-centimeter) layer of topsoil and meet the horticultural requirements for Class A topsoil.

10.1 Softball fields

Base length minimum is 65 feet (19.8 meters).
Foul line minimum distance is a 250 feet (76.2 meters) radius.
Home plate to backstop distance is 20 feet (6.1 meters).
Drainage catch basins or manholes should not be located within the field of play.

Figure 10: Softball field design

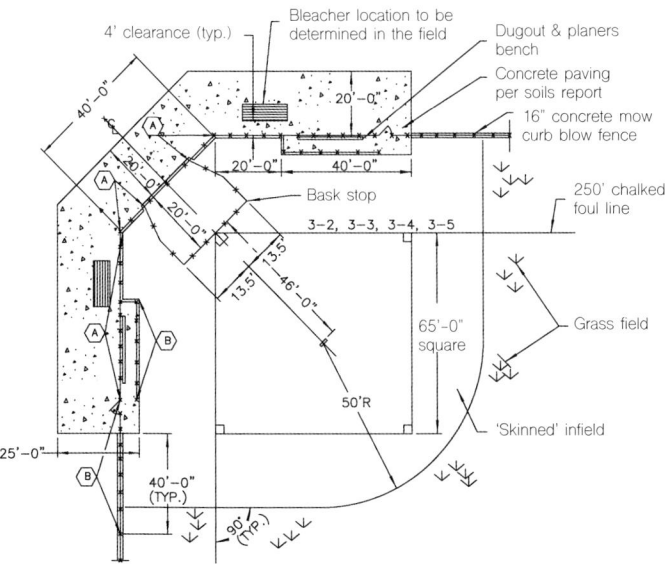

Softball field

Notes:
1) Backstop area is symmetrical about the center line, except as noted above.
2) Dimensions are to center line of fence posts.
3) Contractor shall install home plate and place guineas at base locations for future bases (bases by others).
4) Tie backstop in as part of fence, see backstop notes.
A) 12-foot (3.7-meter) high black vinyl chain-link fence.
B) 8-foot (2.4-meter) high black vinyl chain-link fence.

10.2 Field orientation

The preferred orientation places the batter facing the pitcher in a northerly direction with a line from home plate to the pitcher's mound not deviating more than 20 degrees east or west of north, and the first base line running in a west–east orientation. However, optimum utilization or configuration of the site may require deviation from the preferred orientation.

10.3 Field drainage

The fields will typically be crowned in the center with drainage to the sides. Certain sites and field overlay situations would make this drainage pattern unacceptable. In such cases, other drainage patterns or drainage devices will be considered and approved by the park project manager. In all cases, there will be positive drainage away from home plate.

10.4 Softball field infield mix

Softball field infield mix shall meet the following requirements. See table 4 for grain size distribution/percent passing.

10.5 Certification of the infield mix requirements

Certification shall be provided by the contractor to the resident engineer or project manager at the time of project submittals. Infield areas shall not be amended with soil conditioners used for planting areas.

10.6 Infield dust control

Infield dust control provides two quick coupler valves in the lawn area just beyond the perimeter of the infield. These valves should to be at the finish grade. Additionally, a manually controlled system of high-speed rotors at the perimeter of the infield will wet the infield evenly and quickly.

10.7 Fencing and backstop

Detailed data is shown in figure 11 and figure 12 on the next page.

10.8 Access to softball field lighting

Maintenance access to the lights shall be provided by concrete walkways (concrete designed for heavy equipment), or 12-foot-wide (3.7-meter-wide) access gates shall be provided in the fencing.

10.9 Electrical requirements

Verify location for the electrical outlet for the use of a pitching machine with the sports park's design team. The outlet can be located in a lockable stainless-steel box behind the backstop or the backstop fence or provided adjacent to the pitcher's mound in a lockable waterproof box within an 8-inch (20.3-centimeter) gate valve box.

10.10 Softball bleachers

Softball bleachers shall be hot dipped galvanized steel, three rows minimum or five rows typical, and 15 feet (4.6 meters) long. Bleachers with five rows require a guardrail. Specify spot welding of seats and foot planks to bleacher frame (free of burrs and sharp edges). Bleachers shall be placed a maximum of 4 feet (1.2 meters) from the fence line of the backstop.

10.11 Soccer fields

Preferred size is 225 by 360 feet (69 by 110 meters) with a clear zone of 9 feet (2.7 meters) on all sides. (Soccer field size may vary depending on site constraints.) The playing surface shall not overlay onto the skinned infield of a softball field. The field area shall be free of drainage catch basins and manholes.

10.12 Soccer field orientation and placement

Preferred orientation is with the long axis north–south. Multiple fields placed adjacent to one another shall be placed side by

Table 4

Sieve size	Minimum	Maximum
No. 4	100%	
No. 8	90%	100%
No. 16	85%	95%
No. 30	65%	85%
No. 50	35%	55%
No. 100	20%	35%
No. 200	10%	25%

Clay content shall be 10 to 15 percent.
Sand equivalent shall be 15 to 25 percent, as per test method.
Ph levels shall be 6 to 8.5.
Color gold is preferred. Red is acceptable.
Depth of infield mix shall be 4 inches (10.2 centimeters) to 6 inches (15.2 centimeters).

Figure 11

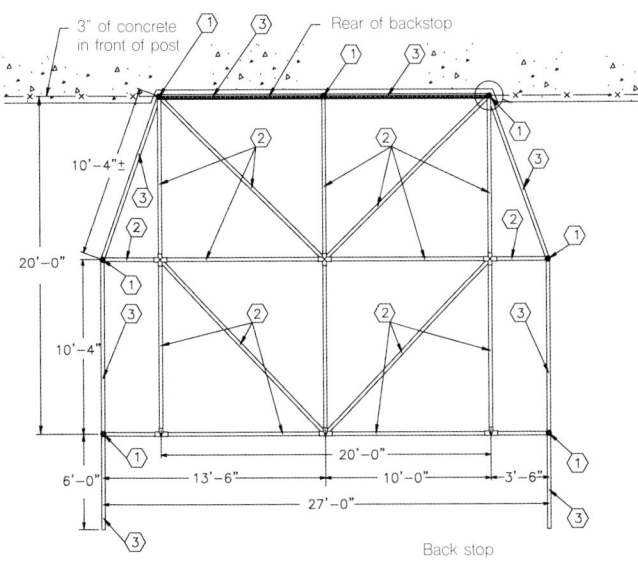

Notes:
1) 2.5-inch (6.3-centimeter) galvanized iron pipe hubs 30-inch (76.2-centimeter) deep at base of each post (total 7) with concrete footing, see detail 3-5.
2) 1.5-inch (3.8-centimeter) galvanized iron pipe (typ.).
3) 2-inch (5.1-centimeter) galvanized iron pipe (typ.).

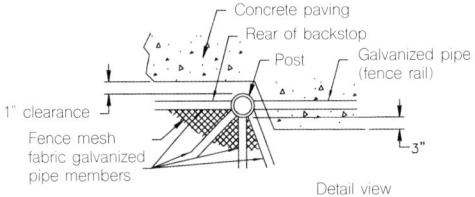

Figure 12

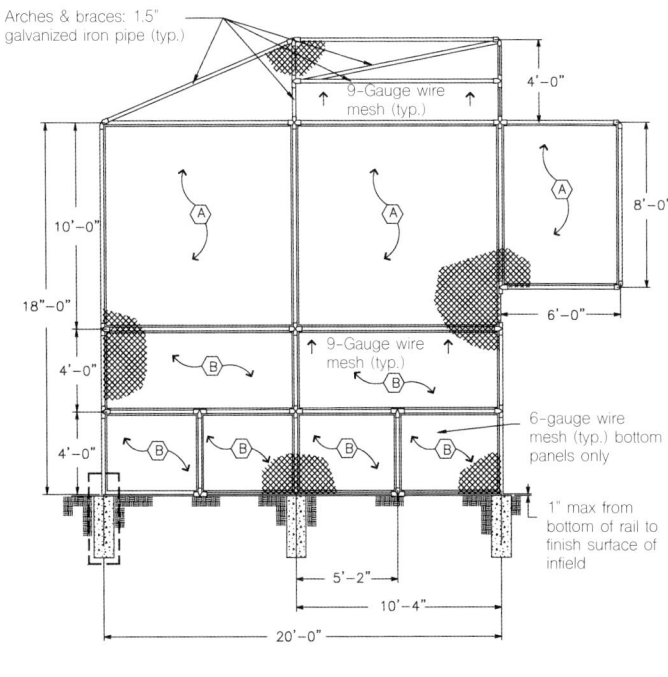

Notes:
1) All pipe frame to be 2-inch (5.1-centimeter) galvanized iron pipe, except as noted above.
A) 3/4" x 3/16" tension bar with 1" x 14-gauge bands 12" on center (typ.).
B) 3/4" x 3/16" tension bar with 1" x 14-gauge bands 8" on center (typ.).

side. Fields may be offset to facilitate field layout, but may not be end to end.

11 Playgrounds and equipment

11.1 General play area requirements

Play areas for preschool children (ages two to five years) shall be separated from play areas for school-age children (ages five to 12 years).

Barbecues, hot-coal receptacles, and plant materials with thorns or stickers, or that attract bees, or other potential hazards shall not be located adjacent to play areas. Trees are not allowed to overhang safety zones of play equipment. Play areas with sand surfacing shall not be located adjacent to a gymnasium or recreation center, to prevent tracking of sand indoors. Drinking fountains shall not be located adjacent to play areas with sand surfacing, but in close proximity.

Current ADA requirements are now adopted federally, and though the requirements are for about a third of the equipment to be disabled accessible, the sports parks and recreation department prefers to maximize ground-level play components and to provide resilient accessible surfacing to a minimum of 50 percent of the play equipment.[3]

Provide seating close enough to play areas for adults to supervise children. Seating shall be designed to meet disabled people's requirements, and shall be designed or located to discourage skateboard damage. Seating shall be designed to meet ADA requirements.

11.2 Active recreation areas

Active recreation areas provide for physical activity either as an informal group or as an individual. Opportunities can include exercise stations, kick-about areas or other active elements that encourage or facilitate physical activity.

Table 5

Park size \ Types	Citywide sports parks	Citywide waterside parks	District recreation parks	District waterside parks	Local sports parks
One large kick-about area	164 by 229.7 feet (50 by 70 meters)		164 by 229.7 feet (50 by 70 meters)	164 by 229.7 feet (50 by 70 meters)	98.4 by 131.2 feet (30 by 40 meters)
Two small kick-about areas	98.4 by 131.2 feet (30 by 40 meters)	164 by 229.7 feet (50 by 70 meters)			
			plus one multipurpose half court with hoop and backboard, or one rebound wall and court		plus one multipurpose half court with hoop and backboard, or one rebound wall and court

Standard requirements

For sports park size and types, refer to table 5.

Example alternative solutions

Citywide and district sports and waterside parks must provide at least one kick-about space of 37,673.7 square feet (3500 square meters) which has no dimension smaller than 131.2 feet (40 meters), plus at least two other active recreation elements (see examples below).

Local recreation parks must provide a kick-about space not less than 4,305.6 square feet (600 square meters) with no dimension smaller than 65.6 feet (20 meters), plus at least one other active recreation element.

Examples of active recreation elements include:
- informal sports fields;
- active recreation sites for youth such as BMX track, jump park, skate park or sports courts;
- horizontal climbing and bouldering walls;
- basketball courts/half courts;
- dog off-leash exercise areas (fenced);
- running tracks;
- outdoor 'gyms' using fixed exercise equipment;
- dedicated fitness trail or multiple use of the parks internal path network as an exercise trail;
- waterway access points for canoeing and other paddle sports (waterside parks only); and
- an area for older residents to congregate and take part in a shared activity such as a bocce court, outdoor chess areas, or outdoor exercise equipment.[1]

Other requirements for alternative solutions

Design and construction should address public safety and maintenance costs and include consideration for fencing where the kick-about area may lead to children running onto roadways; the likely ages and preferences of residents to be serviced by the park should be considered in determining the provision of appropriate embellishments within the park.[1]

11.3 Play space and adventure playgrounds

The provision of spaces for play is fundamental to recreation and waterside parks. The scale of the play space and unique features (such as adventure play, water play and play sculpture) can help define a park as a destination for residents and visitors and contribute to the diversity of experience on offer to the community. However, providing successful play spaces combines numerous elements such as landscaping, location, and play equipment. Citywide and district sports parks need to accommodate a range of ages and abilities, while local parks should cater for the needs of residents within the local catchment.

Standard requirements

For citywide sports parks:
- one themed adventure playground (nominal size 328.1 by 328.1 feet [100 by 100 meters]) on either a flat (150 maximum grade) or terraced site incorporating a range of play equipment for children aged two to 12;
- shade structure;
- seating (two tables and four bench seats);
- soft-fall;
- fenced toddler play area; and
- child cycle circuit.

For district recreation parks and citywide waterside parks:
- one themed adventure playground (nominal size 196.9 by 131.2 feet [60 by 40 meters]) on either a flat (150 maximum grade) or terraced site incorporating a range of play equipment for children aged two to 12;
- shade structure;
- seating (two tables and four bench seats);
- soft-fall; and
- fenced toddler play area.

For local sports parks and district waterside parks:
- one play space (nominal size 65.6 by 49.2 feet [20 by 15 meters]) on either a flat (150 maximum grade) or terraced site incorporating a range of play equipment for children aged two to 12.[1]

Example alternative solutions

For citywide sports and waterside parks:
- adventure play space for older children 12+ (which could include a skate park, mountain bike trail, BMX jump park or similar);
- play sculpture (meaning sculpture that provides artistic and interactive play elements) and interactive landscapes;
- zero-depth water play features (citywide sports parks only);
- play space or multiple spaces integrated into special landscape features of the park; the spaces must cater to at least two different age groups including younger and older children;

- a linear adventure trail providing a range of activities and still visible from central areas;
- opportunistic use of natural features (such as boulders, ridges or slopes) to create informal play landscapes;
- developed edge treatments providing safe fishing platforms or water play opportunities (waterside parks only).

For local recreation parks:
- a play or activity space designed for an older youth demographic as appropriate to the local community, such as a small mountain bike trail, informal BMX area, outdoor gym equipment, climbing wall, adventure playground.[1]

Other requirements for alternative solutions

- Citywide and district parks must provide for a range of ages.
- Play spaces for very young children (toddlers) should have seats.
- Play spaces for different age groups should be physically separate.
- All play equipment should have provision for shade.
- High visibility/casual surveillance of the play area.
- Play spaces and adventure playgrounds should not be located adjacent to high-volume vehicular-traffic areas or roads. However, if play spaces are unavoidably located in proximity to highly trafficked vehicle areas or roads, particularly when they cater for very young children (toddlers), then fencing or effective barrier landscape should be provided to limit wandering out of the play space.

The provision of spaces for play and active recreation are complementary objectives for sporting parks. These provide additional value to local residents and visiting users, and allow for efficient multiple uses of public parks.

Standard requirements

One play space (nominal size 65.6 by 49.2 feet [20 by 15 meters]) on either a flat (150 maximum grade) or terraced site incorporating a range of play equipment for children aged two to 12; shade structures and soft-fall.

Example alternative solutions:
- numerous play events provided close to each other with shade, soft-fall and appropriate landscape elements;
- activity sites combining play and adventure (such as an adventure playground);
- a combination of play space and outdoor recreation or active recreation elements such as an informal BMX track, climbing walls, exercise equipment catering to two to 12 year olds and older youth;
- play sculpture and interactive landscapes.

Other requirements for alternative solutions

- For sports parks it is considered that the provision of sporting and practice facilities provides for adult and older youth activity, and therefore play opportunities appropriate to children between the ages of two and 12 is preferred.
- All play equipment should be shaded with natural shade (preferred) or structures.
- High visibility of play areas from the surrounding park space to enable carers a clear view and encourage casual surveillance is a requirement of all solutions.
- Play spaces or elements should generally not be located adjacent to high-volume vehicular-traffic areas or public roads, unless there is no other feasible alternative and the play space is appropriately fenced. [1]

Figure 13: Play space with active recreation elements in sports park

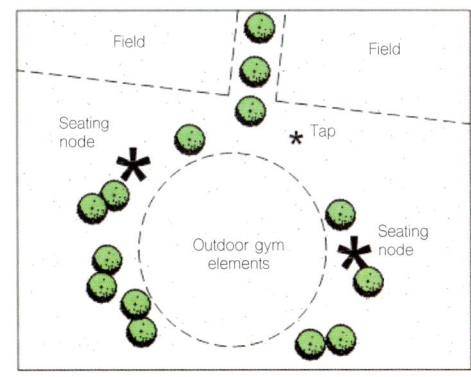

Figure 14: Dispersed play events in landscaped corridor in sports park

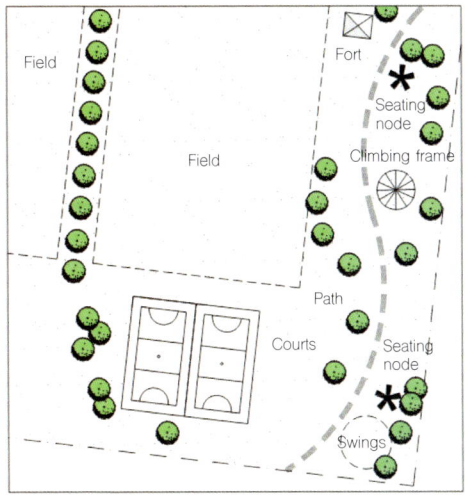

Playgrounds shall be designed to offer the greatest play value possible within the budgetary constraints and physical restrictions of the site. The play experience should challenge the users by addressing their physical, social, and mental development while providing entertainment. The play environment shall be safe, durable, and vandal-resistant, and require minimal maintenance. [1]

11.4 General play equipment criteria

Plastic decks should have center access, unless rails are placed 90 degrees to main access or circulation patterns, and perforations in excess of 0.1875 inches (4.8 millimeters) in decks more than 30 inches (76.2 centimeters) in height.

General criteria are decks that are secured with self-tapping screws; climbing walls in vertical orientation on decks over 30 inches (76.2 centimeters) in height (must be canted); climbers that do not have head clearance; enclosed tunnel-slides or level tunnels (unless made of a mesh material); bubble panels; lexan or plexiglass windows; sectional slides; wood components; metal slides; dark colored plastic slides in any orientation; movable digging shovel toys that do not have a safety stop; whirlers (unless equipped with brakes); see-saws with fulcrum points (springs are acceptable); pinches-type coil spring base animals; swings with heavy animal figures; half-bucket swing seats with chains to secure occupants; vinyl-clad cargo nets (except with non-slip clad, rigid horizontal bars); vinyl-clad swing chains; rigid swing seats; non-reinforced swing seats (must be slash resistant); cable components; and roller slides. Recycled plastic structures are not prohibited, but should be limited to low-volume playgrounds, unless reinforced with metal bracing.

At the time of product submittals, any substitutions of specified play equipment on construction plans must fit the designed play area. Shop drawings or catalog cuts are required in order to make a determination.

All play equipment shall be installed in accordance with the manufacturer specifications. The construction documents shall specify that the play equipment shall be installed as late in the construction process as possible.

The tops of all play equipment footings shall be 12 inches (30.5 centimeters) below finish grade of surfacing material, with a smooth finish, except for spring animals. Spring animals shall have footing edges chamfered at 45 degrees or rounded with a 2-inches (5.1-centimeter) minimum radius and exposed bolts cut at the nut and spot welded, and be 3 inches (7.6 centimeters) to 6 inches (15.2 centimeters) below finish grade.

Steel or aluminum play equipment shall be colored by electrostatically applied powder coating or hot dipped galvanized steel with fused vinyl coating, minimum thickness of 0.0047 to 0.0070 inches (0.12 to 0.18 millimeters).

11.5 Play area drainage and construction

The play area subgrade shall be sloped to a subsurface drainage system (1.5 percent minimum) for all play area surfaces. Concrete sub-base for poured-in-place rubber surfacing shall slope at 1 percent minimum towards drain inlet or sump. Subgrade for concrete sub-base shall be compacted to 95 percent minimum.

A subsurface drainage system shall be provided for all play surfaces. This system shall be designed for positive flow for the play area square footage. The drain lines shall contain a clean out before it empties into a storm drain. Leach lines or sumps may be considered if a storm drain is not available. If sumps are needed, design them outside of the play area, if possible, to minimize the amount of drainage rock that infiltrates the play area in the event children dig down and pull up the filter fabric, or repairs to the play equipment require digging.

New play areas of sand or engineered wood fiber shall be contained by a concrete walk that is a minimum of 4 feet (1.2 meters) wide, with a deepened footing set at a continuous elevation. Sand shall be a minimum 4 inches (10.2 centimeters) below the adjacent paving. Engineered wood fiber may be flush, or up to 4 inches (10.2 centimeters) below adjacent paving, after settlement. The area surrounding the play area shall be graded so that runoff flows away from the play area. If the play area is contained with a wall adjacent to a turf area, the wall shall include an 8-inch-wide (20.3-centimeters-wide) concrete mow edge at the base of the wall, sloped at 2 percent away from wall.

A concrete walkway of a minimum of 4 inches (10.2 centimeters) wide shall be provided around all play areas. At existing concrete containment curb or low wall, the walkway shall be installed with an expansion joint adjacent to the concrete containment curb or wall. Walkways shall provide a 1.5 percent gradient away from the play area.

11.6 Safety standards for play equipment

Platforms on modular equipment shall be punched steel with 0.1875-inch (4.8-millimeter) diameter holes on decks over 30 inches (76.2 centimeters) in height (to prevent fingers protruding up from below being crushed from above and minimize potential for hood drawstrings to be caught in larger deck openings at the top of slides) with non-skid surfacing and 6 feet (1.8 meters) maximum height. Low (less than 30 inches [76 centimeters]) steps and transfer stations may have larger holes to aid grasping for transfer from wheelchairs. Decks may be taller if the unit is fully enclosed with no potential for falls from the greater height. Do not incorporate tunnels or lexan or plexiglass windows or panels in the modules. Posts shall be at least 0.5 to 3 inches (1.3 to 7.6 centimeters) in diameter of steel or aluminum, or recycled plastic with aluminum framing for structures built for children aged two to five; and 5 inches (12.7 centimeters) minimum diameter steel or aluminum for structures built for five- to 12-year-old users. Swings shall have steel or aluminum posts of 5 inches (12.7 centimeters) in diameter, or galvanized steel posts of 0.5 to 3 inches (1.3 to 7.6 centimeters) in diameter. Posts shall be aluminum or recycled plastic with aluminum framing within 1 mile (1.6 kilometers) of the coast or bay.

Rungs or climbing bars shall be cylindrical, smooth, and sized per local consumer product safety commission's guidelines. Non-slip coating is acceptable. Light colors are recommended for plastic climbers (yellow or tan), even in coastal areas. Rockwall chains may be coated with non-slip heavy-duty coating.

Swings These shall be free-standing, with four posts minimum for stability, and not attached to composite structures. They should cater for two separate age groups (two to five and five to 12). Swiveling swing attachments, which minimize chains wrapping around the top bar, are preferred. No more than two swings shall be hung in each bay of the support structure. Preferred surfacing below swings is manufactured wood fiber, with minimum 1-inch-thick (2.5-centimeter-thick), 4 by 4 feet (1.2 by 1.2 meters) rubber mats, 6 to 8 inches (15.2 to 20.3 centimeters) deep, secured with duckbill anchors. If space does not permit 10 feet (3 meters) minimum separation between wood fiber and sand, then a combination of sand and rubberized surfacing is acceptable. Swing chains shall be 4.0-gauge galvanized steel (no vinyl coating allowed on chains).

Swings shall be provided with seats that accommodate preschool children (bucket seats), as well as school-age children (belt seats). If space permits, specify a swing set for each age group of children. Belt and bucket seats shall be provided in different bays of the swing set. Belt seat swings shall be slash proof. Fully enclosed bucket seats shall be molded rubber, reinforced with steel. Hard seats are not acceptable. Half-bucket seats with chain restraint is not acceptable.
Swing safety zones provide a safety zone for the swing set equal to two times the height of the top rail in front and in back of the centerline of the swing, and 6 feet (1.8 meters) clear between the support posts and other structures.

Slide structures Free-standing and attached slides shall be single-piece units with plastic beds. Decks at the head of slides shall have no openings in excess of 0.1875 inches (4.8 millimeters) in any direction. Light colors are recommended for slide beds (yellow or tan), even in coastal areas. Install minimum 1-inch-thick (2.5-centimeter-thick), 4 by 4 feet (1.2 by 1.2 meters) rubber mats, 6 to 8 inches (15.2 to 20.3 centimeters) deep, secured with duckbill anchors at exit region of slides.

Stairways and ladders shall have continuous handrails on both sides and be placed at a height that will allow the child to stand erect over each step.

The preferable orientation for slides is facing north to northeast. All slide exits shall be located in uncongested areas with a clear safety zone.

Spring animals Spring animal bodies shall be constructed of cast aluminum. Spring animals shall only be mounted on cinches spring bases or non-pinching coils.

Horizontal ladders/overhead grasp bars Rungs on horizontal ladders shall be 0.25 to 1 inches (0.6 to 2.5 centimeters) of galvanized steel, spaced at intervals of 11 inches (28 centimeters). Maximum height of horizontal ladders shall be 7 feet 6 inches (2.3 meters). Minimum height of horizontal ladders shall be 6 feet 6 inches (2 meters).

Track rides The minimum height of track rides shall be 6 feet 6 inches (2 meters); the maximum height shall be 7 feet 6 inches (2.3 meters), equipped with ladders on each end.

Safety zones All safety zones set by the most current local consumer product safety commission guidelines take precedence over all noted safety zones in this book.
Roof heights on modular structures shall be set at a minimum 6 feet 6 inches (2 meters) clear height from deck or adjacent step tread.

A permanently mounted sign indicating age-appropriateness for each play area shall be set. Verbiage shall include that supervision is required for children aged two to five, and recommended for children aged five to 12. The signage may be incorporated as a panel on a modular structure. Stickers may be applied with the initial installation to supplement permanent signage, but should not be the only means of identifying age-appropriateness. Stickers stating compliance with fall surfacing requirements must be provided upon completion of installation.

11.7 Play area surfacing materials

Acceptable surfacing material includes sand, engineered wood fiber, loose rubber fill or rubberized paving to a depth of 12 inches (30.5 centimeters). If both sand and engineered wood products or loose rubber fill are used in the same play area, then they shall be separated from each other by a minimum of 10 feet (3 meters) of paving or rubberized surfacing.

Sand Shall be imported, clean, double washed, manufactured #20 silica sand, free of deleterious organic material, loam, clay and debris, with a mean effective size between 0.55 inches (1.4 centimeters) and 0.65 inches (1.7 centimeters), and a mean uniformity coefficient between 1.00 and 1.54. Sand shall only be used with a filter fabric and drain system. Depth shall be 12 inches (30.5 centimeters) minimum, and shall be of a thickness sufficient to attenuate falls.

Engineered wood fiber Shall be an energy-absorbing protective surfacing manufactured for playground installations. The manufactured fibrous crushed wood product (tumbled, with blunt ends) shall consist of random-sized wood fibers comprised but not limited to soft wood such as ponderosa pine, douglas fir, spruce and/or white pine. The particle size shall be between 0.5 and 3 inches (1.3 and 7.6 centimeters) in length, and not less than 0.4 inch (1 centimeter) in width or 0.078 inch (0.2 centimeter) in thickness. At least 85 percent by volume of the manufactured wood product shall be the sizes specified. It shall be non-toxic, and free of bark and organic materials.

Loose rubber fill Shall meet the requirements of local consumer product safety commissions for play areas. Color shall be brown or tan. Rubber shall be clean, with no fiber or steel radial remnants. Depth shall be of a thickness sufficient to attenuate falls. A ramp for disabled access shall be provided.

Interlocking rubber pavers Shall meet the requirements of local consumer product safety commissions for play areas.

Only pavers that have joints that will not trap sand or dirt in the process of expansion and contraction are allowed, similar or equal to Play Matt as (no known equal). Pavers may be placed on asphalt or concrete sub-base, and shall be of a thickness sufficient to attenuate falls.

Poured-in-place rubberized paving All rubberized paving shall be installed on a concrete sub-base. Colored ethylene-propylene-diene monomer (EPDM) layer shall be 0.5 to 0.63 inches (1.3 to 1.6 centimeters) thick. Buffing layer shall be of a thickness sufficient to attenuate falls. A thickened color layer shall be keyed into the surface adjacent to transition to concrete pavement. Thirty degree cant into adjacent sand play area shall be keyed into concrete sub-base.

12. Parking areas

Parking for district and citywide sport, recreation, and waterside parks is normally provided on-site with a combination of surfaced and unsurfaced overflow areas. All formal parking areas are required to provide sufficient parking spaces as required by the planning scheme. Local recreation parks are primarily 'walk to' parks serving local catchments generally within a 1640.4-foot (500-meter) radius, and therefore only on-street parking needs to be provided. When designing the surrounding road network and development adjacent to local recreation parks, consideration should be given to increasing the availability of on-street parking where practical. Indented parking within the road reserve fronting the park can be provided in an integrated manner with streetscape and park design outcomes. Development forms that reduce the number of vehicle cross-overs, such as those accessed via rear laneways, increase on-street parking capacity and are encouraged. Linear parks are linked across urban areas via adjacent road and path networks and no on-site parking is required.

12.1 Standard requirements

For vehicle parking, normal sports parks design guidelines require the following internal parking to be provided (see table 6).

Table 6

Park type	Surfaced (paved and line marked)	Overflow (grassed reinforced or other)
Citywides ports (500 cars peak)	250 cars and four coaches	250 cars adjacent to formal parking areas
Local sports (150 cars peak)	100 cars and four coaches	50 cars adjacent to formal parking areas

12.2 Example alternative solutions

A range of alternative solutions for parking provisions are possible. However, the peak loads indicated in table 6 must still be accommodated. Alternative solutions may include avoiding large areas of 'sterile' car park by breaking up parking areas to service different nodes within the park, which may be preferred for citywide recreation, sport, and waterside parks; providing some of the parking as on-street spaces, where local city council considers there is sufficient parking space capacity within the surrounding street network; and reducing the extent of hardstand by increasing the amount of overflow parking on reinforced grassed areas.[2]

12.3 Further requirements

- Location of parking areas should seek to minimize internal road networks by being located close to the perimeter or adjacent to a key facility that requires its own driveway access.
- Parking areas must consider access to key facilities and make provision for people with limited mobility.
- For citywide sports parks, consideration should be given to the provision of parking for cyclists.
- Providing multiple parking nodes with separate street entries will only be considered if deemed acceptable relative to traffic circulation and safety and is supported with appropriate signage.
- A calculation of likely demand is required to support any case for a park proposal where the number of spaces to be provided is less than that required.[1]

Sports parking area paving provides a pavement section on the construction plans based on R-values and the project manager's pavement recommendations. Sports parking area geotechnical tests shall be conducted to provide a paving section design for the sports parking lot and all vehicular access paths. The paint utilized for striping and markings shall be based on the local environment-friendly materials specifications. To compensate for vehicular overhang, provide wheel stops in parking spaces or provide a concrete walkway of at least 6 feet (1.8 meters) wide to allow operation of lawnmowers when vehicles are parked. (Refer to figure 15.)

13 Irrigation

13.1 General requirements

The irrigation system must be designed with water conservation standards and equipment. The irrigation design shall be based on accurate pressure information and produce an irrigation system that efficiently applies uniform water throughout the site. The irrigation design must also have sufficient residual pressure and flow to accommodate site conditions, field changes, and unforeseen future demands as well as anticipated future demands, if it is a phased project.

For most sports parks there are two primary considerations:
1. to assure that the irrigation design will meet the time constraints of the sports parks' required operation needs;
2. the system must be able to apply the volume of water necessary to achieve the evapotranspiration rate (ETO) for the highest demand month within the following criteria: four days per week, eight-hour irrigation window, 10.00 pm to 6.00 am (America, San Diego time).[3]

For sports parks with active sports fields, it is critical that the irrigation design is adequate to irrigate the site within the irrigation window and the recreational schedule of the sports fields. The irrigation design must be able to irrigate the complete site within one eight-hour irrigation window. This cycle must be able to supply the volume of water needed in a peak summer condition following two consecutive days of no water. A typical condition at most sports field complexes requires that the fields not receive irrigation on Friday or Saturday nights in preparation for community use on the following morning, and therefore the irrigation design must

Figure 15: Mixed parking solution using on-street and grassed overflow area

Note: Car park design is indicative only. Design of off-street car parking is to be in accordance with AS2890.1.

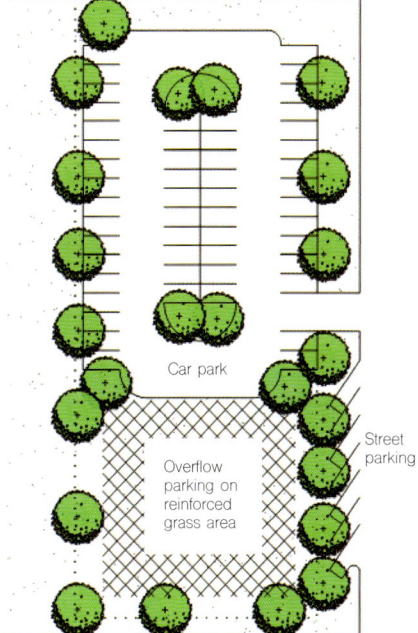

apply three days of irrigation on a single night. To carry overtime for this condition is NOT effective.

In developed areas, the residual pressure shall be 15 percent, and in undeveloped areas the residual pressure shall be 25 percent of the required operating pressure. Irrigation systems for ballfields shall be separated from other lawn areas of the sports parks.

Irrigation lines shall run horizontally (level and parallel to the slope contours) to reduce line drainage and pressure loss. The supplemental irrigation specifications shall be implemented in the irrigation design and selection of irrigation materials, and shall be provided in the plans.

13.2 Reclaimed water

The irrigation designer shall verify with the appropriate water district if the project requires irrigation products for reclaimed water or future reclaimed water. All above-grade irrigation equipment is required to be integral colored purple and embossed with the 'Reclaimed water—Do not drink' symbol on all materials; purple paint is not acceptable. Reclaimed water irrigation sprinkler heads shall have integral color purple caps.

Cross-connection test station shall be a cast-bronze globe valve with stainless-steel fittings, 0.75 inches (1.9 centimeters) female thread, and shall be installed in a concrete valve box with cast-iron locking lid.

The maximum water meter size is 2 inches (5.1 centimeters). If the irrigation system requires a larger service, provide an additional water meter. Provide separate meters for irrigation and domestic uses. The preferred location is in a shrub or groundcover planting area rather than a lawn area. A reduced pressure backflow preventer is mandatory per the municipal code. The installation is to include a stainless-steel enclosure (free of burrs and sharp edges) on a concrete pad.

13.3 Irrigation controllers

Automatic irrigation systems should be installed for lawn, shrub and groundcover areas. Controller locations shall be approved by the project manager. Preferred locations are within the park and recreation storage room of a comfort station.

All pedestal-mounted irrigation controllers shall be installed in vandal-resistant, weather-proof, stainless-steel enclosures on concrete pads. All exterior wall-mounted irrigation controllers shall be installed in a stainless-steel enclosure. Rain shut-off devices shall be automatic and provided for each controller. Irrigation controllers shall be specified to have on–off switches and electrical receptacles. A concrete pull box to loop the 110 service into before sweeping into the controller enclosure shall be provided. All new controllers shall have a phone jack installed as part of the installation for future central control systems.

Pressure-regulating valves

Provide a pressure regulating valve if the static pressure is over 85 psi at time of construction. The pressure-regulating valve shall be in line, below grade, and within 10 feet (3 meters) of backflow device.

Master control valves and flow-sensor devices

Master control valves and flow-sensor devices provide a 'normally open' master control valve after the backflow preventer and the pressure-regulator valve. It shall be wired independently and have a separate station at the controller. The flow sensor shall be located downstream of the master control valve. Installation shall be per manufacturers' recommendations. All transitions from mainline depth to valve box depth shall be accomplished by the use of 45-degree coupling.

Isolation valves

Provide isolation valves along the mainline at appropriate locations to divide the irrigation system into controllable units, at stub outs for future systems, prior to crossing expansive pavement, at each remote control valve or manifold, and for each quick coupler. All isolation valves shall be bronze globe valves, unless the line size is more than 4 inches (10.2 centimeters), then a bronze gate valve may be used. For all mainline applications, install line-size globe valves. For all remote control valves or valve manifolds, install a globe valve the same size as the remote control valve or the largest valve in the manifold. For quick coupler applications, install a 1-inch (2.5-centimeter) globe valve.

Remote control valves

The maximum remote control valve size is 2 inches (5.1 centimeters) with a maximum flow of 80 gallons (0.1 stere) per minute. Remote control valves shall be installed in manifolds where feasible (maximum four remote control valves per globe valve). Install individual boxes for each remote control valve. In multipurpose fields, locate remote control valves along the fence line, outside the field of play. All other remote control valves shall be located in shrub or groundcover areas where possible. Plastic valves are not acceptable.

Quick coupler valves
Quick coupler valves provide 1-inch (2.5-centimeter) locking rubber cover quick couplers with a 1-inch (2.5-centimeter) globe valve at a maximum of 150 feet (45.7 meters) on center. Minimum mainline size is 0.5 to 1 inch (1.3 to 2.5 centimeters) to quick coupler valve. All quick coupler valves shall be set and installed in shrub or groundcover areas.

Irrigation boxes
All irrigation boxes shall be concrete with a cast-iron locking top. The preferred location for irrigation boxes is in shrub or groundcover areas adjacent to walkways. Irrigation boxes for remote control valves shall be set parallel to each other, and perpendicular to adjacent paving or concrete curb. The contractor shall paint the identification number of the valve box on the cover. The paint shall be white or yellow 100 percent acrylic epoxy waterproof paint.

Irrigation heads
Head coverage Provide head-to-head coverage for all lawn, shrub, and groundcover irrigation heads. All heads shall be spaced at 50 percent of the maximum rated diameter of coverage.

Overspray All irrigation heads shall be installed and adjusted to avoid overspray onto buildings, walkways, play equipment, etc.

Anti-drain valve/excess flow valve Every irrigation head, regardless of change in elevation, shall have an anti-drain valve/excess flow valve installed in the riser of the head assembly.

Pop-up head locations Irrigation heads in an 'accessible area' or prone to vandalism, as determined by the local city project manager, shall be pop-up heads. All heads directly adjacent to walkways, curbs, sports parking areas, or pedestrian-accessible areas shall be pop-up heads.

Lawn heads These shall be pop-up spray heads or rotors. Pop-up spray heads shall have a 4-inch (10.1-centimeter) or 6-inch (15.2-centimeters) riser height, depending on lawn type and mow height. Pop-up rotors shall have a 4-inch (10.1-centimeter) riser height and stainless-steel risers.

Shrub or groundcover heads Pop-up heads shall have a 6-inch (15.2-centimeter) or 12-inch (30.5-centimeter) riser height depending on the adjacent shrubs or groundcover. Fixed heads shall be on 6- to 12-inches-high (15.2- to 30.5-centimeters-high), Sch. 80 PVC risers.

Bubblers Two bubblers are required for each tree per detail, in lawn areas, two bubblers per tree in shrub and groundcover areas. Bubblers shall be on a separate valve from other irrigation heads.

Trenching
No shared use of trenches will be allowed between various trades and for incompatible uses. Pipes shall not be installed directly over one another. A minimum of 2 inches (5.1 centimeters) horizontal clearance shall be provided between parallel lines to allow for accessing all pipes.

Warning tapes shall be a minimum of 3 inches (7.6 centimeters) wide and shall run continuously for the entire length of all constant pressure mainline piping and low-voltage wire. The tape shall be installed in the trench 12 inches (30.5 centimeters) below finish grade. In a mainline trench, containing low-voltage control wire, the trench marker tapes shall be installed side by side.

13.4 Piping

All systems shall be designed to operate at a water velocity not to exceed 5 feet (1.5 meters) per second (fps). PVC pipe shall be a minimum of 0.5 to 1 inches (1.7 to 2.5 centimeters) in diameter with Sch. 40 fittings. Anything larger than 5.1 centimeters (2 inches) in diameter shall be Class 315 PVC pipe with Sch. 80 fittings. Fittings for 3-inch (7.6-centimeter) pipes and larger shall be solvent weld.

Non-pressure lateral pipe shall be Sch. 40 PVC pipe with Sch. 80 fittings. All end runs, regardless of head type, shall be 0.75 inches (1.9 centimeters) line size minimum, or 1inch (2.5 centimeters) if the head inlet is 1 inch (2.5 centimeters). On-grade piping is only allowed with the sports park design manager's approval.

Sleeving
Sleeving is required for all plastic irrigation pipe and electrical lines below paving. Extend sleeves a minimum of 12 inches (30.5 centimeters) beyond the paved surface above. All sleeves for irrigation lines shall be Sch. 40 PVC pipe two times the diameter of the pipe to be enclosed.

All sleeves for electrical lines shall be 2 inches (5.1 centimeters) Sch. 40 PVC pipe unless the wire bundle diameter exceeds 1 inch (2.5 centimeters). Size the sleeve accordingly to achieve pipe size for the sleeve to be twice the diameter of the wire bundle.

Wiring

A minimum of two spare control wires shall be run along each mainline branch to the furthest valve manifold. Bundle and tape 10 feet (3 meters) of additional wire and install in a pull box adjacent to the valve manifold. All control wires shall be color coded.

No splices will be allowed on runs of less than 500 feet (152.4 meters). On runs of greater than 500 feet (152.4 meters), splices are to be made with an approved splice unit, soldered, and installed in a concrete pull box.

14 Planting

14.1 General requirements

Planting design shall be appropriate for the site and climate conditions and shall aesthetically enhance the sports park site and the sports park user's experience.

All planting shall be located to permit the proper operation of irrigation systems and the effective use of mechanized maintenance equipment. Plant locations and spacing shall permit normal plant development without undue crowding or trimming. Shrubs, groundcover and vines should be spaced at half of their mature diameter from all walkways.

All existing and manufactured slopes greater than 4:1 and more than 5 feet (1.5 meters) in height shall be revegetated.
All sports parking areas shall provide a minimum of 5 percent of the sports parking area as landscape area. Within the sports parking area, one 24-inch (61-centimeter) box tree shall be provided within 30 feet (9.1 meters) of each sports parking space. The required trees shall be located in a minimum of 40 square feet (3.7 square meters) of landscape area. Sports parking areas that are adjacent to public rights-of-way shall provide a 30-inch-high (76.2-centimeter-high) screen. Plants may be used to screen the sports parking area if the plants selected will provide a 30-inch-high (76.2-centimeter-high) screen within two years. Curbs (minimum 6 inches [15 centimeters]) are required to protect all landscape areas within sports parking areas.

Plants in lawn areas shall be spaced to permit the most effective use of mechanized maintenance equipment and operation of irrigation system. There shall be 12 horizontal feet (4 meters) between trees and other vertical objects in the sports parks. For all trees installed in lawn areas, provide a non-lawn area of 2-foot (60-centimeter) radius from the baseline of each tree trunk to the edge of the lawn area. The radius around the tree trunk shall have a layer of mulch to prevent weed growth. There shall be no mulch on the crown of the tree. Dense tree groves should be excluded from lawn areas, or provide a continuous surface of bark mulch under the grove.

Ornamental shrub beds in sports parks and around sports parks buildings may be provided with approval from the local city project manager. Shrubs/vines adjacent to building walls should have a mature height that preserves visual access. Provide a 2-foot (60-centimeter) layer of shredded bark mulch in all shrub areas.

Groundcover shall be planted with triangular spacing at a distance that will typically ensure 100 percent coverage within one year of installation. Lawn shall be used for passive and active recreation. Lawn areas should be of a size and configuration to permit the most effective use of mechanized maintenance equipment and reduce lawn edging. Small, decorative lawn areas are discouraged.

Non-planted areas must be covered with a 2-foot (60-centimeter) layer of shredded bark mulch.

Plant material used adjacent to coastal bluffs shall be native or naturalized to minimize the need for irrigation beyond initial plant establishment. Existing exotic and other plant material that requires regular irrigation should be removed and replaced with native or naturalized plant material.

14.2 Plant selection

Plant shall be those species that are considered relatively disease- and pest-free and require minimal trimming to be maintained in a safe and attractive condition. The sports parks and recreation department retains the right to prohibit any plant material generally known to require excessive maintenance, because of factors such as, but not limited to, disease, pest control, troublesome root development, ultimate size and difficult growth habits. Non-native invasive plants shall not be used unless approved by the sports parks and recreation department.

Trees shall be selected to provide a succession of growth, enhance the uniqueness of the site, and provide shade and seasonal interest. To provide a succession of growth, an even mix of fast-growing and slow-growing trees shall be provided (e.g. a mix of acacia trees with oak trees). To enhance the uniqueness of the site, tree species shall be selected that create a sense of place (palm trees at beach locations or sycamore trees for inland areas). To provide shade and seasonal interest, an even mix of evergreen and deciduous trees shall be provided.

The use of drought-tolerant or native-plant material that is particularly compatible with the local environment is encouraged to promote water conservation and reduce maintenance costs.

The preferred lawn species is one that is drought-tolerant and stays green throughout the year.

All non-irrigated seed mixes shall be installed in October to February (in temperate continental climate area) only.

14.3 Installation criteria

Horticultural suitability soil tests The consultant shall obtain a horticultural suitability soil test on the site soil and incorporate the results and recommendations into the construction plans and specifications. The test results shall determine the type and rate of soil amendments, whether leaching is a requirement, and the post-maintenance requirements.

Tree staking Trees shall be staked.

Root barriers Trees located within 5 feet (12.7 centimeters) of walkways, walls, etc. shall be installed with root barriers. The root barrier shall be installed adjacent to the walkway or wall and not around the rootball. The length of the root barrier shall be a minimum of 10 feet (3 meters) from the center of the trunk in both directions of the tree and 24 inches (61 centimeters) deep. Root barrier shall be made of a rib system, polyethylene material with a minimum thickness of 0.08 inch (2 centimeters).

Tree grates Grates shall have expandable center openings and they must meet accessibility requirements. Concrete tree grates are not acceptable.

Lawn installation Seeded lawn areas shall have a germination/establishment period of 120 days prior to acceptance, and sod shall have a growth period of 90 days prior to acceptance.

15 Lighting

15.1 General design requirements

All designs shall comply with the applicable local city requirements, including, but not limited to, traffic signal and street lighting requirements. Light fixture and plant locations should be coordinated so that plants and trees at maturity do not obscure the lights.

Exterior lighting design
During the design phase, the designer shall provide to the sports parks project manager point-to-point drawings showing illumination levels of the playing surfaces, extending 150 feet (45.7 meters) beyond the playing surface in all directions. The drawings will be used to verify the amount of spill lighting, or trespass light outside the playing area.

Interior lighting design
Interior sports lighting systems shall consider the use of tubular-type skylights to minimize the use of artificial light during the day. The designer shall evaluate gymnasium sports lighting systems including use of pulse start metal halide and multi-ballast fluorescent fixtures.

During the design of all lighting systems, the designer shall consider the merits of using occupancy sensors and automatic lighting control systems to switch lights. This includes but is not limited to automatic lighting controls, day lighting controls, and programmable lighting controllers to minimize energy consumption from lighting.

Exterior lighting spill and glare requirements
All exterior lighting systems shall have internal reflectors to reduce light pollution. All security lighting and parking-lot pole-mounted lighting shall be cut off. The other exception is sport lighting; this type of lighting shall be 1500 watt metal halide. All lighting systems shall use internal reflectors and exterior louvers to reduce light pollution.

Underground conduit improvements shall be in Sch.40 PVC pipe, minimum size of 1 inch (2.5 centimeters). Above-ground conduit improvements shall be in galvanized, rigid, steel pipe. When adjacent to a sidewalk, the conduit shall be installed parallel to the sidewalk, 6 inches (15.2 centimeters) beyond the edge of the sidewalk.

Pull boxes shall be placed in the sidewalk or within concrete areas where possible. Pull boxes must be a minimum of 10 feet (3 meters) from all drainage inlets. Pull boxes are required at each light standard when light standards are placed further than 50 feet (15.2 meters) apart. Pull boxes shall be concrete with a bolt-down cover. All light poles located in lawn areas shall have a concrete mow curb around the base.

Light poles and irrigation head layout shall be coordinated to allow for full irrigation coverage and to avoid spraying poles. The bottom anchor bolts and nuts for all light poles shall be grout covered. Metal shrouds provided by the manufacturer shall be installed. A midget ferrule fuse shall be provided in the base of each light pole. All outdoor lighting facilities shall be flush mounted and installed in lockable and vandal-proof enclosures.

Local city maintenance trucks must have access to all light poles for relamping and maintenance purposes. New lights are installed with a boom mounted on a truck. A typical truck weighs 12 tons with outriggers extending to 14 feet (4.3 meters). All new paving and walkways shall be designed to provide access and support the maintenance trucks. All software needs to change times or zones.

15.2 Security lighting

All sports parks shall be designed with security lighting along the walkways and sports parking areas (where possible, security lights are to be mounted on building walls). The minimum amount of lighting along all walkways and in sports parking areas shall be 0.5-foot (15.2-centimeter) candles, with a uniformity rate of 6.

The refractor shall be UV stabilized, prismatic acrylic, or polycarbonate. The mast-arm type shall be the slip-on type. Each fixture shall be individually switched by means of a twist-lock photocell. Lighting circuit shall be energized by means of a timer, so that each system has the capability of being switched off at a pre-determined time.

15.3 Multipurpose field and court lighting

Lighting shall meet the skill level of the highest play activity that is being provided. The design shall use the least number of light fixtures and electrical energy required to provide the specified lighting intensities. Spill and glare shall be minimized. Photometric data and lighting density calculations must be provided at plan check phase. (Refer to table 7.)

Tennis courts
50 foot-candles—measured at the net.
30 foot-candles—measured at the baseline.

Basketball/volleyball courts
If lighting is provided, light level should be evenly distributed across the courts. Optimum is a 30 fc minimum.

Table 7

		Horizontal	Vertical	Uniformity
Soccer	Recreational	20 fc	15 fc	3.0 max. to min.
	Amateur	30 fc	25 fc	2.0 max. to min.
Softball	Infield	30 fc	25 fc	3.0 max. to min.
	Outfield	20 fc	15 fc	3.5 max. to min.
Baseball and Little League	Infield	50 fc	40 fc	2.0 max. to min.
	Outfield	30 fc	25 fc	2.4 max. to min.

Tennis court and multipurpose court light switches

Control of sports lighting shall be accomplished with an 'on' button only, triggered by a timer, which shall turn lights off after a set time. Verify all court lighting requirements with the local city project manager. Each tennis court shall be lit independently. Individual 'on' buttons shall be located adjacent to each tennis court.

Multipurpose field light switches

Multipurpose field light switches shall be activated by means of an on–off switch located in a separate lockable (padlock) vandal-resistant enclosure. The 'on' switch shall be triggered by a timer. The clock shall turn the lights off at a predetermined time. Lighting for each softball and soccer field shall be on a separate system. Relay switches (contactors) of more than three poles or any other exotic switching equipment shall not be used.

Multipurpose field and court light pole standards

Lighting poles shall be a maximum height of 70 feet (21.3 meters). Field lighting poles shall be located outside the fenced play areas.

Lighting (other than for playing surfaces)

The provision of lighting enables appropriate recreational activities to be undertaken within parks outside of daylight hours. Lighting can help prevent crime through environmental design outcomes within public parks by illuminating areas of parks to increase casual surveillance and reduce the likelihood of inappropriate behavior in those areas, and conversely to discourage the public use of other areas outside of daylight hours.

Standard requirements for lighting (other than for playing surfaces)

For citywide sport and recreation and district sport parks, light all internal roads, parking areas, and primary pedestrian paths. For district recreation parks, light primary pedestrian paths.

Example alternative solutions
Within any park, lighting is provided to primary pedestrian paths or recreation nodes within the park where after-hours use is to be encouraged, or where there is a specific need for lighting in regards to equipment or facilities safety and security.

Constraints on alternative solutions
- The lighting should not extend use of the park or parts of the park that would result in detrimental amenity impacts (e.g. through light or noise disturbance to nearby residents or lead to inappropriate use of the park).
- The lighting must ensure safety in the park in situations where adequate illumination is not provided by an alternative source (e.g. street lighting).
- The lighting must be located, directed and shielded so as to avoid nuisance to nearby residents.[1]

16 User facility

16.1 General design standard

For citywide sports parks
- Spectator facilities adjacent to the main field, oval, or court provide a pavilion or earth bank/tiered seating (shaded by trees or structure).

Figure 16: Possible shade treatments for sports parks

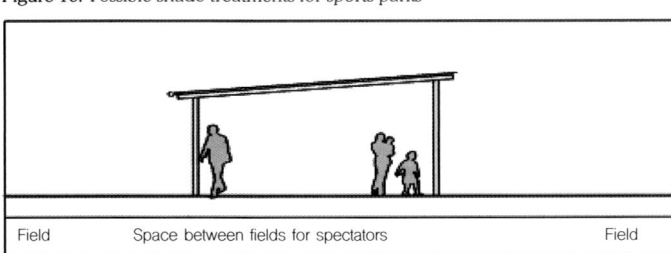

- A clubhouse (painted/colored block construction with custom orb roof, including two change rooms, first-aid room, referee room, meeting room, canteen, store room and public amenities incorporating five cubicles (unisex and disabled) each with toilet and washbasin).
- Overland stormwater flows pose no risk to facilities or increased risk of erosion on batters or playing areas.
- One free-standing public amenities building incorporating five cubicles (unisex and disabled) each with toilet and wash basin.

For local sports parks
- Spectator facilities and shade trees of approved species planted around the perimeter of fields or courts.
- A clubhouse (painted/colored block construction with custom orb roof, including two change rooms, first-aid room, meeting room, canteen, store room and public amenities incorporating five cubicles (unisex and disabled) each with toilet and wash basin).[1]

16.3 Examples for alternative solutions

Shaded spectator facilities
- Multiple small built structures providing clear views of the main playing areas.
- A series of raised mounds planted with shade trees or sloping areas or terraces providing shade from trees and views of competition areas. (Refer to figure 16.)

Club and player facilities
- Provision of change and toilet facilities to service competitors and officials, plus a shared (multiuse) meeting, storage and general use space(s), which can also provide officials or first-aid rooms during competition, provided as a separate building to the change and toilet facilities.
- An integrated 'amenities hub' providing for toilets, changing, meeting, kiosk/canteen and other spaces in a single building.[1]

16.4 Other requirements

All buildings must comply with relevant building codes and regulations. (Refer to figure 16.)
- Sufficient spectator shade should be provided to ensure that there is at least 430.6 square feet (40 square meters) per field and 269.1 square feet (25 square meters) per court.
- Built shade solutions should be low maintenance and consistent with any applicable city design or style guidelines.
- Location of player and spectator amenities must be central to playing fields and courts and designed for multiple users.[1]

17 Concessionary areas

To allow for the hosting of events and providing discretionary services to larger numbers of people, the provision of 'concessionary areas' within citywide sports parks is desirable.

17.1 Standard requirements

Three paved concessionary areas (nominal size of each area 16.4 by 26.4 feet [5 by 8 meters]) adjacent to internal roads in close proximity to activity areas or as extension to the car park.[1]

17.2 Examples for alternative solutions

Alternative solutions that may be considered include:
- alternative hardening treatments such as subsoil reinforcement instead of paving/roadway;
- a basic kiosk or kitchen space provided as part of an amenities hub available for casual hire by food/product vendors during sports events; and
- dedicated spaces within or close to the car park that can be reserved for concession uses.[1]

17.3 Constraints on alternative solutions

- Power and water should be available within 33 feet (10 meters) of any concessionary site.
- Sites should allow for safe user access without conflict with vehicles.
- Where provided in a car park, the site does not detrimentally affect the safe operation and function of the car park, and required levels of parking are maintained.[1]
(Refer to figure 17.)

18 Skate parks

18.1 Types of skate parks

The citywide skate park is the largest and highest order skate park (±19,400 square feet [±1800 square meters]). It is centrally located and attracts users from across the city. The citywide skate park will serve users of all skill levels; however, emphasis will be on intermediate to advanced skill users.

District skate parks are smaller in size than the citywide skate park (±9700 square feet [±900 square meters]). They are ideally located in a district park and/or near a community center and attract users from larger geographic regions of the city. District skate parks will serve users of all skill levels.

Neighborhood skate parks are the smallest in size (±2100 square feet [±200 square meters]). These skate parks are a local facility that focuses on introductory skateboarders and serves only the immediate community that the skate park is located within. The number of neighborhood skate parks will be determined on an as-needed basis, neighborhood by neighborhood.[1]

18.2 Skate park design

Site selection

Skate parks are considered a common public recreation facility that is of a similar order to an outdoor basketball court or outdoor tennis court. Where possible, skate park development should be included into larger park-improvement projects. The location must serve the proposed users within the service area. The location must be accessible to the proposed users. There must be a sufficient number of users in the service area to warrant the skate park development, where youth population approaches or exceeds 5000. There must be public amenities nearby to support skate-park users. Required support amenities include public transit, accessible pathways, trees,

Figure 17: Concession sites using car park space or reinforced grass area

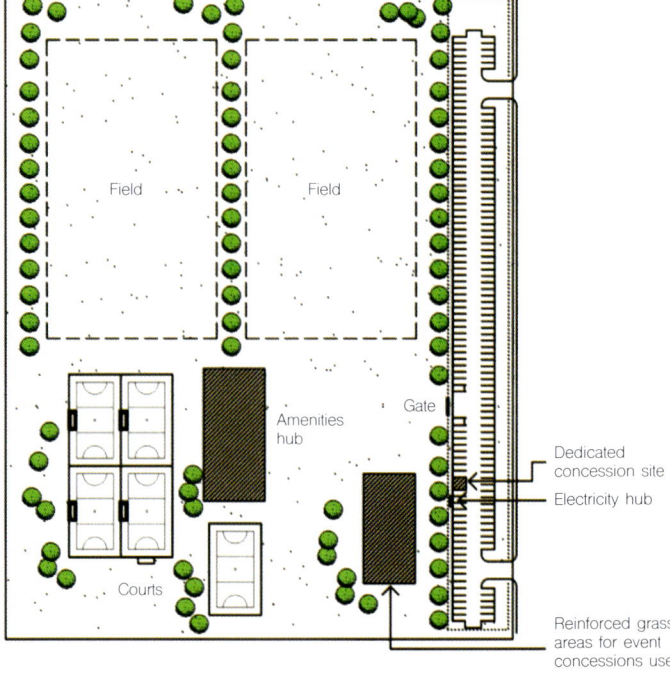

Note: Car park design is indicative only. Design of off-street car parking is to be in accordance with AS2890.1.

and benches. Within a reasonable distance, washrooms and vehicle parking shall be available. Optional support amenities include community centers. If there is a deficiency in required supporting infrastructure, there should be the ability to construct necessary supporting infrastructure (spatial and funding).

The skate park is compatible with the existing community and other park uses, as the well as overall area character. The park designated is a district park and/or contains a community center. If necessary, there are mitigating measures for addressing incompatibility (e.g. skate-park facility design, enhanced setbacks greater than 98 feet [30 meters]) with neighbors and/or other park uses, landscape treatments etc.

Graffiti

Skate-park graffiti tagging is subject to current policies and practices. These bylaws are being updated to a 'zero tolerance' standard. Such graffiti will be actively removed from skate parks. Graffiti-style murals that meet the local city's public art policies may be permitted at skate parks.

Design consultation

In determining the design of any new skate park or the expansion of an existing skate park, the skateboard community and other stakeholders shall be consulted.

Unique skate-park elements shall be considered for any new or expanded citywide or district skate park. The size, scale, and design of neighborhood skate parks may vary from location to location, based on community needs and site compatibility.

The minimum setback required between a skate park and a private residential property is 98.4 feet (30 meters). The minimum setback required between a skate park and other recreation facilities in sports parks is 49.2 feet (15 meters). Skate parks should be visible from one or more public streets.[2]

References

(1) Ipswich, Australia
Ipswich City Council (Australia) Implementation Guideline No. 27 Guidance on Recreation Range and Opportunity Outcomes Arising from Embellishment of Public Parks
www.ipswichplanning.com.au

(2) City of London, UK
Outdoor Skate Park Implementation Strategy
www.london.ca

(3) City of San Diego, USA
Consultant's Guide to Park Design and Development
www.sandiego.gov

St Kilda

Location /
St Kilda, Australia

Area /
4.5 acres (1.8 hectares)

Completion date /
2012

Landscape design /
CONVIC

Client /
City of Port Phillip

The Marina Reserve skate space is located on Marine Parade, St Kilda, approximately 6.2 miles (10 kilometers) from Melbourne's city center. The Marina Reserve is a triangular open space that abuts the St Kilda Marina, the foreshore to the south. The design process included an extensive period of community consultation and feedback workshops to address the contentious nature of the project due to the prime location of the development, as well as environmental site constraints.

The design team responded directly to the local residents and park users, taking account of the broader St Kilda Marina, as a pivotal node and parkland space, to the more extensive foreshore promenade, breathing life into and reinvigorating a desolate pocket of space abutting the St Kilda Marina site. The transformation of this vestige of land has been successfully achieved by creating a central hub of ongoing community and pedestrian activity. The space is focused on catering to the community's young people and engaging them in this waterfront destination in a holistic manner, providing integrated circulation and a promenade pathway along the boundaries of the space to openly connect the bay, marina, and street.

This is the latest open-space addition to the City of Port Philip's ongoing development of the St Kilda foreshore. The St Kilda Marina Reserve will evolve with changing interests, needs, and trends, and will provide a versatile and integrated space for future generations of young people. This stage of the Marina Reserve project was commissioned by the City of Port Phillip as a master plan in 2009, with the opening in February 2013. The City of Port Phillip decided to update the Marina Reserve to revitalize a coastal public open space to become a more inviting community recreational environment with the inclusion of a skate facility.

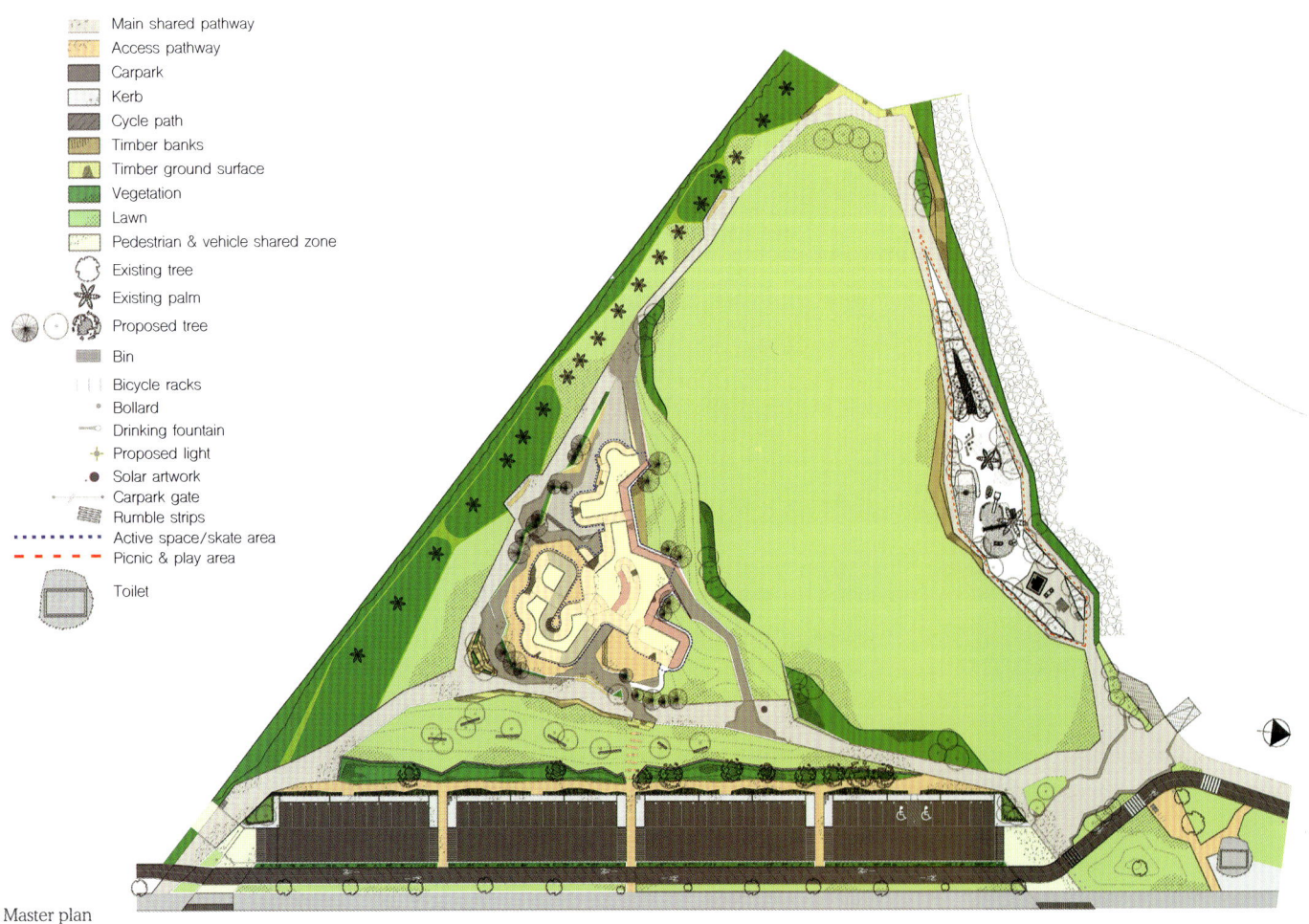

Master plan

01–03
/ Aerial photos of the whole park

The Marina Reserve skate space is a space for everyone, with a focus on unstructured passive and active recreation catering for all age groups, skills, and abilities. It sits as a pivotal open space and bookend activity node to the St Kilda Esplanade. The public open space is focused on a highly textured, colored, and fluid skate facility. The Marina Reserve design plays on the sites angularity and three view aspects to create an inviting and welcoming open space, broadening appeal of the bay foreshore, and catering to the breadth of the community.

The progressive approach to social sustainability recognizes the importance of providing for young people in areas other than structured sport and education. The St Kilda Marina Reserve is a great example of creating a central, accessible public open space that provides a range of active, passive, and social pursuits for all ages, which can adapt over time to meet evolving interests and needs of young people.

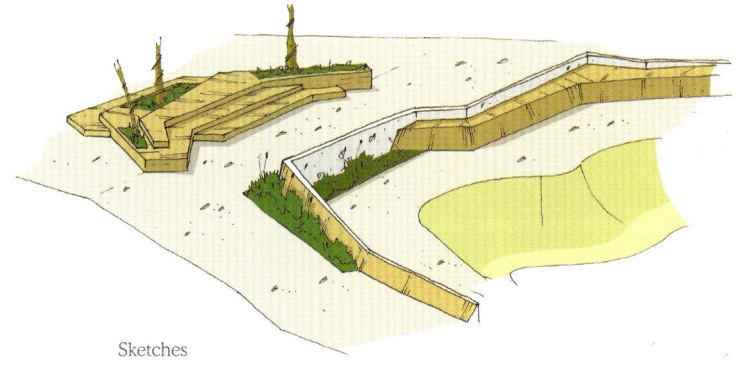
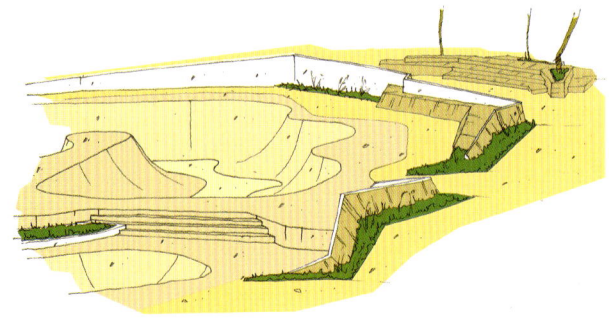

Sketches

04
/ Aerial photo of skating area
05–07
/ Local people enjoy time in the park

Blandan Park

Location /
Lyon, France

Area /
50 acres (20 hectares)

Completion date /
2013

Landscape design /
BASE mandator Landscape designer + Explorations architecture + OGI + ON + CSD

Budget /
€23 million

Photography /
Bruce Buck

In the heart of Lyon, on the old Sergent Blandan barracks from 1830, a new public space of 50 acres (20 hectares) opened in 2013. On this unusual site, which was ignored for a long time, new urban, contemporary and exclusive uses have been planned for the wider community of Lyon. The issues to consider are memory and military history, plant revitalisation and urban renewal, sharing and appropriation, and sports and games. Around the central fortifications, the ancient logic of defensive fronts and bastions is transformed. New spaces of discovery, escape, and meeting are organized among the expansive plains, horticulture, parade grounds, ramparts, and many areas that give rise to specific uses, all of which resonate with the history of the site.

The first part was completed in 2013, and turned this site into the third urban park in Lyon. Very open and based on specific uses, sport and sustainability, this first part offers exclusive, athletic and playful activities. It also gives rise to singular spaces where the waste lands mingle with the historical vestiges and modern equipment, while still remaining accessible to the public (skate park, playground, sport ground, and so on). The parade ground, a new public space of 4 acres (1.6 hectares), can be accessed 24/7. It is in front of the university campus, and served by tram T4, so it has quickly become a new social theatre, a meeting place, and a popular spot for spontaneous gatherings, though it is also liable to flood on rainy days.

① Chateau
② Bastion solarium
③ Central pelouse
④ Bastion nature
⑤ Glacis
⑥ Skate park
⑦ Badminton
⑧ Halle area
⑨ Mini-foot

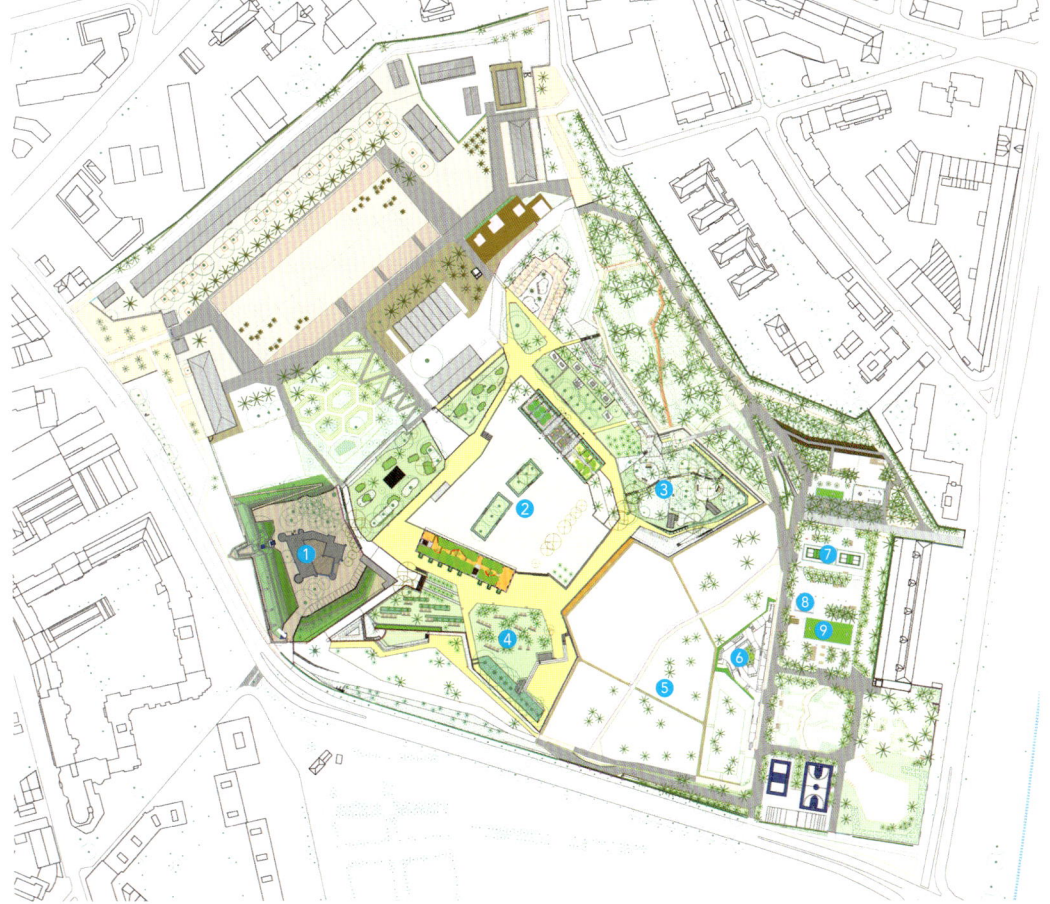

Master plan

01
/ Panorama view of whole Blandan Park

02
/ Table tennis area

03
/ Aerial view of paths in the park
04
/ Local kids enjoying time in the park
05
/ Badminton field
06
/ Local kids playing sports in the park

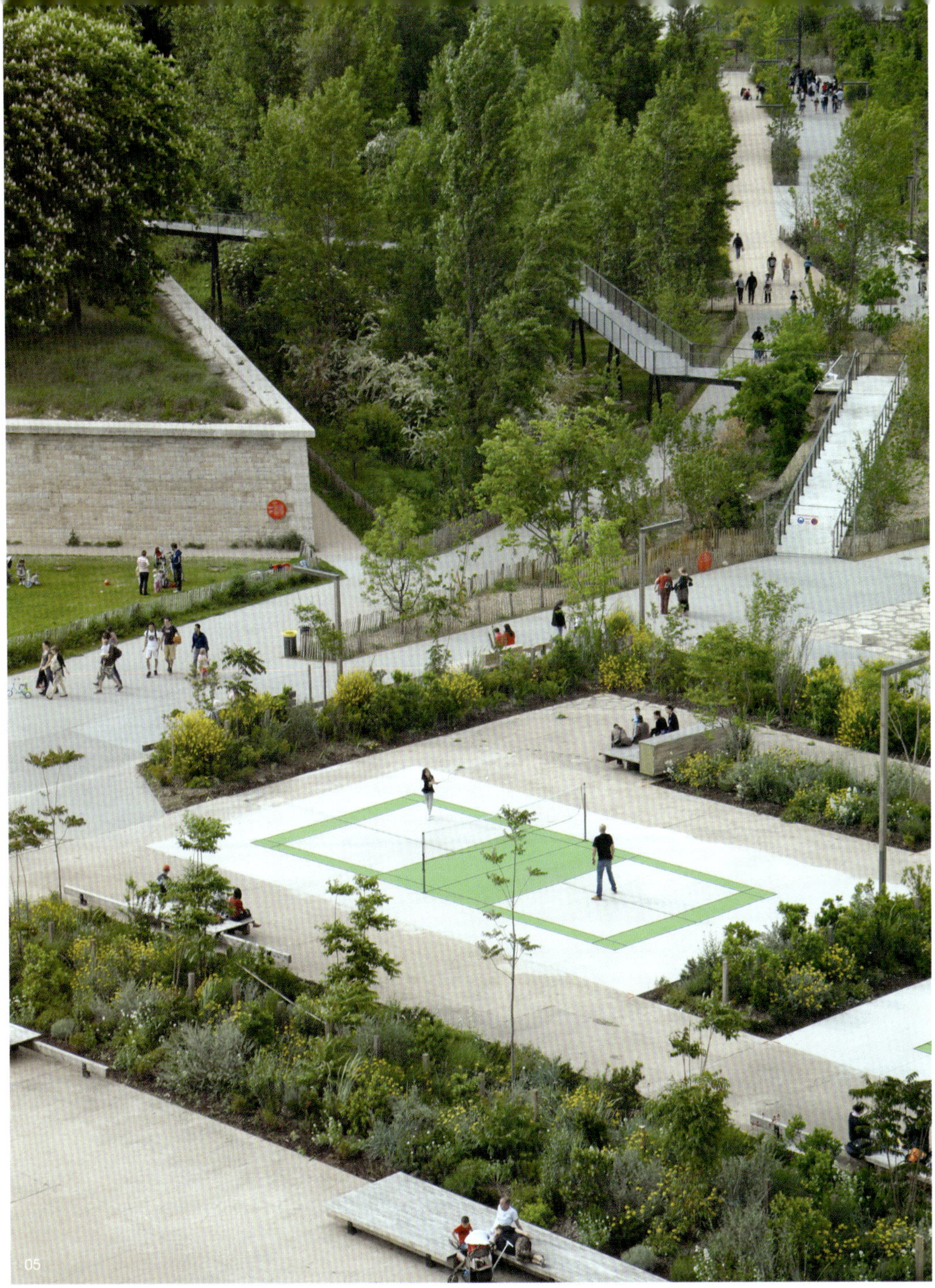
05

06

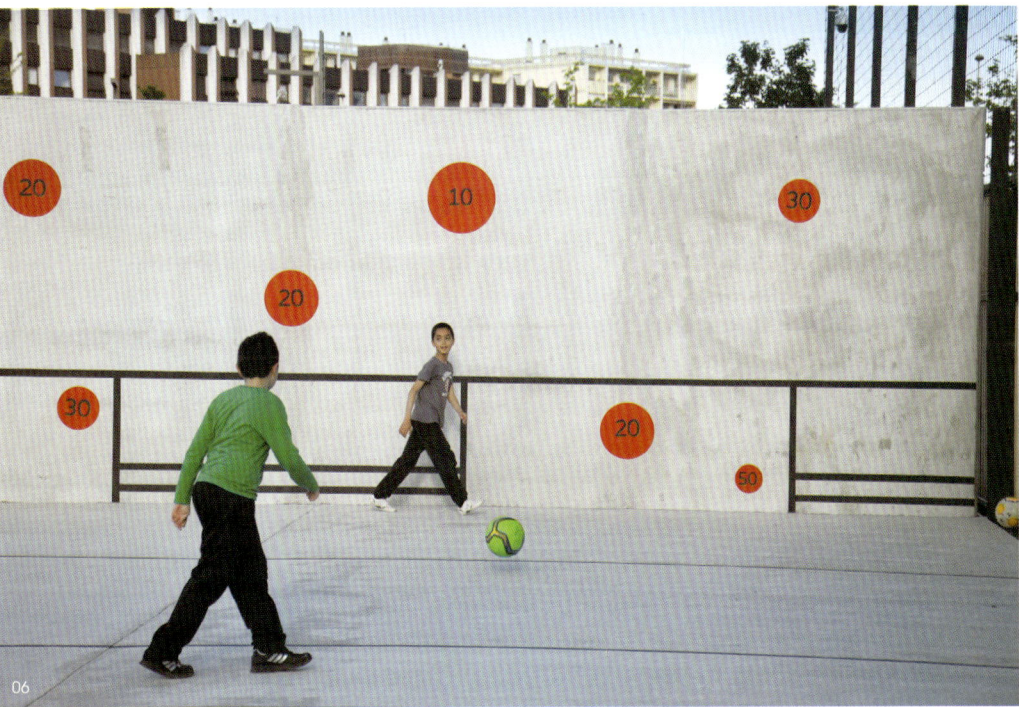

07

08

44

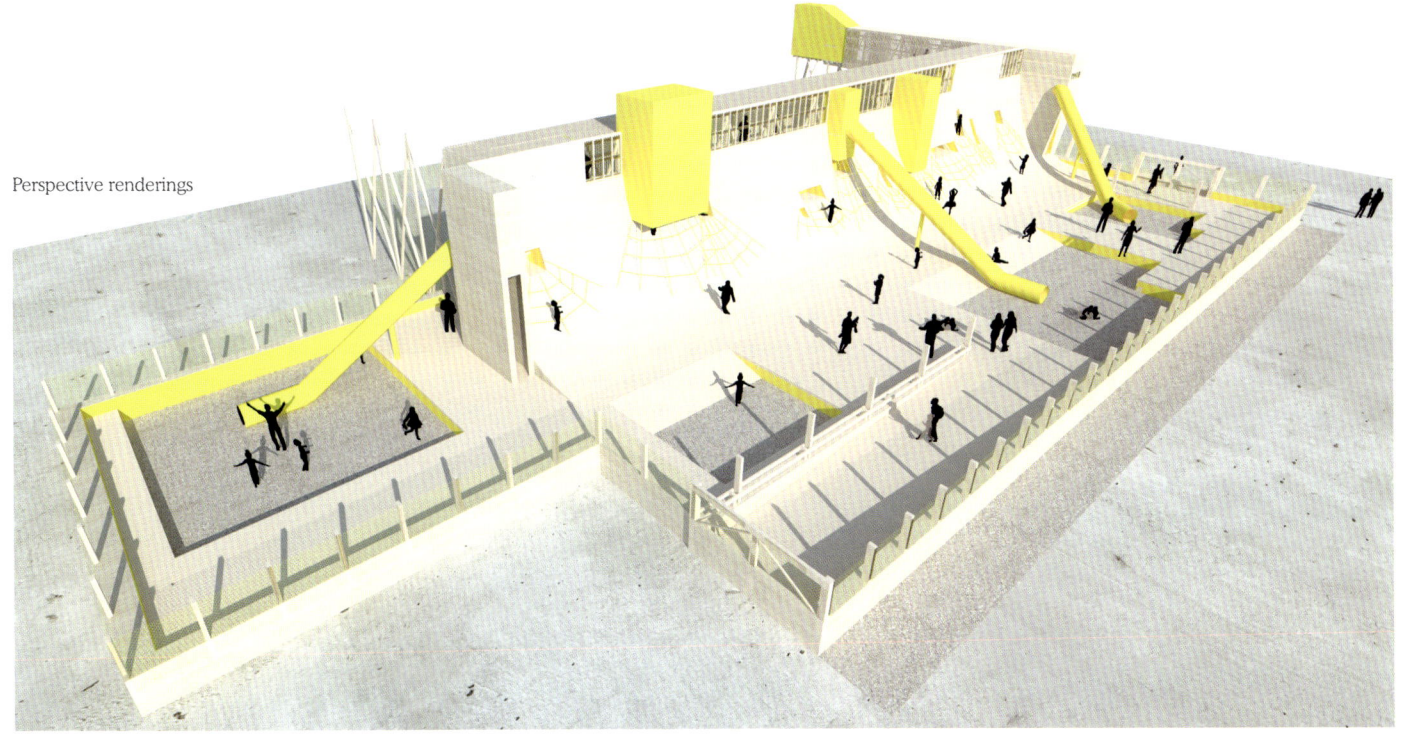

Perspective renderings

07–08
/ Climbing facilities for children of all ages
09–10
/ Wooden facilities are safe for children to play

11

11
/ Aerial view of planting area
12
/ Local residents love to spend free time in this park
13
/ Aromatic plants turn into blossoms
14
/ Kids playing on the bench in the park
15
/ Wooden bench provides resting places

Chinguacousy Sports Park Redevelopment

Location /
Brampton, Ontario, Canada

Area /
**37,350 square feet
(3470 square meters)**

Completion date /
2012

Architecture design /
MacLennan Jaunkalns Miller Architects

Budget /
CA$14,650,000

Photography /
Shai Gil

Client /
City of Brampton

Awards /
**Athletic Business Architectural Showcase Facility of Merit Design Award
Ontario Association of Architects (OAA) Design Excellence Award
Brampton Urban Design Award of Excellence**

The Chinguacousy Sports Park Redevelopment project comprises a new chalet/clubhouse for the ski hill, an outdoor volleyball complex, a skateboard and BMX park, the renovation of the tennis/curling club, and a new Park Amenity and Boat Pavilion, which is integrated into the watercourse within the park. The new facilities are all linked by new landscaping and a pedestrian pathway system. Chinguacousy Sports Park is a civic landmark in Brampton, a local and regional destination, that hosts numerous park activities. The goal of the redevelopment is to create a welcoming community hub capable of sustaining year-long recreational activity, and to transform the park into a beautiful sequence of indoor and outdoor spaces. The new facilities have been designed using a consistent vocabulary of forms and palette of materials. Each building has a series of terraces and shaded deck areas overlooking the park, reinforcing the indoor–outdoor intentions of the complex.

The new facilities are a core group of structures within the larger park system, designed to modernize the park, develop a consistency in the park architecture, and link the program areas. Sustainable features include natural daylight in all buildings, deep building overhangs for sunlight control, and the use of interior and exterior recyclable materials. The buildings feature highly efficient mechanical and electrical systems, energy management controls, and reflective roofing systems. All buildings within the park and watercourse area have incorporated water retention systems. The tennis and curling facility has adapted and reused the existing curling rink.

The chalet and tennis/curling facilities have revitalized the core commercial aspects of the park and added to the interior programs available, as well as adding features to the park that connected to these buildings. The Park Amenity and Boat Pavilion has added new programs to an under-used area of the park, and supports the playground and picnic area. The redevelopment elevates the architectural and service ambitions in this important and popular park. It is intended that these new core elements will inform the future development of new facilities and programs.

01
/ Skate park and chalet/clubhouse
02
/ BMX park and chalet/clubhouse

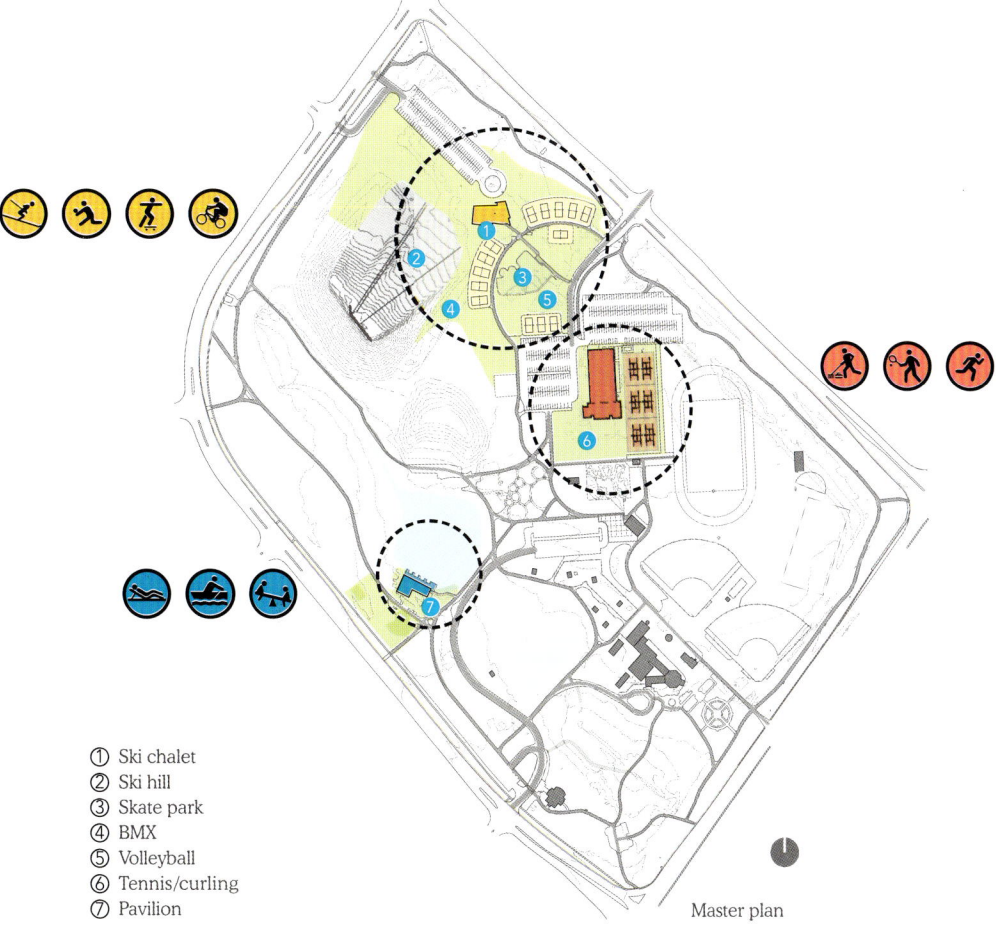

① Ski chalet
② Ski hill
③ Skate park
④ BMX
⑤ Volleyball
⑥ Tennis/curling
⑦ Pavilion

Master plan

03–04
/ Skate park and chalet/clubhouse
05
/ Chalet/clubhouse

Site plan

① Vestibule
② Auditorium
③ Ski shop
④ Concourse
⑤ Concession
⑥ Storage
⑦ Kitchen/bar
⑧ Storage
⑨ Sprinkler
⑩ Lobby
⑪ Ski instructor school
⑫ Reception
⑬ Administration office
⑭ Vending
⑮ Lockers
⑯ Janitor
⑰ Tuning
⑱ Equipment

06–09
/ Paddleboat pavilion

53

Bijlmerpark

Location /
Amsterdam, The Netherlands
Area /
90,417 square feet (8400 square meters) (sports and play zone)
Completion date /
2011
Landscape design /
Mecanoo
Playground design /
Mecanoo in collaboration with Marie-Laure Hoedemakers
Photography /
Harry Cock, Carve
Client /
District Amsterdam Zuidoost

The Bijlmerpark is the main park in Amsterdam's Southeast district, Bijlmermeer. This 1960s and 1970s modernistic suburb of Amsterdam had developed numerous social problems by the end of the 1980s. It was characterized by high-rise residential buildings and disjunctive infrastructural networks for pedestrians, cyclists and motorists, with few services or facilities. A radical, integral restructuring process was initiated. The renewal of the Bijlmerpark was the final chapter in this process. A move from quantity to quality became the policy for the redevelopment. Bijlmerpark was to remain the main park in the built-up area, and was also identified as a new residential environment with a plan for approximately 900 dwellings. The main components would be a park encircling a central sports facility, and residential units along the flanks of the park. The concept reconfigured the spatial and social structure. The new housing faces the park, providing eyes and ears on the park. The central position of the sports park means it is within walking distance of the residents.

The sports and game esplanade in the center of the park was intended as a bypass of the main route, the circular pedestrian and bicycle route. The esplanade embraces several elements: a ball court, the playing strip, the 'king crawler', a skate park, and a water and sand playground.

The paved multisports court includes a stage and ball-catchers with 'professional'-grade boulder routes. A series of yellow frames on bright and sparkling pink safety surfacing forms the playing strip, containing different types of rope bridges and a zipline connecting to the 'king crawler'. The 'king crawler' structure is a multilevel playing wall that incorporates two toilets and facilities for the playground manager. The playing strip is located at the foot of two rolling green hills with trees. On top of the hill, a skate park consisting of two connected pools is hidden, with banks and stairs coming down to ground level again. On top of the other hill there is a water and sand playground, a colorful landscape for younger children, with sandboxes and water jets.

Plan drawing

Sports and game esplanade

01
/ Elegant lanes connect the northern and southern parts of the park

02

03

02
/ Butterfly hill
03
/ View from the butterfly hill
04–05
/ The southern part of the park is a nature park with a lot of water and large fields with colorful plants and bridges
06
/ Elegant lanes and bridges meander alongside solitary trees, water, small islands and loping hillocks

07–09
/ Bijlmerpark is a park for the neighborhood, featuring a great diversity of areas for different interests
10
/ Artisanal braided 'lace' fence work decorated with patterns surrounds the sports fields
11
/ Sports fields for organized activities are located in the middle of the park
12
/ Water play area

60

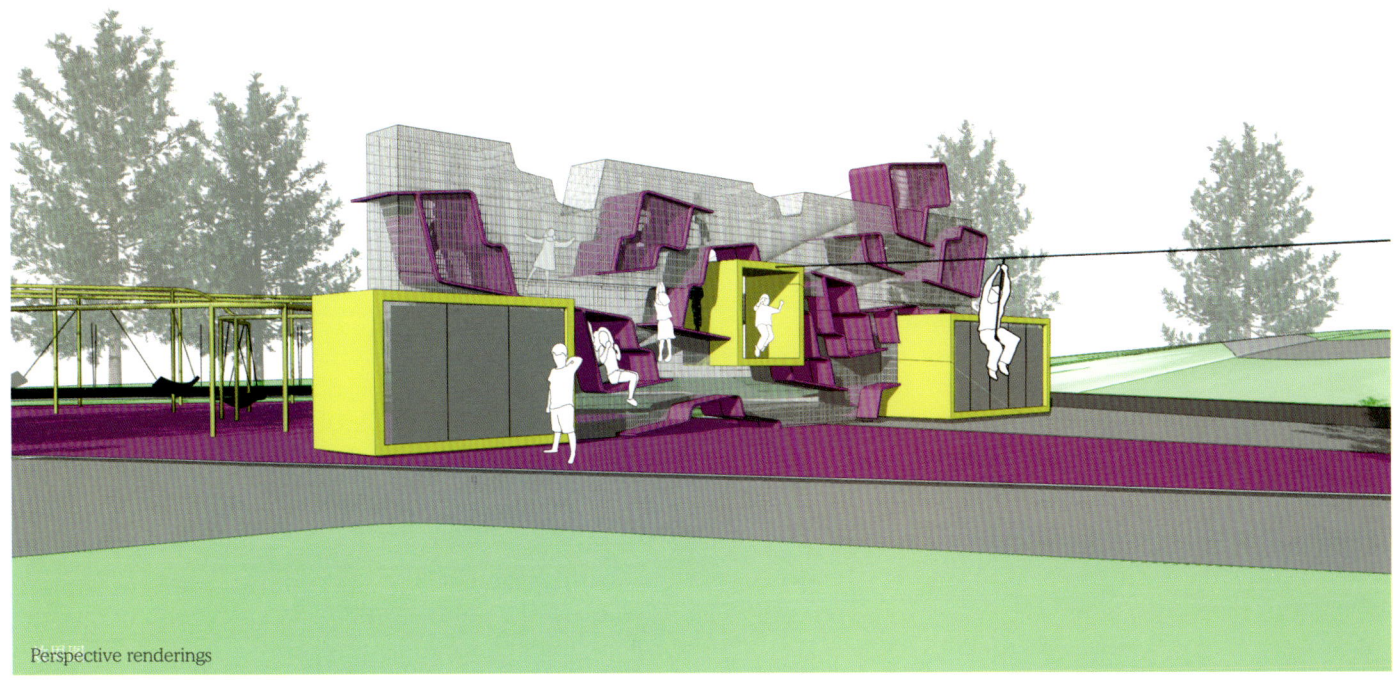
Perspective renderings

13
/ King crawler multilevel playing wall with public toilets and a space for the playground manager
14
/ A zipline connects the king crawler to the other part of the playground
15–16
/ Climbing parkours
17
/ The king crawler contains two slides

Freestyle Park

Location /
Zurich, Switzerland
Area /
**91,493 square feet
(8500 square meters)**
Completion date /
2013
Landscape and architecture design /
Streiff Architekten GmbH
Budget /
4,645,000 Swiss francs
Photography /
Michael Lio, Winterthur
Client /
City of Zurich, Building Department

In response to inadequate facilities for practicing freestyle sports, such as skateboarding, inline skating, and BMX riding, the City of Zurich planned and realized a Freestyle Park. The Freestyle Park Association of Zurich initiated the long and drawn-out political process.

The transition space between the city and a large, open, green common called Allmend offered an ideal location for the project. In three triangular parcels between Allmend Street and the existing sports fields, the Freestyle Park nominates specific uses. The street area serves as a simulation of a dense city, with stairs, ramps, railings, and walls. The central area indicates a flat practice field, ideal for beginners. A monolithic concrete pavilion houses infrastructure that serves the bike park. The bike park is situated on the opposite side of Allmend Street, and is directly connected with an underpass. The pool area is made up of organically shaped pools of varying difficulty, and is accessed over a drivable bridge. The bridge crosses over where the underpass connects to the green common, thereby separating the public space from the sports facilities.

A spectator area is set up over the entire facility on a slightly raised level. An important criterion in the planning of this free-of-charge public facility was to ensure suitability for all age groups, while covering all ability levels. The complex had to offer something for everyone from beginners to professional riders. Up to 80 people can use the facility simultaneously.

The design of the facility is based on a simple, site-specific approach: the far view into the green common from the sports hall and from Allmend Street should not be obstructed by massive or tall obstacles. The result is a continual digging into the earth, sloping down to the lowest point in the center of the complex. The low-lying pedestrian path can be hooked into, offering the riders a natural flow toward the center. When viewed from the Allmend, the green ramps and obstacles reveal the full embedded nature of the skate park. The continuous detailing and material usage (asphalt, concrete, galvanized steel) strengthen the image of the overall complex. With the exception of the bridge and pavilion, all concrete surfaces are allowed to be covered in graffiti. Tree groves and solitary trees punctuate the facility in recognition of the greater design concept: the green common, Allmend.

① Sihl-City
② Bike park, Allmend
③ Freestyle Park, Allmend

Master plan

01
/ Bridge, connecting pool and street area
02
/ Central area
03
/ Pavilion

04–05
/ Overview of the street area
06–07
/ Center of the street area

08

09

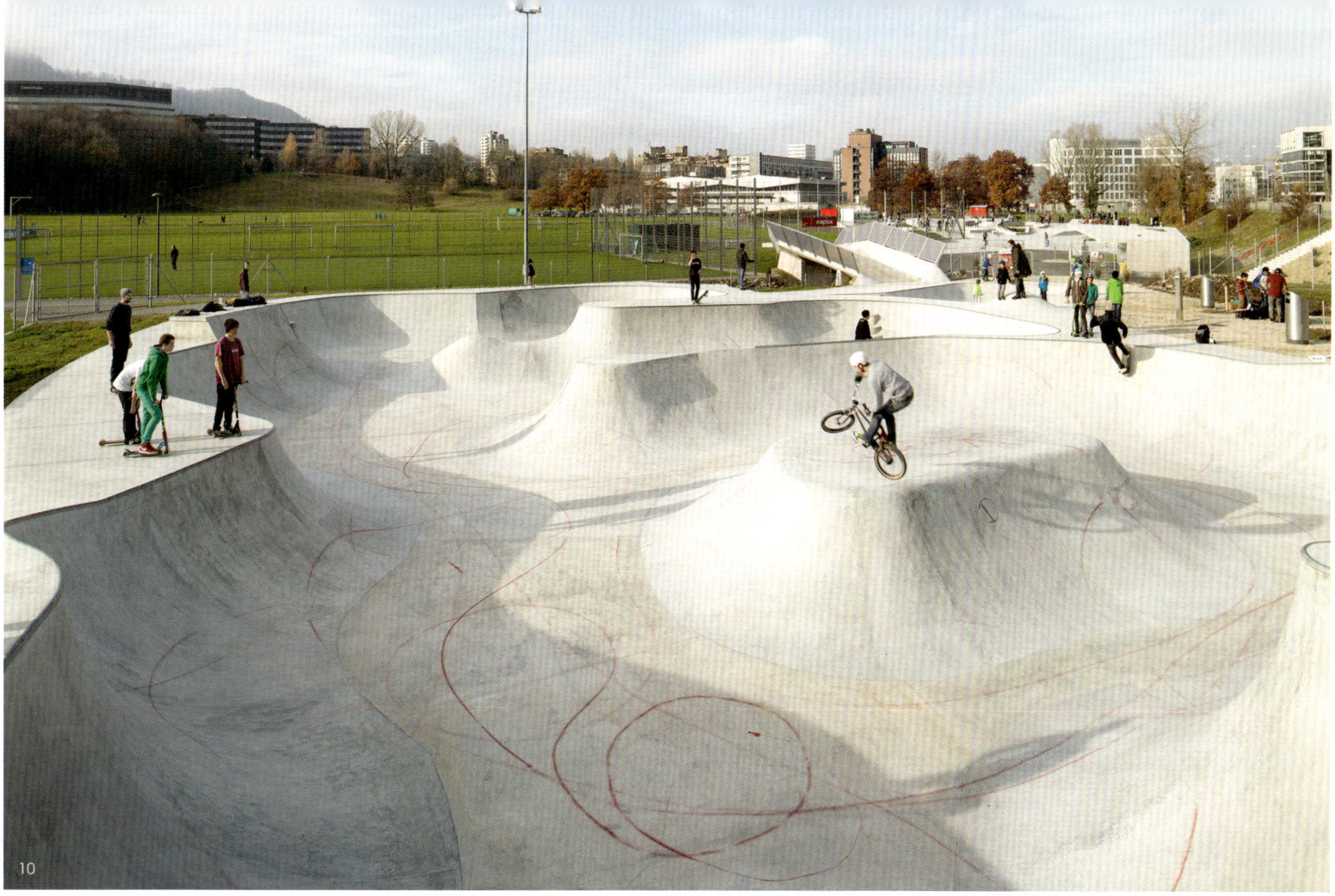

10

11

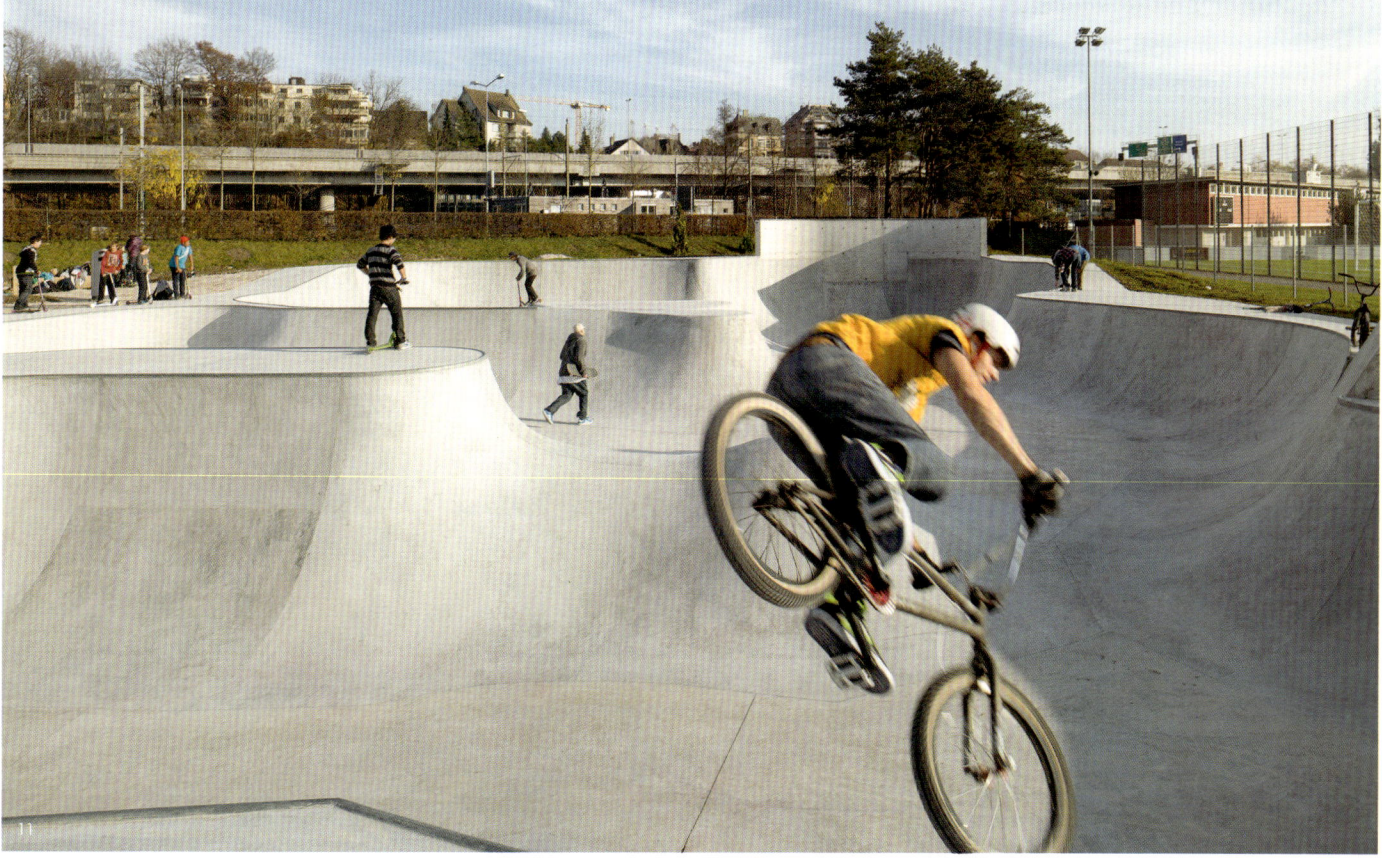

08
/ Pool area
09
/ Pool area, beginner's pool and bridge
10
/ Overview pool area
11
/ Pool area, wall ride in the background

Heerenschürli Sport Complex

Location /
Zurich, Switzerland

Area /
1044 square feet (97 square meters)

Completion date /
2010

Landscape design /
TOPOTEK 1

Photography /
Hanns Joosten

Client /
Park Development Agency

Awards /
Competition 1st prize

The design approach for the Heerenschürli Sport Complex addressed urban design issues that were facing the surrounding neighborhood. This neighborhood at the edge of Zurich is a homogenous community, constructed in the 1950s and 1960s, that found itself deprived of usable public space.

Heerenschürli serves as a hybrid sports complex and public park, giving the neighborhood facilities for organized sports as well as general leisure activities. A public square with seating and a restaurant are integrated into the complex; the lawns themselves are also open to the public—accessible even when the local athletic clubs are closed.

With its right-angle grid base and intense vertical extrusions, the design concept embodies the urban density that the homogenous neighborhood is missing. A strong axial grid of paved roads for pedestrians and cyclists provides access to the complex, joining the southern neighborhood of Mattenhof to Uberlandstrasse in the north, and connecting the new Hirzenbach tram loop in the west with the Stettbach grasslands to the east. The navigational system of the complex echoes a system of downtown alleys, pathways and squares, with the ball courts acting as city blocks. High ball fences accentuate the compact nature of the complex, and are required for safety and spatial division. Heerenschürli's ball fences are not requisite eyesores, but designed objects in themselves: loud, green, oversized and hyper-functional. The fences are doubled to create a visual game, opening and closing the view to the ball fields as the viewer moves.

Visual unity of the complex was achieved by a set of design principles based on color and materiality. The project's competition title, Immergrün, or evergreen, embodies the color concept, which originated from a fascination withthe unchanging, artificial green grass in a sports complex. All metal structures in Heerenschüli up to 19.7 feet (6 meters) in height are painted green. The second principle applies to the concrete constructions and the asphalt, both of which retain their original colors of grey and black, respectively, giving the immense sea of green a solid neutral base. Two shades of green are used throughout the complex, reflecting the separation of indoor and outdoor spaces. The colossal, doubled green fences are unique to Heerenschürli, and create a dynamic moiré, veiling the sports fields, and exposing the spectators for what they are: participants in fleeting athletic voyeurism.

Master plan

01–02
/ Panorama views from different sides

03

04

70

03
/ Food and beverage area
04
/ Audience seating area
05
/ High ball fences
06–07
/ Football field

Aqua Soccer

Location /
Hamburg, Germany

Area /
6727 square feet (625 square meters)

Completion date /
2013

Landscape design /
TOPOTEK 1

Budget /
€45,000

Photography /
Hanns Joosten

Client /
International Garden Exhibition Hamburg

The Aqua Soccer installation at the 2013 Hamburg International Garden Show aspired to take a conventional game and introduce it in a new context. The Aqua Soccer installation offered a fun twist on the traditional sport. Conventional soccer is played on a flat, rectilinear lawn with wide, straight shots made to the opposing goal. At the Aqua Soccer installation, the field conditions of soccer were intentionally inverted; everything that was once simple became a struggle: fast movements were difficult, straight shots were nearly impossible, the goals did not align with each other, and the playing field was drastically narrowed. Most importantly, the field surface was rubberized and filled with water.

Playing this revitalized game of soccer became a provocative adventure, guided by new rules and free thought. The hybrid game contextualized soccer as a water sport, bringing humour and transgression to the conventional game. The imaginations of the players were pushed to find new strategies that would allow them to play the new game successfully. The Aqua Soccer installation pushed the boundaries of traditional play activities in order to revitalize an old game.

01
/ Aqua Soccer, with the Dymaxion Golf behind
02
/ The playground is filled with water

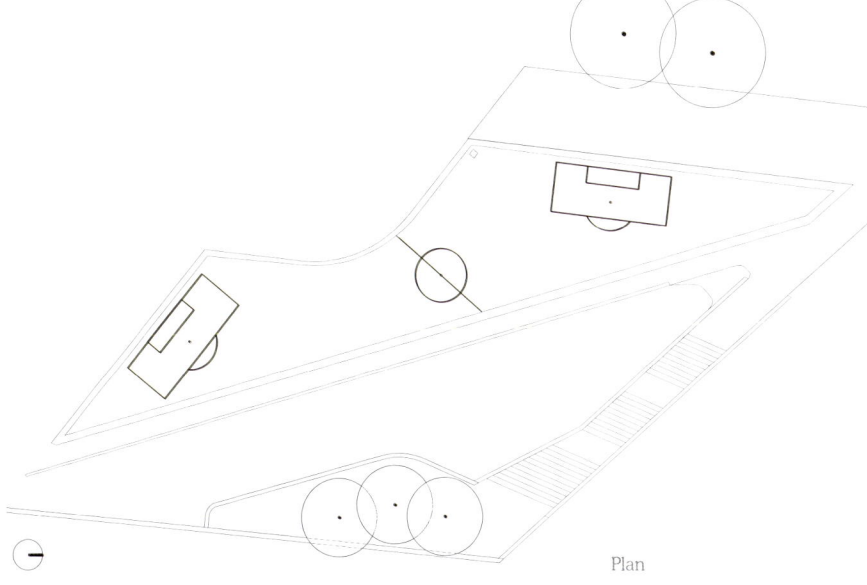

Plan

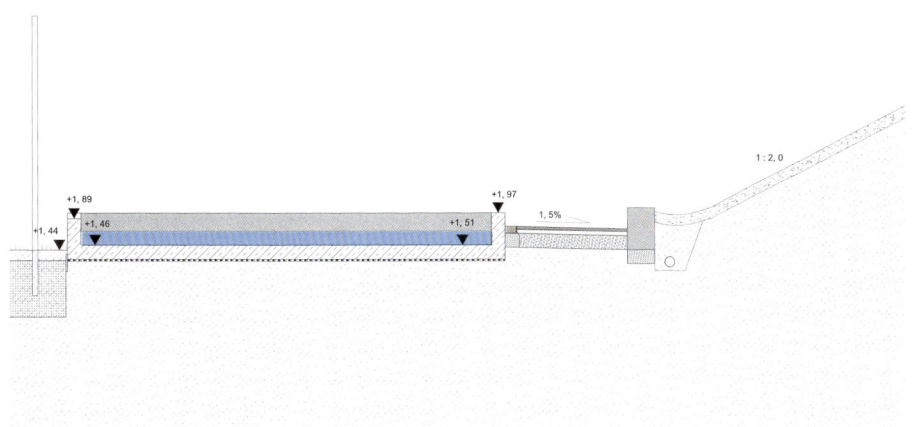

Detail

74

03
/ Aqua soccer game
04
/ Balancing on the border can be fun, too
05
/ The playground used as swimming pool
06
/ Birthday party in the Aqua Soccer field
07
/ Goaaaal!

Dymaxion Golf

Location /
Hamburg, Germany

Area /
6727 square feet (625 square meters)

Completion date /
2013

Landscape design /
TOPOTEK 1

Budget /
€45,000

Photography /
Hanns Joosten

Client /
International Garden Exhibition Hamburg

In 1933, the architect R. Buckminster Fuller created the Dymaxion World Map, a cartographic projection of the globe separated into polyhedrons, which can be unfolded into a two-dimensional map. In 1954, at Lake Maggiore, the first standardized mini-golf course was opened, designed by the landscape architect P. Bongni. The Dymaxion Golf in garden 73 is a combination of these: the Unfolded Dymaxion World Map is the support field for the mini-golf game. Continents and countries are successively played and conquered. As with 'big' golf, water traps create obstacles. The folded triangles of the world map consist of reinforced, lightweight, concrete stilts, hovering over the lawn area.

01
/ Overview of the whole installation
02
/ Detail of the graphical
  interpretation of the European map
03
/ Detail of the folded triangle

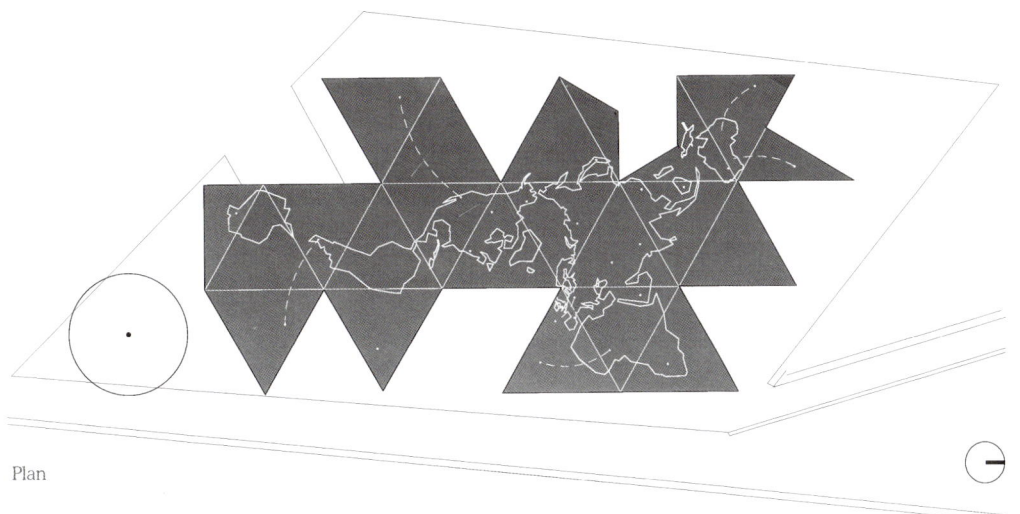

Plan

04

05

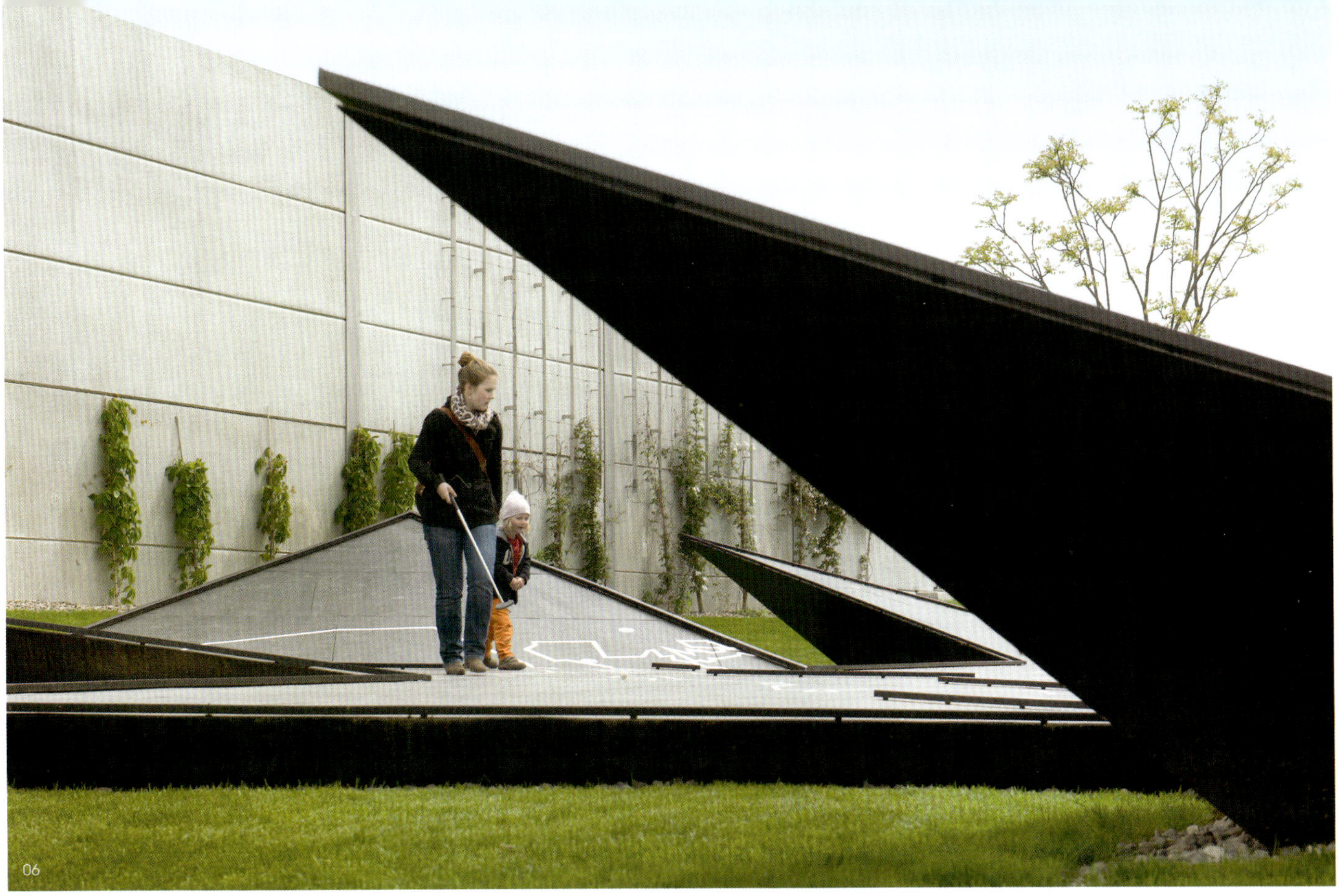
06

07

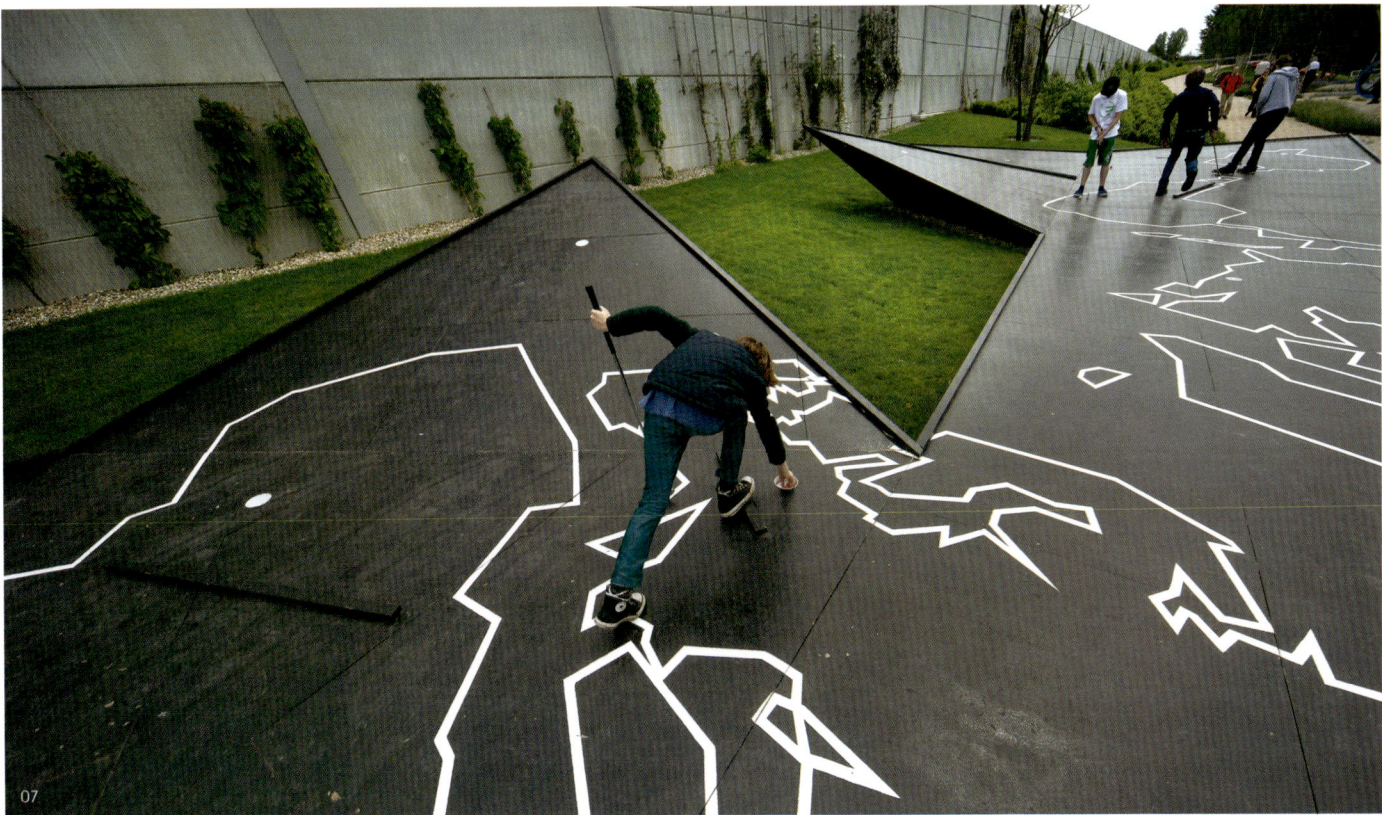

04
/ Big fun for all ages
05
/ Detail of the playing field
06
/ Close-up of a concrete stilt
07
/ View of the folded Dymaxion
World Map

Kavel K

Location /
Den Haag, The Netherlands

Area /
**17,760 square feet
(1650 square meters)**

Completion date /
2014

Landscape design /
Carve

Budget /
€600,000

Photography /
Carve (Marleen Beek)

Client /
Municipality of The Hague

Kavel K is situated on a triangular plot, boxed in by a railway track and a connecting road. It is a skating, sports and youth facility that attracts a wide range of user groups. The public space and the building are designed as a unit; the façade and the skate cradle even seem to melt together.

Kavel K is one of the three skate facilities that were originally planned as part of the urban layout for Leidschenveen-Ypenburg, which started in the 1990s. The location is a typical unused space the tapered terrain is wedged between a railway track and a connecting road, at the edge of one of the largest Vinex neighborhoods in the Netherlands. Previously, only skating was planned here, but because of demographic changes, the need for a youth center grew; young families moved into the neighborhood, and their children grew into adolescents.

Carve was asked to design both the amenities and the building. The designers of Carve thought it was important to create a building that presented itself as at one with its surroundings, both visually and functionally. But how could a skating area, a sports center and a youth center be designed in such a way as to create a whole?

The small strip of land is divided into three zones: skating area, youth centre and sports center. By positioning the youth center in the middle of the zone, a front and back are created, between which the building forms the hub. The entry zone is flanked by the skating facility, which is elevated 19.7 inches (50 centimeters) above the ground. By raising the skating area, a sitting edge is created along the entry zone. Furthermore, the entrance can be reached without getting in the path of the skaters. In contrast, at the front, the multifunctional sports court in the back is sunken, and its edges can be used for activities.

The façade and the integration of the skating facility are an essential part of the design. The cradle—an eye-catcher at the front—is integrated into the façade. By doing so, the façade and skate pool become one entity.

Plan drawing

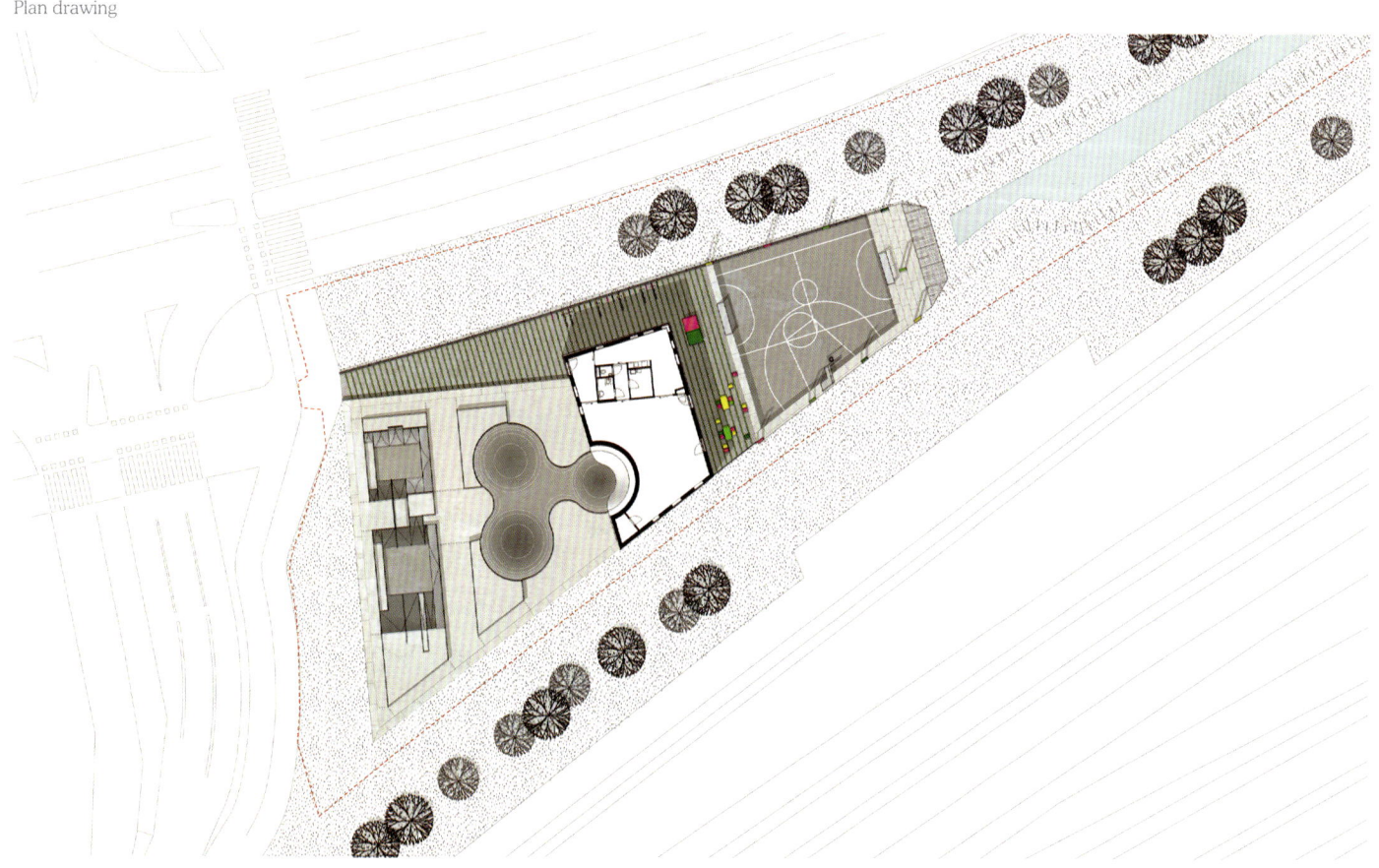

01
/ View of the sports zone

02
/ Entrance area with street skate and a skate bowl

Concept sport court

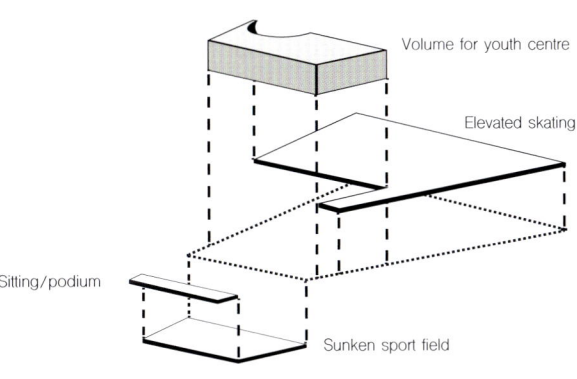

Concept plan

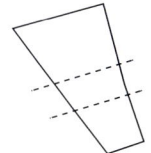 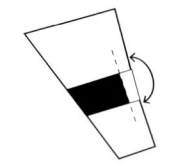

01/ Plot in three pieces 02/ Building as connector

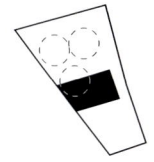 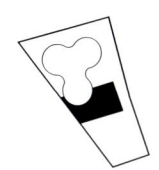

03/ Combining skating functions 04/ Integrating skate in the building

Concept skate pool

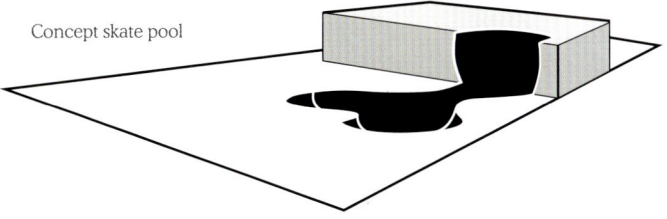

81

A second principle was the acceptance that the façade would be sprayed with graffiti. Instead of seeing this as a problem, the design anticipated this. The façade consists of large concrete elements, in which a braille-like pattern is pressed. The graffiti can be removed, but remains visible in the recessed circles. As a result, the façade turns into a canvas, in which an ever-changing color pattern reflects the history of the site.

A third principle was the building's flexibility in regard to what it could be used for; this was especially important in designing the floor plan. The interior was designed in collaboration with the future users, and was kept robust and simple. Core and floor were designed in a contrasting color, the walls lined with durable underlying panels. Large sliding doors around the core create the possibility of dividing the space in various ways. In addition, the building features an entrance at both the skating and sports sides. Currently, only one entrance is open, but in the future both can be used. In doing so, different user groups can enjoy the facility independently from each other: skaters, youth at risk, women who come for typing lessons, and sporting adolescents.

Remains of graffiti in sunken dots

03
/ Artist impression of the sports zone
04
/ The sports zone is slightly sunken and contains custom-designed basketball stands and football goals
05
/ Custom-designed ping-pong table
06
/ Custom-designed seating and tables

07
/ The skate area is a main meeting place for local youth
08
/ The skate bowl is integrated into the building's façade
09
/ View of the skate bowl
10
/ Street skate

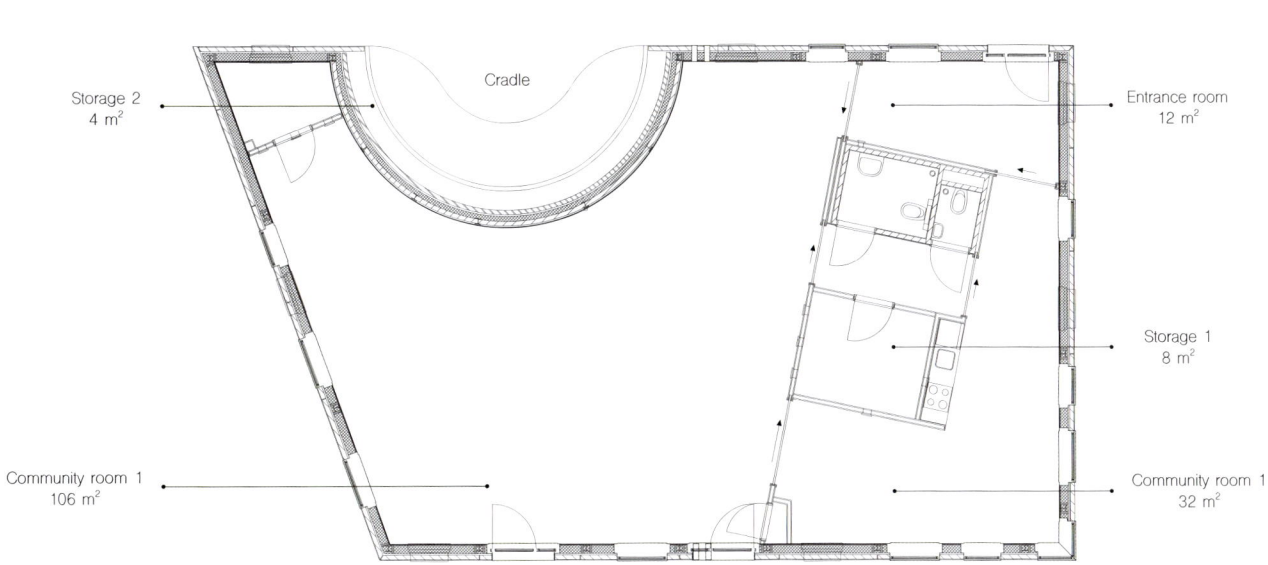

Floor plan and façade

Nieuwegein

Location /
Nieuwegein, The Netherlands

Area /
64,583 square feet (6000 square meters)

Completion date /
2011

Landscape design /
Dijk&co Landschapsarchitectuur (Rob van Dijk)

Skate and play area landscape design /
Carve

Photography /
Carve (Marleen Beek)

The project is the community park for the new district—Blokhoeve. The park was designed by Dijk&Co Landschapsarchitectuur. It is a hilly grassland with sparsely scattered trees. Although it is a new park, the trees are quite old; several years ago, the existing Hungarian oak and linden trees were removed, stored, and replanted back in the park after the construction was complete. The path system has a fluid design that connects all entrances and includes the sports- and playgrounds in a logical but playful pattern. The old location contained a running track that has been integrated into the new design. It is now a fresh running and skating track that encloses the new sports and play areas. The skate and play area landscape was designed by Carve. The skate objects 'stick' to the inside edge of the track, and are made of light-colored concrete that forms a nice contrast with the dark asphalt of the track. As this is a neighborhood park with a sporty character, the choice was made to integrate games and sports into the playground, too. The play area, with its forest of vertical wooden posts, balances the vertical direction of the mature trees in the park. The play cubes, which hang tilted between the posts, are designed from the scale and viewpoint as if perceived by a child. The exterior of the same objects, however, are boulder walls, which challenge parents to climb on them. The play cubes are placed quite high to prevent small children from climbing on the outside. Nevertheless, children can crawl and climb from one cube to the other through elevated climbing paths. Two worlds are united in one object; they don't blend but they do meet. With this, the children's playground also becomes a playground for adults.

Master plan

01
/ The playground is integrated
  into the park

02
/ The skate objects 'stick' to the
  inside edge of the running track

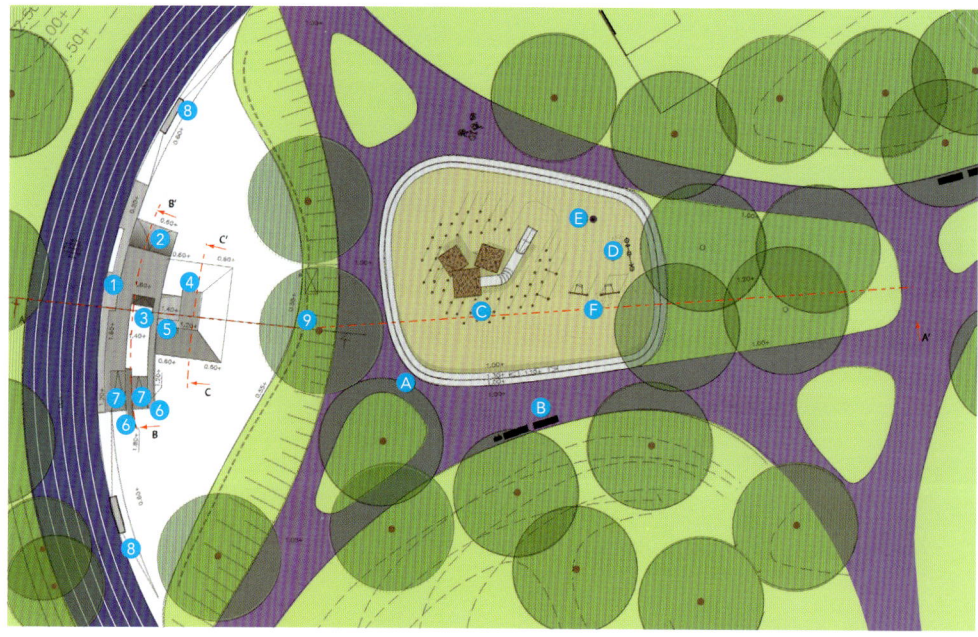

The skate objects and the playground

Skate facilities

1. Curb with gap
2. Transition
3. Flat
4. Pyramid
5. Wembly gap
6. Ledge
7. Bank
8. Grind box
9. Drainage

Play facilities

A. Concrete edge
B. Entrance
C. Tree trunk forest with play objects
D. See-saw
E. Spinner bowl
F. Swings

03
/ The path system can be used for strolling around

04–06
/ The skate objects are made of light-coloured concrete, creating a nice contrast with the dark-coloured running track

07–08
/ The running track can be used for various sports
09
/ The play cubes hang tilted between a trunk forest
10
/ The play cubes are interconnected by crawling tunnels
11
/ The skin of the cubes can be used for professional bouldering

Spectrum

Location /
Lugano, Switzerland

Area /
**10,764 square feet
(1000 square meters)**

Completion date /
2014

Budget /
€4000

Photography /
Zukclub

Client /
City Lugano

The site of Moscow-based art-group Zukclub's outdoor exhibitions in Lugano, Switzerland, is a 10,764-square-foot (1000-square-meter) pool renovated into a skate park. It is impressive for its incorporation of light and spectrum art to create an active and distinct skating space. And it's even a sundial. Zukclub has honed its craft in a large number of outdoor street-art expos, and the Lugano Skate Park is a large, robust reflection of their talent for the randomness of urban street art. Initial impressions of the skate park reverberate with a graffiti aesthetic; multiple contrasting colors from across the spectrum lie next to each other, terrifically out of place amid the greenery of Switzerland's central European mountainscape. Yet whereas the tone of discontent from which graffiti art arises lies in its continual accretion and accumulation over time, perhaps by many artists, Zukclub controls that chaos and cuts right to the rebellion. The rush for time that might leave street art hastily scrawled onto an urban surface is gone; Zukclub has perfected the stark transitions from color to color that are more chaotically displayed on walls in the back alleys of European cities.

Rainbows rim one of the edges, while the outline of a skull arises from an interlocking backdrop of black and white streaks arranged into a complex diamond pattern. The central, conical ramp of the park utilizes the same black and white shades without the complexity of that diamond pattern, which redefines the use of those colors and lends innovation to the pool as a whole; the two sections are distanced by a sea of other designs, allowing them to be taken on their own without too much undue cross-referencing on account of their similar colors. Elsewhere, a red-and-white checked pattern is overlaid with a gray one, creating a delightful confusion of shapes and colors. This confusion contributes to the spectrum pattern of the artwork, which is created by overlying shadows. Horizontal transitions from color to color create the dynamic of the skate park, but vertical transitions from shadow to shadow lend character. Zukclub also plays with the light directly, as the time of day can be deduced via the sundial function that the pool serves. Morning light passing through the pool is dispersed into the color spectrum, and adds further levels of geometry to the design. Zukclub showcases the gallery-level potential of street art, but keeps it from the confinement of galleries, laying it bare in the middle of the urban locale of Lugano, and allowing natural light to reveal its myriad perceptive qualities.

Concept

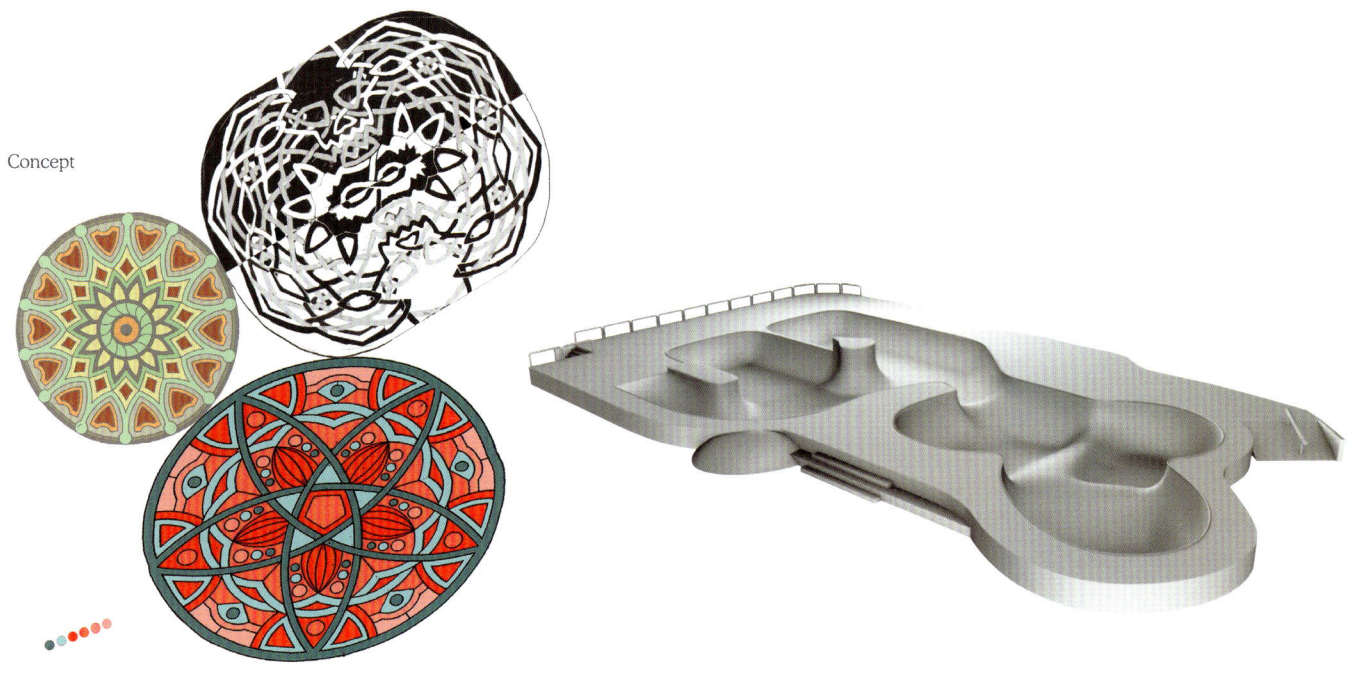

01
/ View from the top
02
/ View from the left side
03
/ Detail

04
/ Panoramic view
05
/ Action
06
/ Sundial
07
/ Mandala

Collie

Location /
Collie, Australia

Area /
8073 square feet (750 square meters)

Completion date /
2014

Landscape design /
Design & Construct – CONVIC

Client /
Shire of Collie

The site for the Collie Youth Facility is located in an idyllic setting of an existing open space, Soldiers Park, with the natural backdrop of the Collie River. This space is the central parkland setting for the broader community, who use it regularly and for community social events. The Collie Youth Facility creates a dynamic relationship between the landscape and recreation features, with the integration of a dry creek bed that weaves through the space. It is a district-level facility that both amplifies and adds value to the Collie River Precinct, while creating a central social and recreational hub for the community.

Acknowledging the existing strength of the BMX, skateboarding and scooter communities, the design of the facility incorporates a tight bowl, a number of transition elements, and several technical street features, a standout being a kicker-to-kicker gap over the dry creek bed. These features are all set within a framework that maintains speeds throughout the whole facility. It caters for a range of abilities, allowing users to progress through the space, developing their skills from a beginner to an advanced level in a safe and creative environment.

The dry creek bed allows for sustainable overland flow and water treatment, while providing an exciting visual and physical connection to the scenic Collie River. This creek bed, along with terraced concrete seating walls, frames a grassed central gathering space that can be used for a number of community activities. The palette of diverse textures, colors and materials engages the senses and reflects the rich character of Collie. This interesting combination of landscape and recreational facilities culminates in an iconic space, holistically integrated, with parkland pockets and spaces for families and groups to gather and take in the spectacle, or relax and enjoy the scenic Collie River atmosphere.

Site plan

01
/ Aerial photo of the whole park
02
/ Skate path in the park

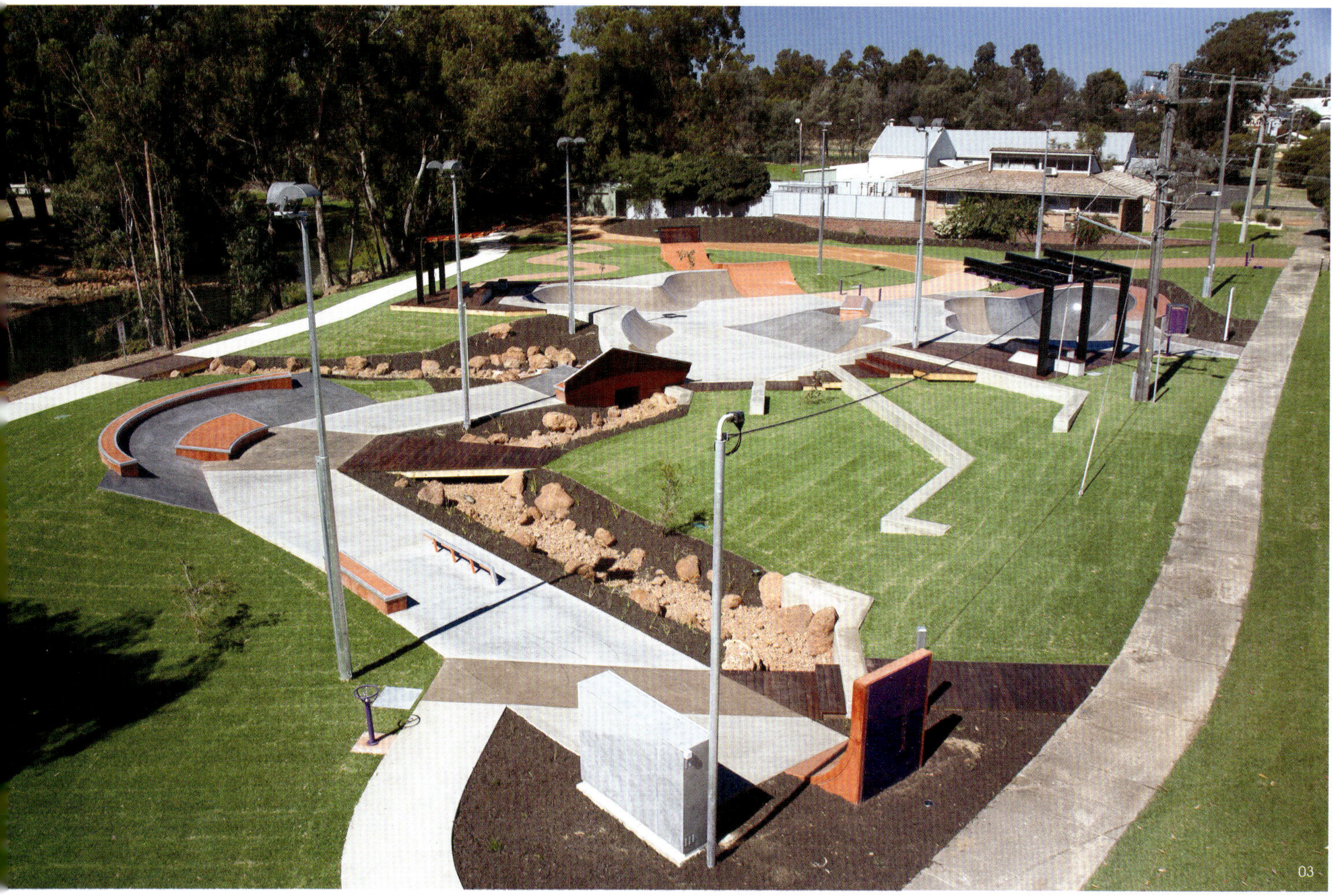

03

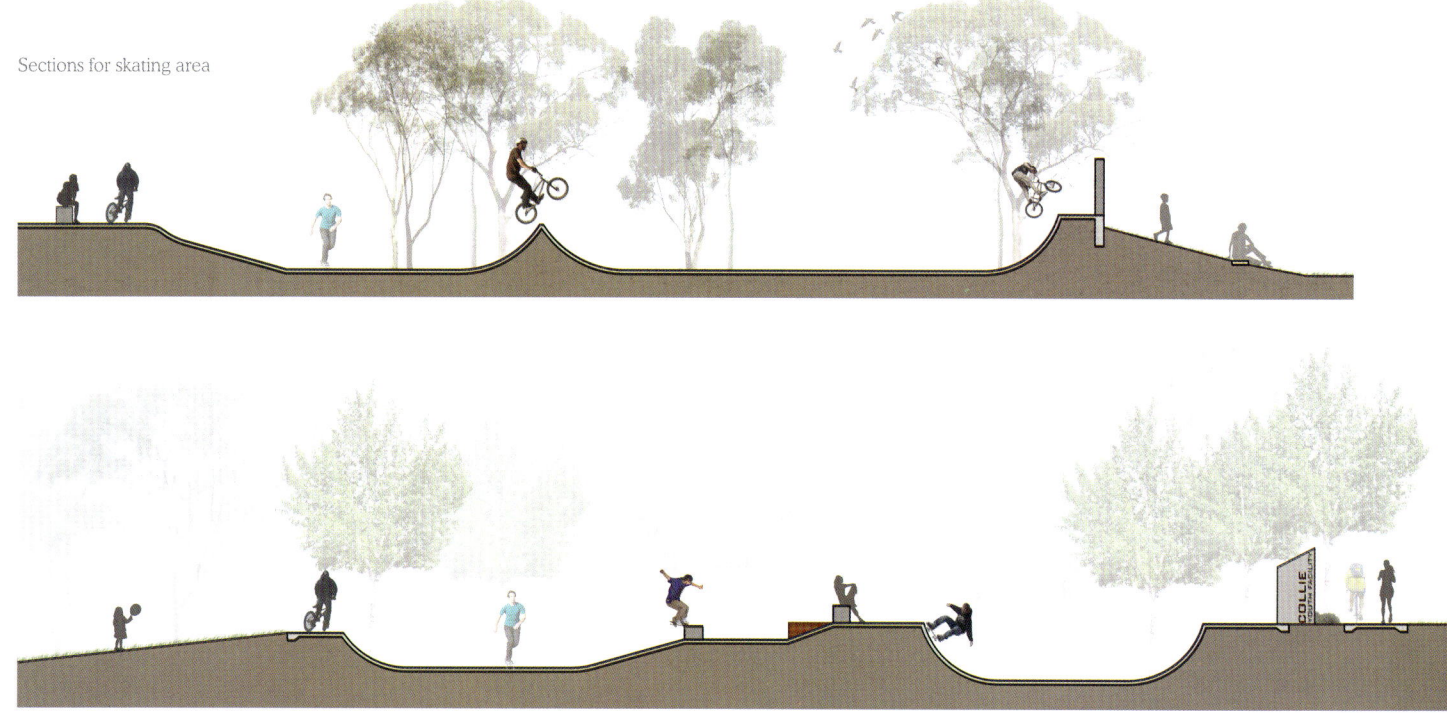

Sections for skating area

03
/ Aerial photo of skating zone
04–06
/ Skating zone

07

08

100

07–08
/ Resting pavilion
09–10
/ Paths in the park can be used as skating zones

Bahndeckel Theresienhöhe

Location /
Munich, Germany

Area /
4.2 acres (1.7 hectares)

Completion date /
2010

Landscape design /
TOPOTEK 1

Budget /
€2.6 million

Photography /
Hanns Joosten

Client /
City of Munich

The Bahndeckel Theresienhöhe provided an opportunity for a unique design. The site—a Bahndeckel, literally 'train cover'—is a constructed landscape for a public open space, located in central Munich on a former exhibition ground. Artificiality in landscape architecture is long established, and is dominated by the idea of replicating nature. It is epitomized by the English landscape garden. Bahndeckel Theresienhöhe was conceived to encapsulate what it means to replicate landscapes today.

Trains passing under the Bahndeckel depart from the Alps and terminate at the North Sea in a matter of hours, connecting the two landscapes through travel. The top of the Bahndeckel is a recreation of these landscapes, brought together by the abstract link of the train journey. In fact, the entire landscape of the Bahndeckel, with mountains on one side and sandy shores on the other, is German poet Kurt Tucholsky's *Das Ideal*—the German dream view, with the Alps in the background and the sea in the foreground. The conceptual image behind the Bahndeckel is not new, but is newly realized. The old romantic dream is reiterated through a contemporary pastiche of compartmentalized sand dunes, Styrofoam hills, and sawhorses grazing on Astroturf. The artificiality of idealism is liberated from romanticism by its creation.

The form of the Bahndeckel follows the curve of the rail tracks below, marked prominently by the bright, orange bumpers containing the sand dunes, grass moraines, and hills. The entire space is a continuous and interactive sculptural form. Pine trees, native to the sandy regions of Germany, line the park space, forming a neat line in front of adjacent housing, and standing in a grove with a slightly more irregular pattern on the wider, north side of the site. The reality of the Bahndeckel is an artificial construction. With this project, the notions of abstraction and replication are reinterpreted into a design that revels in its own artificial topographies.

① Wall element
② Restraining strip type1, perforated base, galvanized, 1.4 inches (35 millimeters) wide, screwed to the wall
③ Drainage channel, 2.4 by 5.9 inches (60 by 150 millimeters) V2A stainless steel
④ Foam glass aggregate 10/50 as drainage layer, min. 12cm
⑤ Modelling: Styrofoam blocks, rigid polystyrene foam, stepped arrangement and sizes
⑥ Steel edging profile
⑦ Copolymer Astroturf, 13mm, fixed with restraining strips
⑧ Densely textured lightweight concrete LB 16/18 with embedded reinforcement, reinforced steel mesh R 188 A
⑨ Restraining strip type 3a, galvanized, 1.4 inches (36 millimeters) wide
⑩ Soil substrate
⑪ Moisture retention protection layer
⑫ Fleece slip membrane

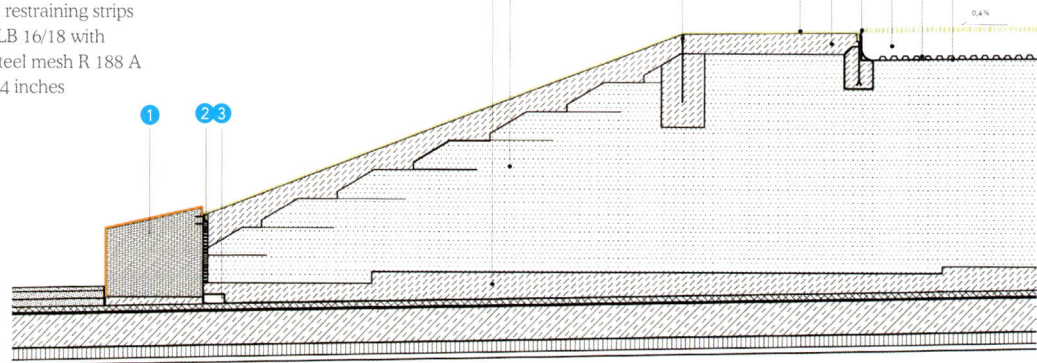

Green mound

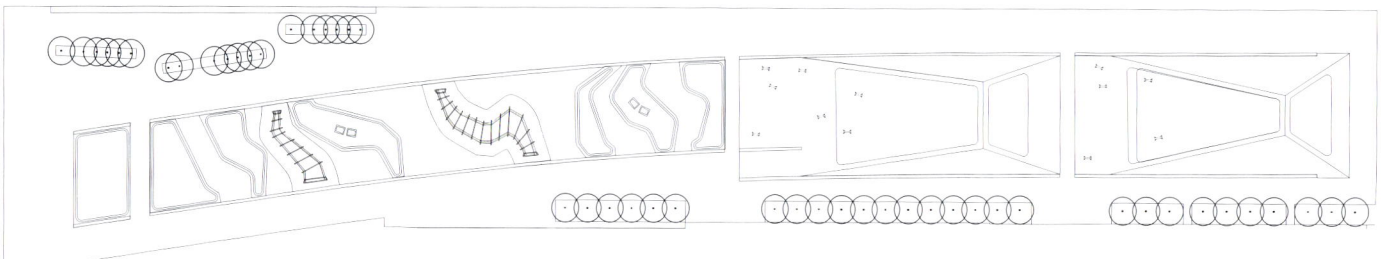

Master plan

01
/ Panorama view of the whole park
02
/ Entrance path to the park

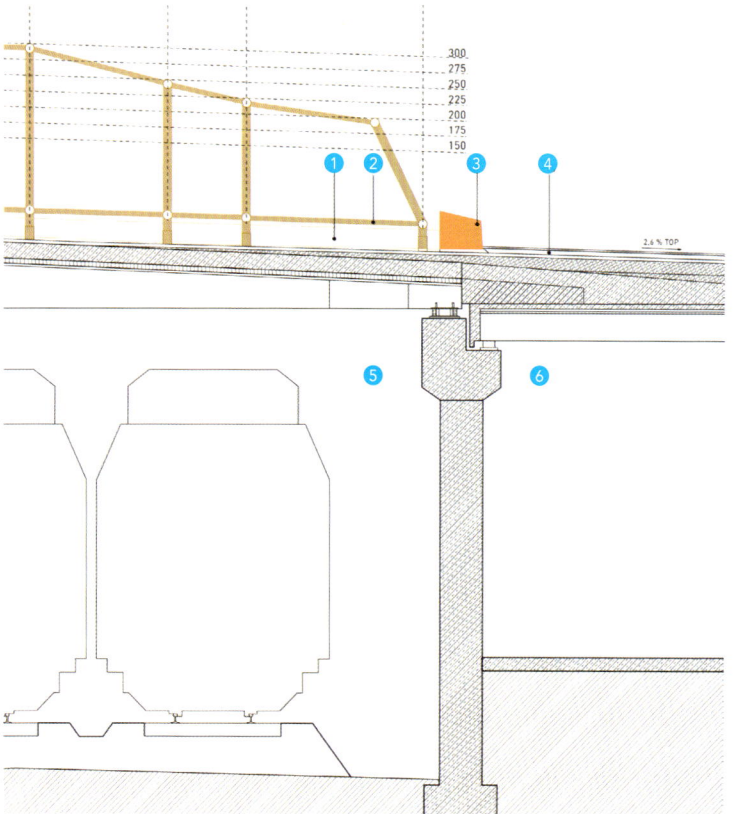

① Gravel
② Frame constructions, climbing frame dunes
③ Walls
④ Asphalt
⑤ Railway line
⑥ Underground structure

Detail section of railway cover bridge structure with fall-softening gravel surface

03
/ Hills and sand dunes
04–05
/ Hanging net facilities for children to climb

Plan and elevation of small climbing dune with hanging net structure

① Swing seats
② Climbing knobs

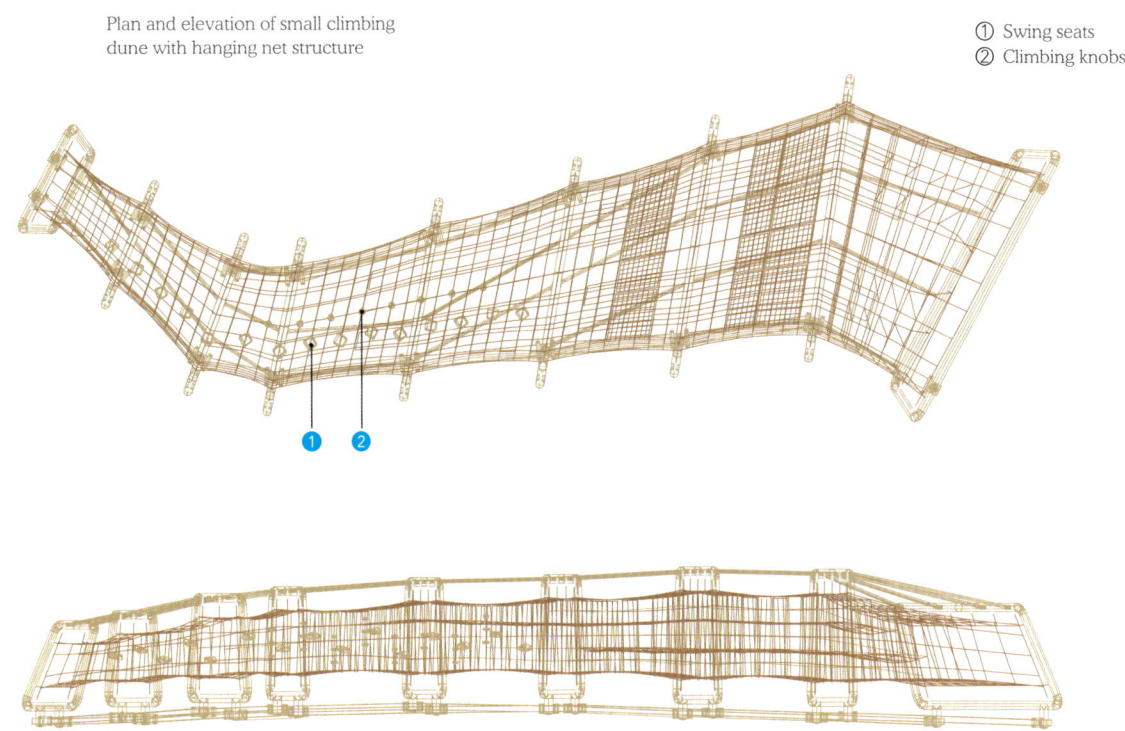

06
/ Pommel horse
07
/ Spray and foot shower
08
/ Playing facilities
09–10
/ Playing area edges can be used as resting benches
11
/ Children playing in the park

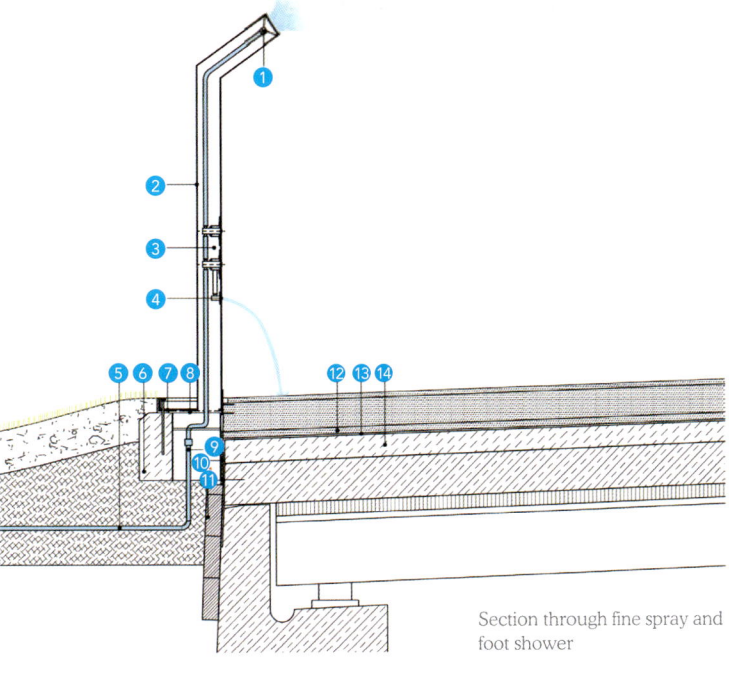

① Shower head
② Steel frame shower
③ Shower button with valve timing gear, flush-mounted in steel frame
④ Water dispenser
⑤ Connections to the existing water supply
⑥ Inspection hatch on a concrete foundation
⑦ Inner hatch frame
⑧ Inspection hatch, shut-off valve for water supply and water return facility for draining in winter
⑨ Flexible hose
⑩ Fleece-backed drainage matting, bonded to railway cover
⑪ Filter blocks
⑫ Poured asphalt
⑬ Welded polymer bitumen sheet
⑭ Blind concrete, varying height

Section through fine spray and foot shower

3D Athletics Track

Location /
Alicante, Spain
Completion date /
2010
Landscape design /
Subarquitectura
Budget /
US$1.3 million
Photography /
Subarquitectura

As an artificial landform, a running track located away from the growth of the City of Elda becomes a part of the landscape; it provides full sports equipment and fills a functional need for comfortable and attractive sporting areas. The idea is to create, as a complement to the standard track, an extra area that represents a new challenge for the runner, and requires a greater effort, generating a rush of action, and increasing competitiveness and personal sacrifice.

With a 'bending action,' the designers generated a three-dimensional folded track, banked, with a varied slope, that becomes a privileged viewpoint for sport events. It can also be considered as a spontaneous grandstand, an alternative route, or a summit to conquer, as part of the daily training. But this usable surface is, at the same time, the covering for the indoor spaces of 3767 square feet (350 square meters) that include two changing rooms, two stores, the gymnasium, and the public toilets. Between the planar and the sloped tracks, and with a space for 300 people, the grandstands are located in the west area to protect the users from the sun and bring a privileged view of the athletics track. The mountains are always in the background of the action. The project explicitly refuses luxurious materials for the entire building.

Location

01
/ Aerial view
02–03
/ The track in context

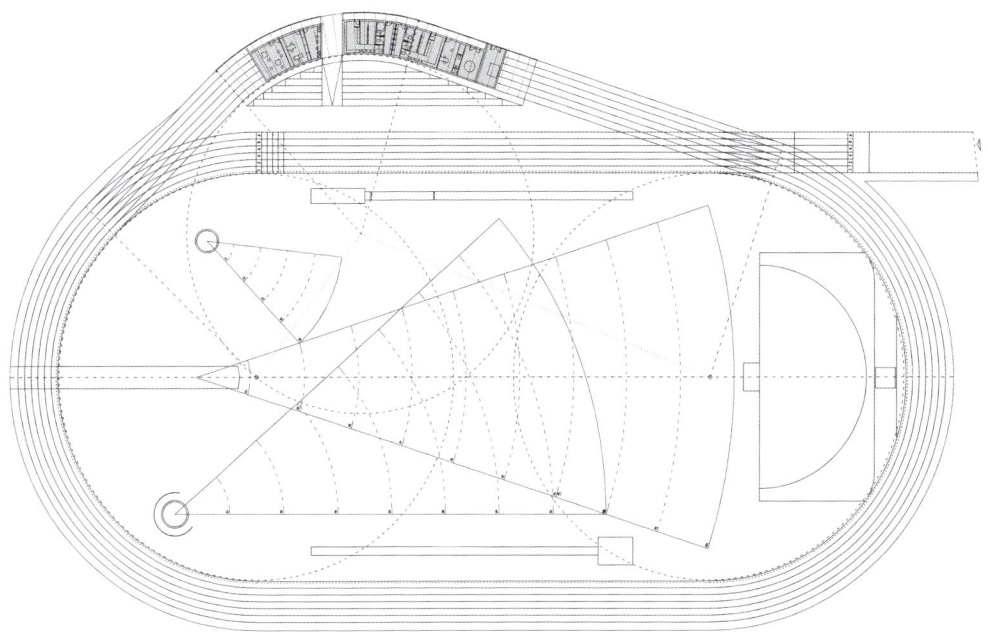

Plan view

109

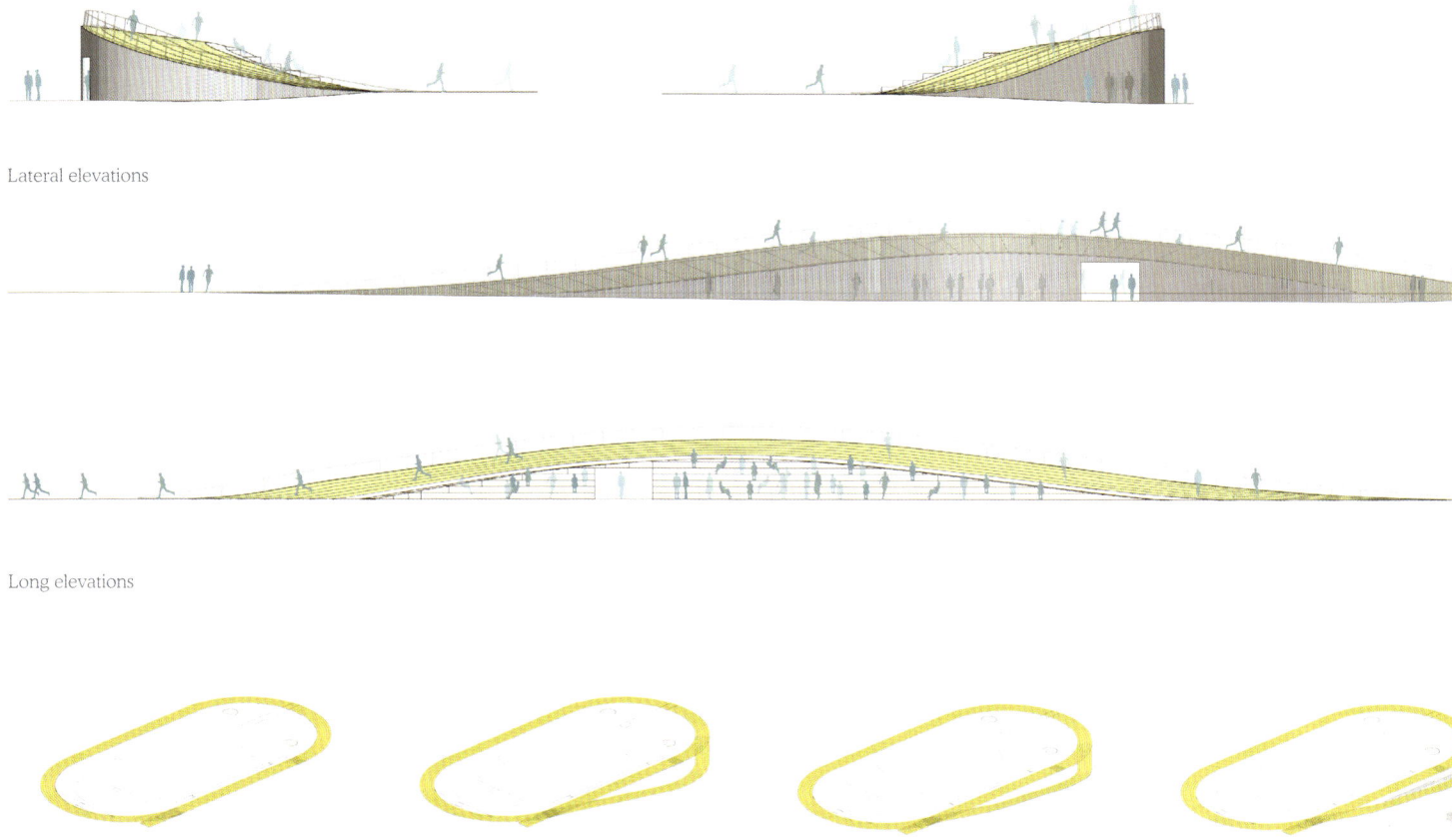

Lateral elevations

Long elevations

| Standard track | Extended track | Three-dimensional | Program |

Sequence

04
/ Elevation from within the circuit
05
/ Spectators stand
06–07
/ Running track

Along the entire west façade, a steel lattice allows visibility of the landscape from the inside, and protects the spaces from the horizontal sun. The competition track and the sloped path are of the same red synthetic-rubber surfacing, making no distinction between them. This track turns into an optimal solution for disabled people. By using soft slopes, it's possible to reach any point in a wheelchair. But the designers also intended to incorporate a new kind of accessibility; they wanted this to be a facility that attracts people who are not necessarily professional, promoting the idea that sport is reachable to everyone, of any age and ability.

Right to the end

Constructive detail

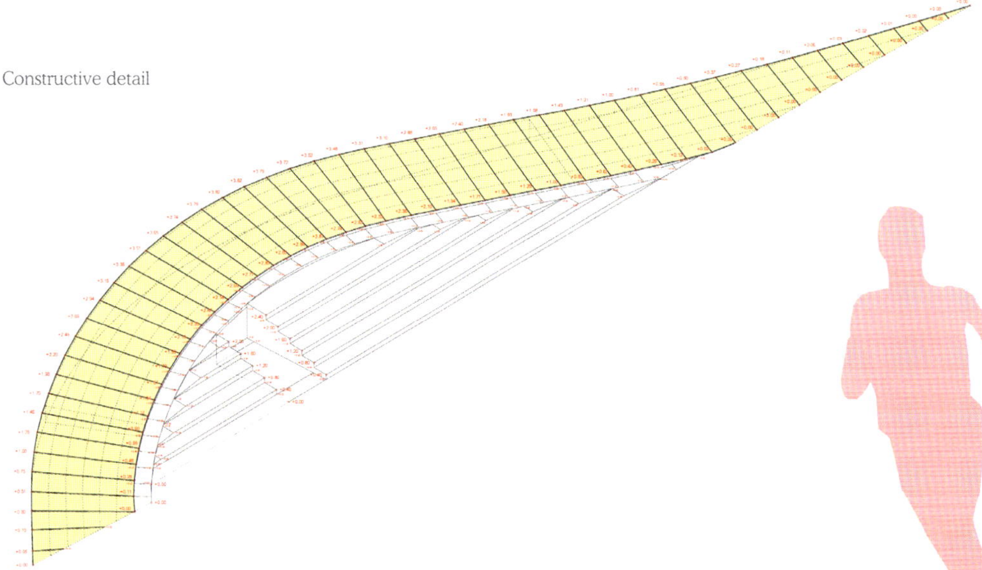

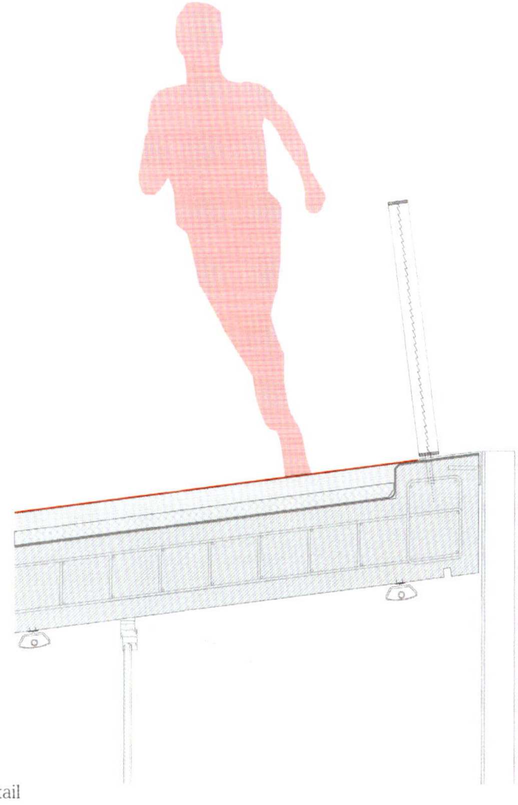

Constructive detail

112

08–09
/ Raised track
10
/ Inside the sheltered facility
11–12
/ Raised track

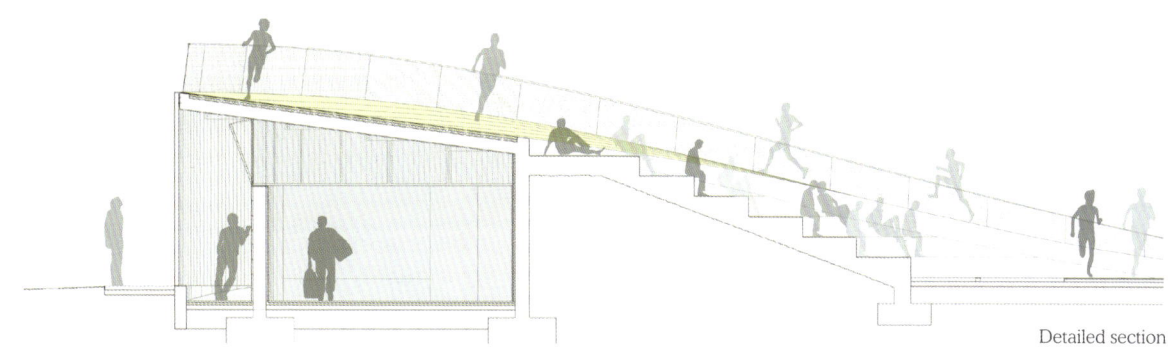

Detailed section

The Lawn on D

Location /
Boston, Massachussetts, USA

Area /
2.7 acres (1.09 hectares)

Completion date /
2014

Landscape design /
Sasaki

Budget /
US$1.5 million

Photography /
Christian Phillips Photography

Client /
The Massachusetts Convention Center Authority

The Massachusetts Convention Center Authority (MCCA), in partnership with a Sasaki-led design team (including HR&A, Inc.), conceived of the Lawn on D—a flexible, vibrant, and temporary urban space—to be an 'early arrival' on D Street, setting the tone for civic impact and expressing the ambitions of a new district.

This new district, anchored by the Boston Convention and Exhibition Center (BCEC), occupies a critical midpoint between South Boston, the Innovation District and Liberty Wharf, and the Fort Point and Channel Center neighborhoods. This new district, inspired by art and events and inclusive of many constituents (residents, workers, conventioneers, tourists), aspires to be interactive, flexible, and technologically advanced. The Lawn on D demonstrates and pilots these ambitions, testing spatial configurations and programming that will eventually be deployed to a future event space that will become the heart and focus of the new district along D Street.

Composed of two parts—the plaza and the lawn—The Lawn on D is a hub of activity for community events. The Plaza's paths blaze trails from D Street to the side entrance of the BCEC; its signature lights describe a right-sized space for gatherings; and its bright, playful, movable furniture invites visitors to make the space their own. The lawn at The Lawn on D, sited where 4 feet (1.2 meters) of urban fill used to block views and preclude access, now provides a gracious forecourt to the BCEC along D Street and hosts a range of short-term art installations and projects.

01
/ The plaza at The Lawn on D is a hub of activity—bright furniture and signature lighting circumscribe a human scale

02
/ The Lawn on D serves as a temporary pilot project to test a new type of landscape event space and express the ambitions and character of the growing district along D Street

03
/ Integrating a large institution with the surrounding community, The Lawn on D creates an opportunity for neighbors, locals, and visitors to come together

The Lawn on D was conceived as a framework for flexible programming, a multiplicity of users, comfort throughout the year, and scalable events—allowing for easy transformation over time

① BCEC
② MCCA Trailer
③ Claflin Street
④ Limit of work
⑤ Element Hotel
⑥ Aloft Hotel
⑦ 411 D Street
⑧ D Street

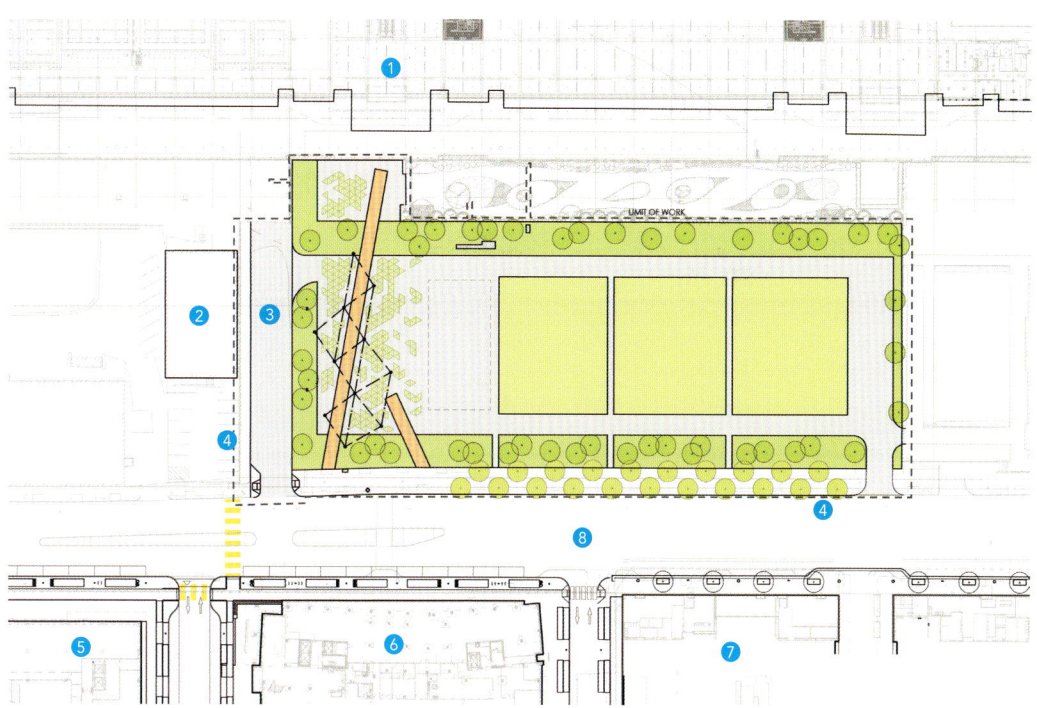

115

04
/ The lawn at The Lawn on D—sited where 4' of urban fill used to block views and preclude access—plays host to art installations, music, furniture, and events

05
/ The Lawn on D is a comfortable background to, and incubator of, strong design—hosting a range of shorter-term installations and projects

06
/ Movable furniture and games let visitors make the space their own, moving things around to suit their needs

07
/ The plaza's signature paths blaze trails from D Street to the side entrance of the Boston Convention and Exhibition Center

05

06

07

117

The Esplanade Youth Plaza—Fremantle

Location /
Fremantle, Western Australia
Area /
0.75 hectares (1.85 acres)
Completion date /
2014
Landscape design /
Design & Construct – CONVIC
Budget /
AU$1.6 million
Client /
City of Fremantle

The Esplanade Youth Plaza, situated in the heart of Fremantle City and the historic parkland setting of the Esplanade Reserve, is an urban oasis catering to the existing community's needs of a junior play space, open parkland amenity, and event space. Embodying the principles of social sustainability, the youth plaza offers opportunities for all visitors, participants, and users. It is a central community hub providing a range of active and passive pursuits, engagement, events and social prospects, and pursuits for all ages. The makeup of community and its recreational needs are changeable over time. The FEYP design response is for an adaptable space to meet the evolving needs for healthy and safe activities of a diversity of users and visitors with differing interests and abilities. The plaza offers a facility for skateboard/BMX/scooter users and extends its appeal for parkour, ping pong, and other informal recreational opportunities.

The plaza is a manifestation of the very essence of Fremantle's culture. These interpretative layers are interwoven through the space, using a range of materials and features to represent the story and rich history of the city, in particular its working past. This is manifest with the repurposing of a reclaimed marine buoy into an iconic skate element and re-adapting a shipping container into a bouldering tower. Complementing this is the strong skating culture within the community, evident in the unique and challenging skate-able terrain that pays homage to the local historic wool stores ledge. This identifies the youth plaza as a key destination for local users and national and international visitors, providing young people with opportunities other than formal sports and structured experiences. The plaza draws on the rich palette of the existing landscape character within the Esplanade Reserve, and incorporates complimentary landscape elements with avenue tree planting, native garden beds, and the use of sympathetic materials to ensure the facility sits comfortably within the unique historic reserve setting. This allows the facility to present itself as a contemporary youth precinct being both responsive and sensitive to the heritage significance of the broader Esplanade Reserve and urban context within which it sits.

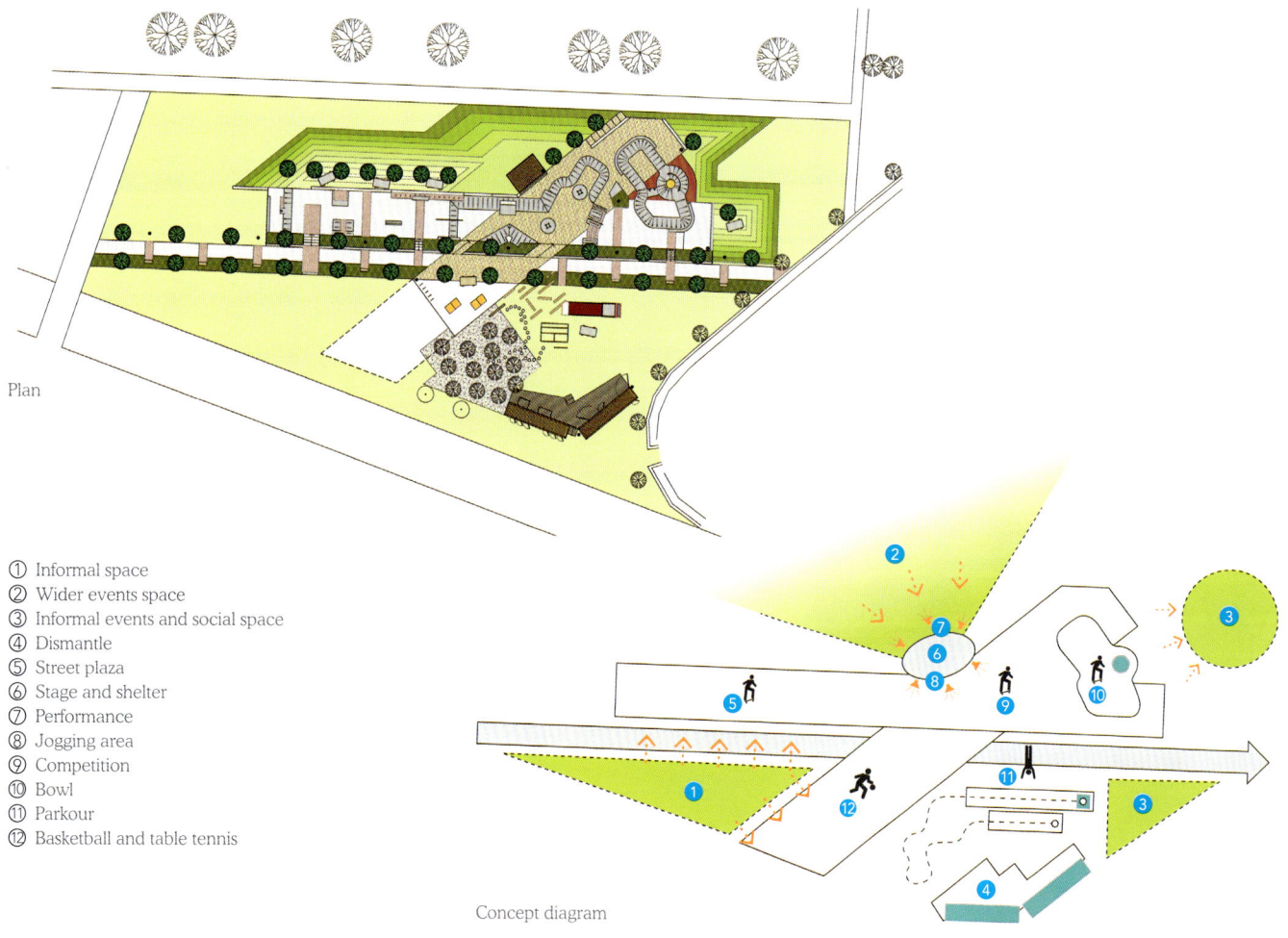

Plan

① Informal space
② Wider events space
③ Informal events and social space
④ Dismantle
⑤ Street plaza
⑥ Stage and shelter
⑦ Performance
⑧ Jogging area
⑨ Competition
⑩ Bowl
⑪ Parkour
⑫ Basketball and table tennis

Concept diagram

01–02
/ Aerial views of the whole park

03
/ Skating area
04–05
/ Local people enjoy time in the park
06
/ Skating area

① Earth mounding to minimize the amount of structure
② Corten steel balustrade
③ Box extension to top of quarter pipe
④ Ledge that can be used for seating
⑤ Ledge with pop-in, pop-out section

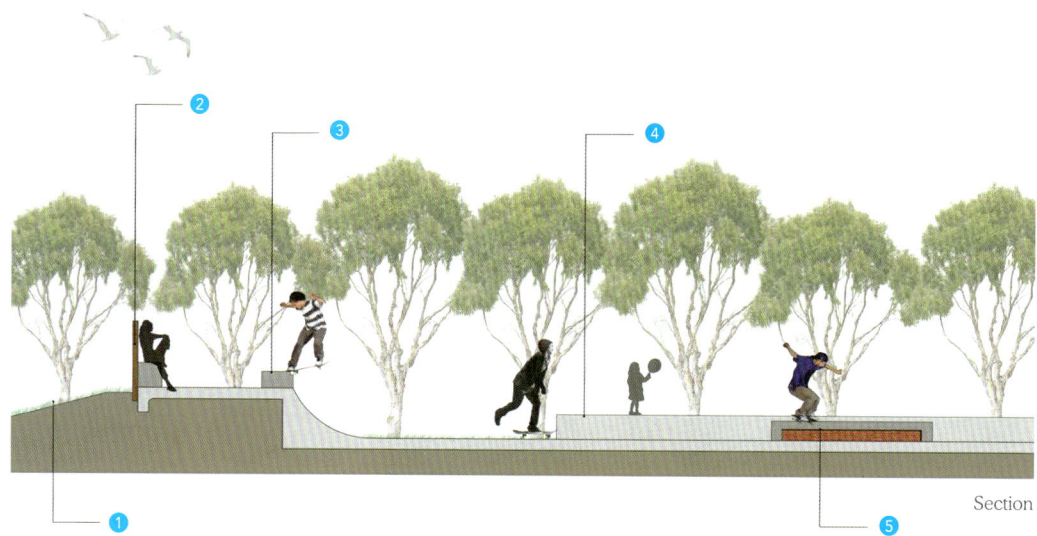

Section

04

05

06

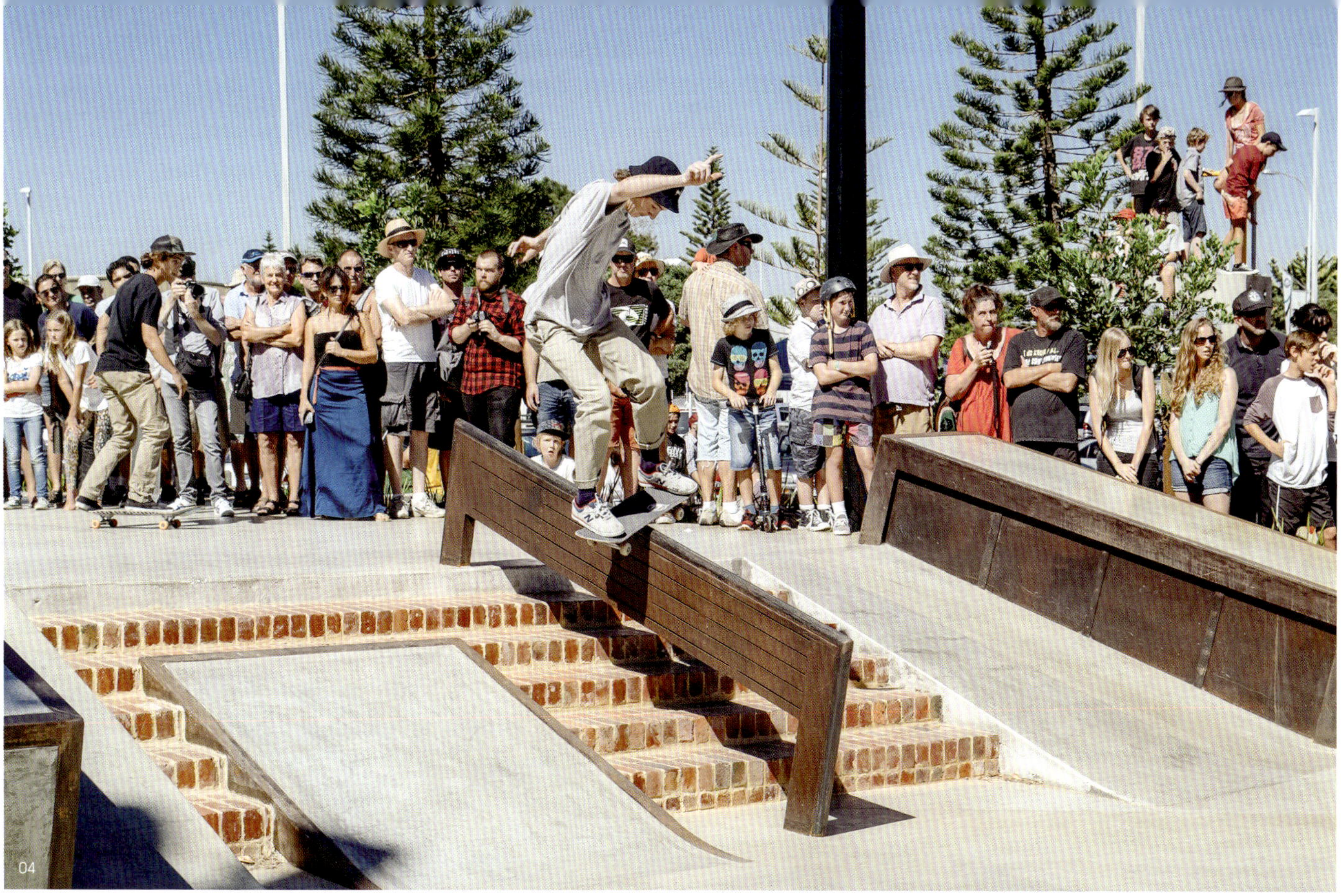

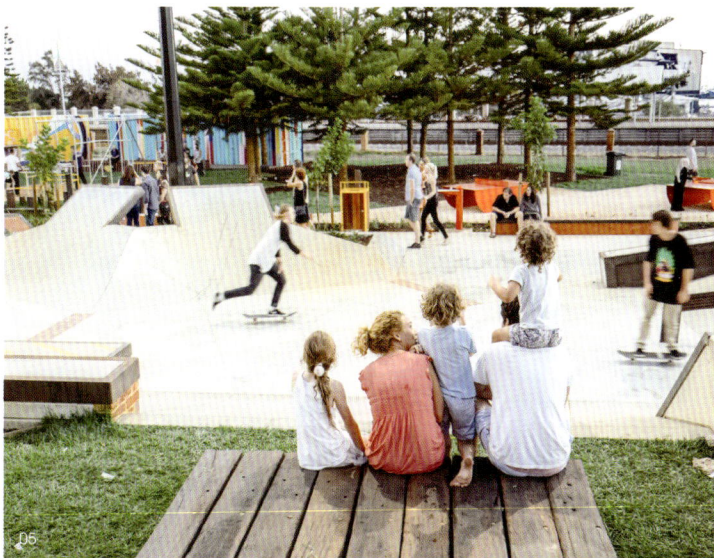

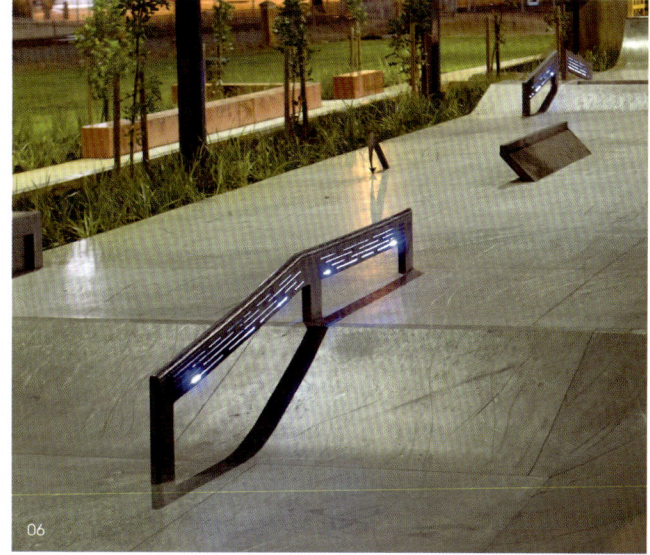

① Earth mounding to minimize the amount of structure
② Ledge to top of bank over lower ledges
③ Ledges and manual pad in low bank
④ Steep cantilevered hip bank
⑤ Avenue of trees and lighting along the central spine
⑥ Raise planter beds
⑦ Seating elements along the central spine

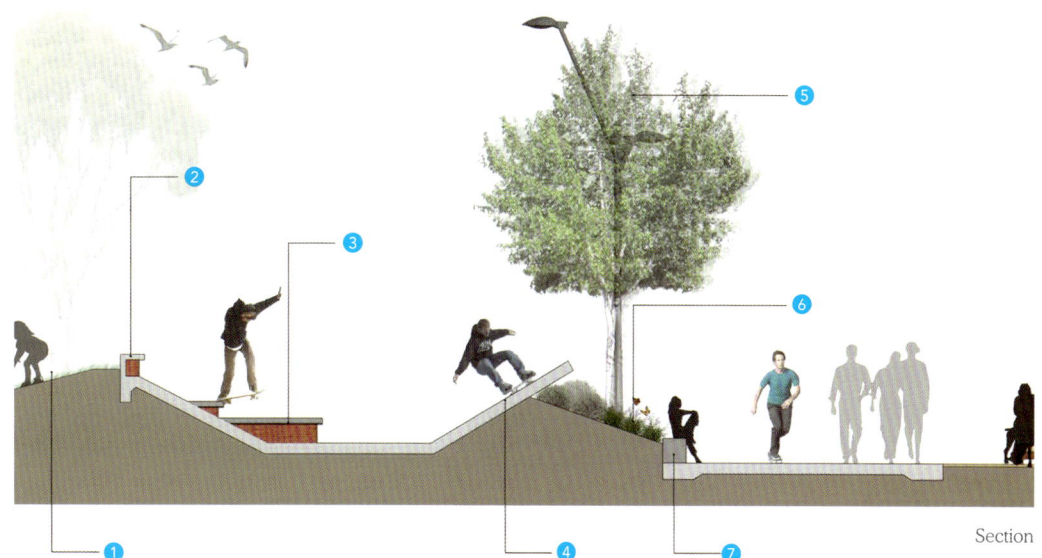

Section

① Garden bed within upper level of skate park
② Deep bowl area
③ Buoy-transition to vert around perimeter
④ Taco around back of buoy

Section

07
/ Skating area
08
/ Local people enjoy time in the park
09–10
/ Mulitfunctional recreation area

11
/ Different kinds of sports facilities
12
/ Resting pavilion
13
/ Local people enjoy free time in the park
14
/ Table tennis
15
/ Local people relaxing in the park

Israel's Square

Location /
Copenhagen, Denmark
Completion date /
2014
Landscape design /
Sweco Architects
Other consultants /
Cobe and Morten Stræde
Photography /
Sweco Architects, Rasmus Hjortshøj
Client /
City of Copenhagen

Israel's Square—the shifting identities

The location of Israel Square is rich in opportunities and stretches between two worlds: the bustling covered market, where thousands of people pass everyday, and the lush H.C. Ørsteds Park, where the people of Copenhagen enjoy the green space in the middle of the city. Israel's Square is placed on top of the historic ramparts, which used to surround the City of Copenhagen, and was in the 1970s rebuilt into a parking lot with Northern Europe's largest underground parking garage. This identity did not involve any aesthetics or invitation to activity—but it was about to change.

The new Israel's Square

The square has wings, as the southwest and northeast corners fold up and create sitting areas while covering the ramp from the underground parking garage. As opposed to the wings of the square, the surface runs downward as a waterfall in the southwest corner into H.C. Ørsteds Park, and thereby blends with the trees that stretch into the square. Across the square, water trickles in a small creek, which continues into H.C. Ørsteds Park, where it ends in stairs created of three oval vessels completing the waterfall.

Depending on the purpose, the light of the pylons on the square can be changed from a dimmed, scattered light to one focused on specific areas during events. Along the edge of the square, small LED-lights are installed to give the illusion of a flying carpet and a hovering surface.

01
/ Israel's Square has granite paving from the façade, with the historically conditioned worn and recycled paving on the streets and in contrast, precisely formed pale granite pavers on the square's raised surface. Areas for games and play are made with surface of rubber

02
/ Israel's Square lies between Ørsted Park and the market halls, created on top of and by filling in the Copenhagen defensive earthworks

03
/ The square contains facilities for skaters and for relaxing on the stairs

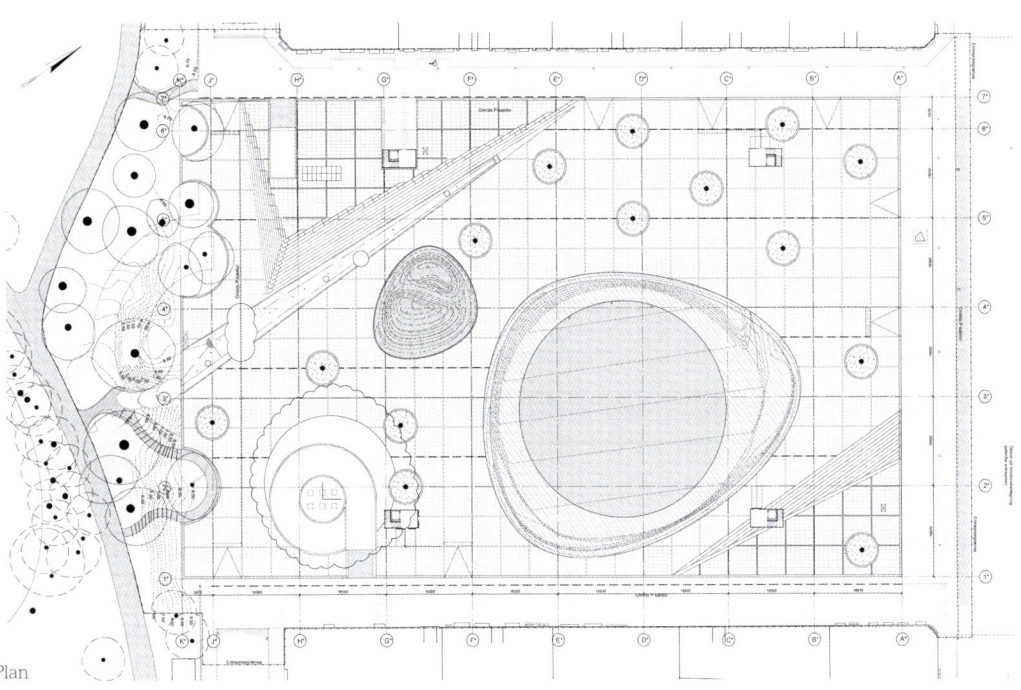

Plan

04
/ Israel's Square is the city's largest square. The surrounding apartment blocks were built at the end of the 19th century

05
/ Since the renewed square opened to the public in 2014, it have been a popular space for people of all ages, for activities, resting, and recreation

06
/ Israel's Square is sculpturally conceived as a square that rises above the existing surface and the surrounding streets, while two of the corners fold upwards, marking the course of the former bastions and moats' over the square

Elevations

07–08
/ It was important to create an openness and relationship between the square and the park by pulling the square into the park and inviting the park's green elements onto the square
09
/ Collage from the competition project—very close to the final realized shape and outlook
10
/ In the evening, the edges of the square are illuminated by subjacent lighting that reinforces the effect of the square as a floating, folded surface

To create a space, that invites everyone, different features have been created on the surface of the square:

- round holes in the square, which are filled with grass and trees and surrounded by benches thus creating green, urban hangout spots;
- areas that invite the citizens to participate in activities including ball games, skating, and playing; and
- stairs in the corners, which can be used as an observation post from where you can see the activities on the square, the pulsating life of the market place, and the beautiful green areas of H.C. Ørsteds Park.

Elevations

Leyton Open Spaces

Location /
London, UK

Completion date /
2014

Landscape design /
Kinnear Landscape Architects

Budget /
£4.3 million

Photography /
Adrian Taylor

Client /
London Borough of Waltham Forest

Marsh Lane

The main objective of the Marsh Lane project was to re-vitalize this urban fringe area and re-assert its presence in the Lea Valley, supporting a natural landscape that encourages sport and recognizing its role as a place of escape. In this project, we have further developed this idea by creating a new rural marsh lane and by reinforcing the importance of a strong line of poplars, using this line of trees as a visual anchor for the proposed sports pavilion. A radical overhaul of the existing sports facilities was also done to create new, high-quality sports areas.

The design integrates playful landscape elements within a vision for a renewed sense of ecology and the landscape of the marsh. As the site sits in the floodplain of the River Lea, the design encourages adventurous natural play in green spaces, supported by the local population. Play islands will become apparent only when the site is flooded, relating the design proposals directly to the site's flood-risk issues. An existing slope provides an adventurous play area for older children and young people, challenging them to improve their climbing and balancing skills, and offering the excitement of a high swing from the bank. The sculptural forms of the timber climbing spheres and metal rope posts have an intriguing attraction to visitors to the park. This has been designed for different skill levels to cater for all ages up to adult to allow cross-generational play. Ecology was integral to the design of the adventure play, providing a space for children to explore the natural environment.

01
/ Marsh hill
02–03
/ Local people enjoy cycling along the avenue in the park

① Wildflower bund
② Junior grass pitch
③ Synthetic turf pitch
④ The walk to school / bike track
⑤ Trampolines
⑥ Grass waves with play
⑦ Concrete waves with water play
⑧ Timber deck
⑨ Wildflower hill
⑩ Pavilion

Master plan

Abbotts Park

The Abbotts Park project in east London rejuvenated an urban park and encouraged local people to participate in sports. The project was completed in March 2013, footballer Sol Campbell (also a keen tennis player) attended an opening event to promote tennis for children.

The main change in the design was to open up the tennis courts and make a new connection from the pavilion to the park, to reduce antisocial behavior around the pavilion. The Victorian character of this suburban park has been enhanced by the design—the pavilion refurbishment stays true to the character of the original structure, but uses brighter materials and opens up the building to include community facilities and toilets. The tennis courts are improved and expanded to include a provision for children. By changing the layout of the tennis courts and creating a new link between the green area of the park and the pavilion, this underused space is activated, safer, and more inviting.

Section

04
/ Children's play area
05
/ Boulevard in the park
06
/ Water-jets play area

06

Concept rendering

Rendering

07
/ Adventure play
08
/ Wildflowers
09
/ Natural play area
10
/ Adventure play area

11
/ Drapers Field
12–13
/ Riding the wave
14
/ Drapers Field

Drapers Field

Leyton is a key regeneration area bridging the existing east London communities, the new East Village (formerly the Athlete's Village) and the Olympic Park. Drapers Field, which was used during the 2012 Olympics as a service facility, sits at this intersection of new and old. A main aim for the park was to create a place of sport and play on the route to school at Chobham Academy, which is located within the Olympic Village. The brief was to improve sports and play provision—the existing football facilities have been replaced with an upgraded synthetic sports pitch and new football pitch. In extension of the brief, the designers aimed to encourage more children and young people into recreational sport.

The playful route to school includes a bike track with space for obstacles and for basic cycling courses. This relates to the London Cycling Campaign's drive for safe cycling routes to schools and to GLA objectives. Cutting through the corrugated grass plane, the route also encourages spontaneous activity, with trampolines and other play elements located along its route.

Purple Pleasure

Location /
Hamburg, Germany
Area /
6727 square feet (625 square meters)
Completion date /
2013
Sportsfield design /
Carve
Budget /
€45,000
Photography /
Hanns Joosten
Client /
Camphill Ghent, Inc.

The Toolenburg lake in Hoofddorp was caused by a large sand excavation. The lake, which attracts visitors for numerous aquatic sports, is surrounded by beaches, sunbathing areas and two bars. Carve was asked by the municipality of Haarlemmermeer to design a sports and play zone on the northern shore of the lake.

A formation of colored circles with diverse playing elements is a challenging play zone, bordering the restaurant. Children with visual, audio, physical or mental disabilities can play here, without being limited in any way. Because of the 'language' of the circles, both in color and form, curiosity is stimulated, encouraging children to explore the whole zone. Because no 'special' elements were designed there, the distinction between able and disabled children is reduced. The play zone allows all children to play without restrictions.

In many cases, small sports fields in public spaces are designed for playing soccer. At best, it might also be possible to play basketball. The new sport zone in the Kwadrant Park was deliberately designed to not be directive in its use. By designing the edges of the sunken court in a different way, sitting, skating, soccer, and basketball were combined on one site. One edge of the court is a terraced lounge area, while the other side is an edge with several skate elements. Its edges are large, pointy planes, folded onto the elevated landscape. The intense purple color of the lounge area, skate area, and sport court gives the place a unique and recognizable identity in the landscape. This place has become a hotspot for young people from the surrounding area to meet for sports, lounging, or skating.

Master plan

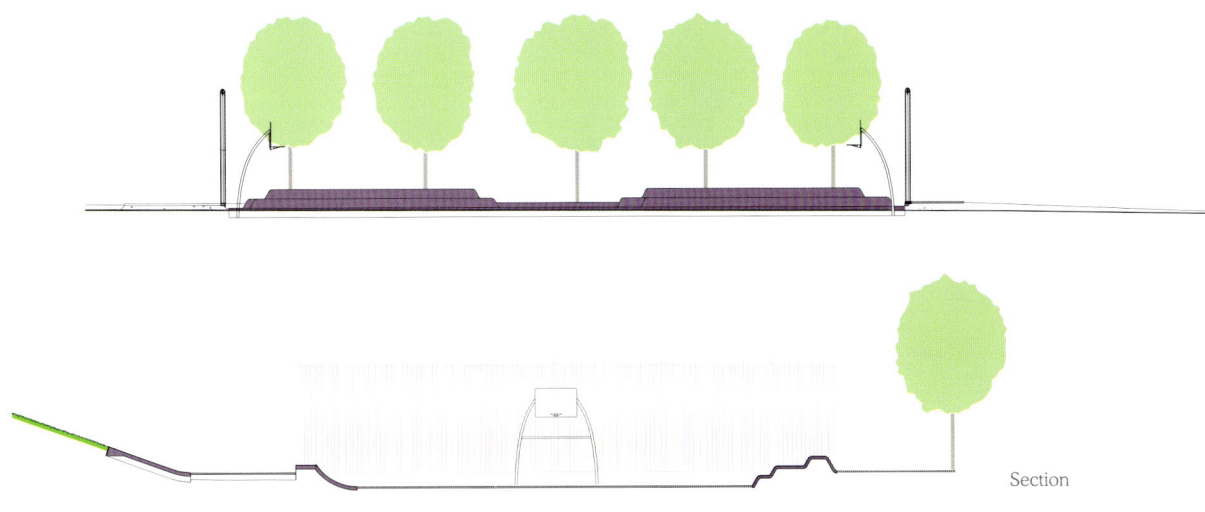

Section

01
/ Panorama view of whole sports zones
02
/ Multifunctional sports zones

03
/ Play zone with multiple play objects
04
/ Climbing net
05
/ Playing facilities for children

Smile Playground

Location /
Island of Mallorca, Spain

Area /
12,378.5 square feet (1150 square meters)

Completion date /
2014

Landscape design /
A2arquitectos

Photography /
Ihobbies

Client /
Hotel Castell dels Hams

In 1967, a small hotel, 'Castell dels Hams', was established on the island of Majorca amid the Mediterranean vegetation. Over time, and through subtle improvements and extensions, it has become one of the most distinctive hotels on the eastern part of the island, a much sought-after tourist destination for its ravishing beaches and turquoise waters. For the last of the alterations, Spanish landscape-design practice A2arquitectos created a new area, an extension of recreational activities and entertainment for the young guests of the hotel.

The vision for the new pool, a big 'smile', focuses on how it can be perceived from different viewpoints and different scales, either at the level of the foot, from the terraces of the hotel or including the aerial and satellite views of Google Maps. The designers opted for circular organizational elements, where the center of the whole is the children's pool. This yellow circle is 39.4 feet (12 meters) in diameter and it differs from the other existing swimming pools in form and color. Around it are different areas with water games for children, showers, sunbeds, etc. Different programs were disguised in the painted circles on the pavement.

The extension also includes a spray play area, as well as a regular play area for toddlers. Using vibrant colors and playful forms throughout, unlike the rest of the hotel, the entire area designated for children stands out from the former sports court and the pre-existing outdoor space.

02

03

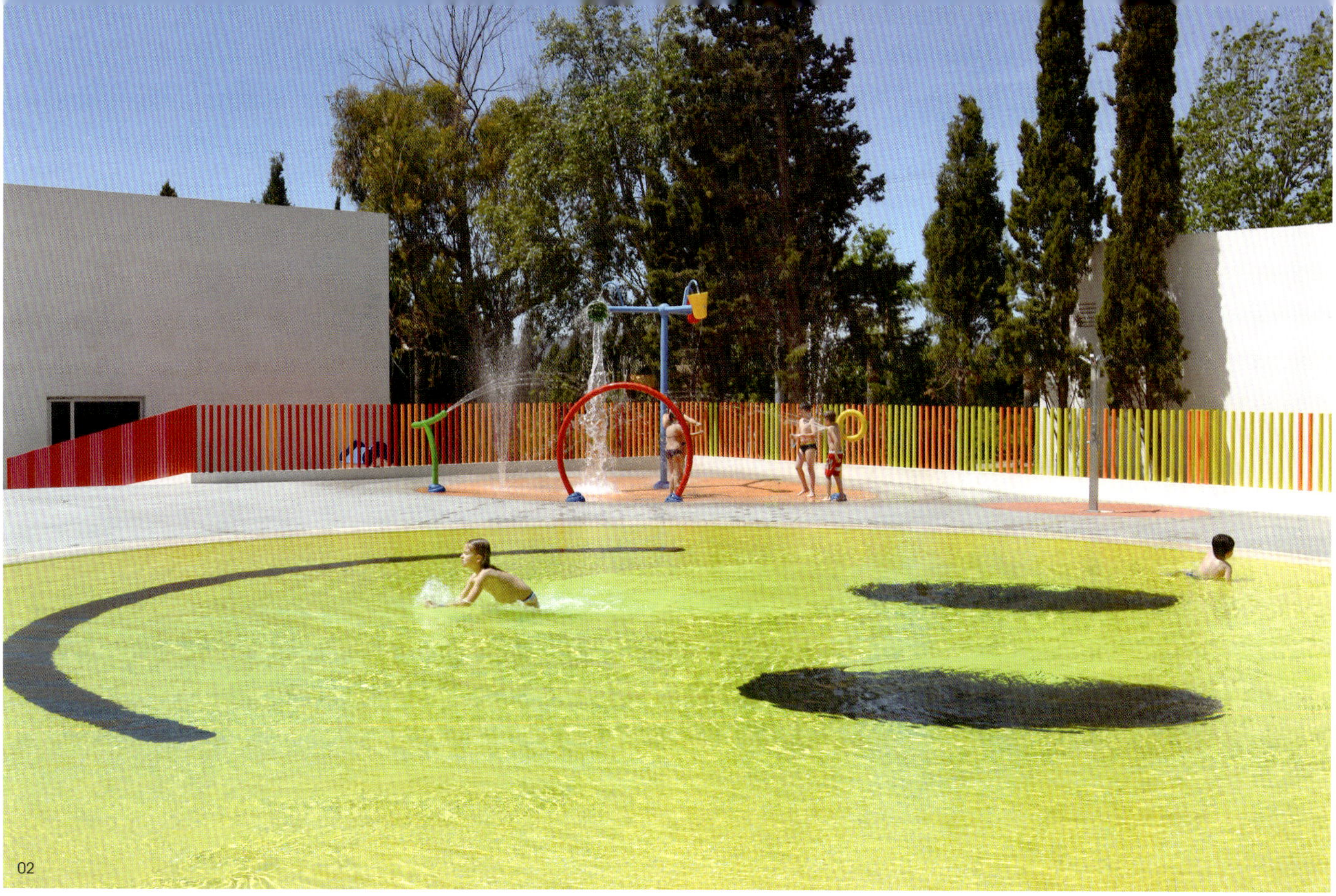

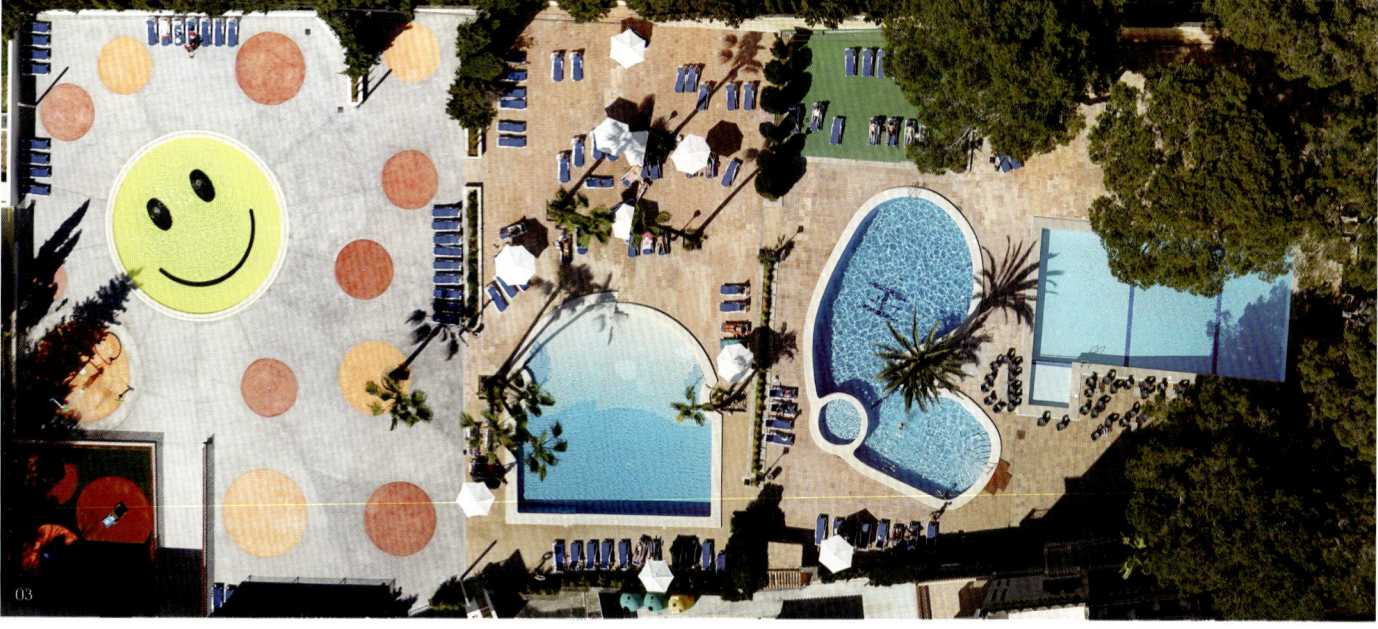

01
/ Aerial view of the smile swimming pool
02
/ Swimming pool and water play facility
03
/ Aerial view of surrounding swimming pools

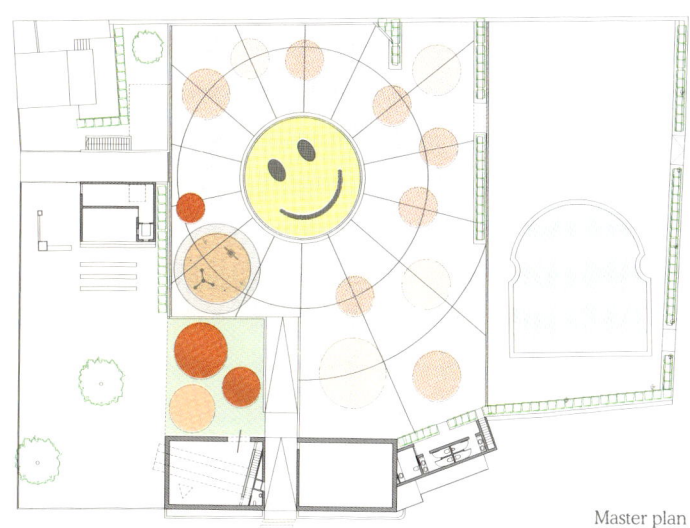

Master plan

04–05
/ Children are enjoying water play in the pool
06
/ Smile swimming pool
07–08
/ Water-play facilities

Van Beuningenplein Sportsfield

Location /
Amsterdam, The Netherlands

Area /
2.3 acres (9500 square meters)

Completion date /
2011

Landscape design /
Carve

Architecture design /
Concrete Architectural Associates

Photography /
Carve

Client /
Municipality of Amsterdam

Old situation

The Van Hallstraat, which passes one side of the Van Beuningenplein, is the demarcation line for this poorer neighborhood, which lacks public facilities. The Van Beuningenplein was hidden from view by cars, fencing, and a poorly maintained green, isolating a former play and sport area from its surrounding context. As a result, this hidden square had become prone to teenagers hanging out there, often vandalizing the area. Residents living around the Van Beuningenplein were strictly opposed to any cutting of old trees, although they didn't make use of the square since it was perceived as a no-go area. The City of Amsterdam decided to construct a parking garage at Van Beuningenplein, removing parked cars from the surface and creating a more open space. On top of the newly constructed parking garage, a new play and sport area was to be built. This was the start for a new Van Beuningenplein.

Aim

The square was safe at night, inviting children to play and citizens to find a personal place to pause, relax, engage, and interact. The most important demand was to keep all the existing large trees around the square, which meant the new parking garage had to be carefully fitted in, leaving more space on street level for public use.

Intervention

The site was designed in collaboration between three offices, each bringing their special expertise. The buildings were designed by Concrete Architectural Associates, the landscape concept came from Dijk&Co, and the inner courts of the square, facilitating leisure areas, the playground and sports, were designed by Carve. Bringing the three offices together to discuss one another's proposals and perspectives has certainly added to the quality of the plan, together with collaborative processes with residents and engaging experts with their particular fields such as the disabled, local kids, and city ecologists as to the preservation of the Amsterdam trees, etc.

Master plan

01
/ View of the play zone
02
/ View of the sports fields

03

04

03
/ The sports fields can be used for various sports like soccer, basketball and panna. Edges are for seating and skating
04
/ Play zone with hammocks
05
/ The water element can be activated by the playground manager
06
/ The edges of the sports zone are used for skating

07

07–08
/ Play tower
09
/ Play zone with play tower
10
/ Detail of how to climb up to the tower

Argenteuil Skatepark

Location /
Argenteuil, France

Area /
13,185.8 square feet (1225 square meters)

Completion date /
2013

Skate park designer /
Spectrum Skateparks Inc.

Landscape design /
Recreation Urbaine

Budget /
€700,000

Photography /
Jim Barnum / Spectrum Skateparks Inc.

Client /
Val-d'Oise Department

Located within a newly developed public park made up largely of expansive pathways and open green space, this park is a juxtaposition of organic, endless circular flow with linear, back-and-forth technical skating.

The flow zone incorporates 'rollout lip' for ease of entry for all skill levels, as well as a vertical pool coping section for the most advanced skaters. The lack of flat bottom is extremely uncommon in skate parks, as is the layout of the park in general, so it's at first arresting and even confusing for the average skater as they are challenged to ride something unexpected. The experience of pure flow, focusing less on tricks and more on movement and generating speed through the park, soon has the rider laughing and having a great time. Parks of this style change the act of skateboarding from performance/goal/trick-oriented riding to an experience of fun and play, with skaters going 'out of their minds' and into their bodies as they experience the flowing sensations. The social interaction changes from a competitive/performance environment into one of play, with skaters spontaneously playing games of 'follow the leader', 'tag', and 'freight train'.

The street zone comprises the simplest shapes, little more than flat concrete and rectangular boxes. The stripped-down nature of this area forces skaters to do what they do best, getting creative with very little, and transforming something incredibly basic and mundane into a playground. While progression in the flow zone generally means more speed and fluidity, and less effort, here it means more and more complex tricks and variations, putting them together in 'lines' where multiple elements are hit one after the other. This results in a very pure street-skating experience in an active environment. The adjacent mature shade trees and snack bar provide respite on long days at the skate park.

Layout of street and flow zones, multisport court, pathways and green spaces

01
/ Street zone with playground in background
02
/ Street zone mirroring adjacent walking path
03
/ Overview of flow zone

Early layout of street zone

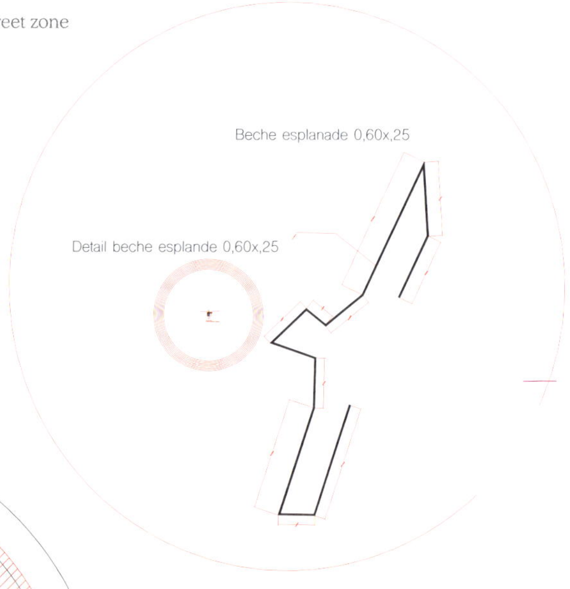

Beche esplanade 0,60x,25

Detail beche esplande 0,60x,25

Layout of flow zone

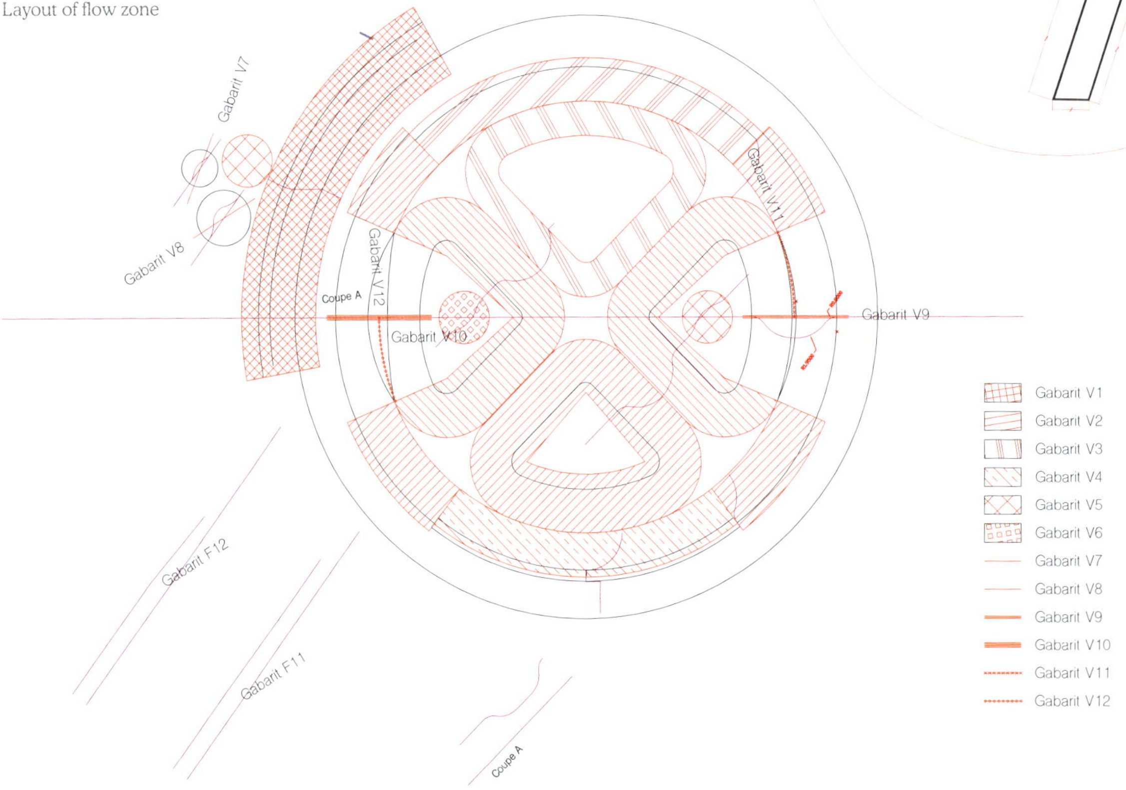

Gabarit V7
Gabarit V8
Gabarit V11
Gabarit V12
Coupe A
Gabarit V10
Gabarit V9
Gabarit F12
Gabarit F11
Coupe A

	Gabarit V1
	Gabarit V2
	Gabarit V3
	Gabarit V4
	Gabarit V5
	Gabarit V6
	Gabarit V7
	Gabarit V8
	Gabarit V9
	Gabarit V10
	Gabarit V11
	Gabarit V12

04
/ Skatepark in the background on the left, playground on the right, Le Ginguette snack bar in the background on the right
05
/ Spectrum's Jim Barnum, FS 50-50 on the pool coping extension
06
/ Spectrum's Jim Barnum, backside carve down the speed line
07
/ The park is suitable for young beginners through to professionals
08
/ The flow zone

Elmira Skatepark

Location /
Elmira, Ontario, Canada

Area /
**8611.1 square feet
(800 square meters)**

Completion date /
2014

Skate park designer /
Spectrum Skateparks Inc.

Budget /
CA$400,000

Photography /
**Jim Barnum /
Spectrum Skateparks Inc.**

Client /
Woolwich Recreation Foundation

Elmira's long, linear layout aligns with the existing grain of the adjacent street. Colored earth-tone concrete and landscaped transition spaces soften the impact of this concrete incursion into the landscape. Entry pathways and viewing areas are defined and delineated as non-skate areas by the different textural language of exposed areas. Elmira is well known as a producer of Canada #1 Grade maple syrup, so the local skaters requested the inclusion of a maple leaf symbol in the park, which was acid-etched into the most towering, daring feature in the street zone—the bank-to-barrier. Designed to take advantage of the existing mature trees, the park feels like it's always been there, offering a comfortable environment for both active and passive users.

The park includes a replica pool and street area. The long, narrow layout of the street zone provides skaters with an expansive skate experience without the costs associated with a large skate park. Long lines are the foundation of street skating, being able to hit multiple features all in one line, travelling in one direction; riding this park feels just like riding down the street, although in this case it's an idealized, enhanced street. While other parks of similar square footage can feel cramped, this park allows skaters to really cover some distance instead of feeling like they are caged. The variety of features across the street area, while tending toward more technical skating, is vast, from the low-to-the-ground, ultra-long manual pad with all the trimmings, to the large set of stairs and the tight transitioned rainbow quarter pipe.

The pool is a non-traditional shape, not kidney or egg shape, but more in keeping with the linear nature of the street area. At 5 feet (1.5 meters) and 8 feet 6 inches (2.6 meters) deep, it provides a visceral grinding experience. The pool draws skaters from hours away due to its unique shape, challenging depths, and the lack of similar facilities in the province.

01
/ Looking east at the Pier 7 manual pad, hubbas and rail
02
/ Looking northwest as a skater rolls through the tech flat ground zone

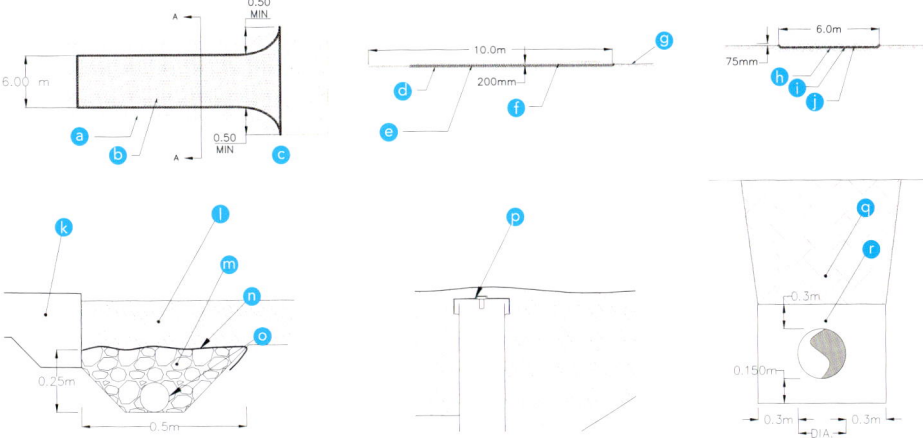

- ⓐ Existing ground
- ⓑ 3.9 to 5.9 inches (10 to 15 centimeters) of rock
- ⓒ Existing pavement
- ⓓ Existing ground
- ⓔ Filter cloth
- ⓕ 3.9 to 5.9 inches (10 to 15 centimeters) of rock
- ⓖ Existing pavement
- ⓗ Existing ground
- ⓘ Filter cloth
- ⓙ 3.9 to 5.9 inches (10 to 15 centimeters) of rock
- ⓚ Skate park
- ⓛ 5.9 inches (15 centimeters) of topsoil
- ⓜ 0.75 inches (19 millimeters) of drain rock
- ⓝ Non-woven filter fabric
- ⓞ 3.9 inches (10 centimeters) of perforated pipe
- ⓟ Clean outs to be buried under ground
- ⓠ Select backfill
- ⓡ Bedding

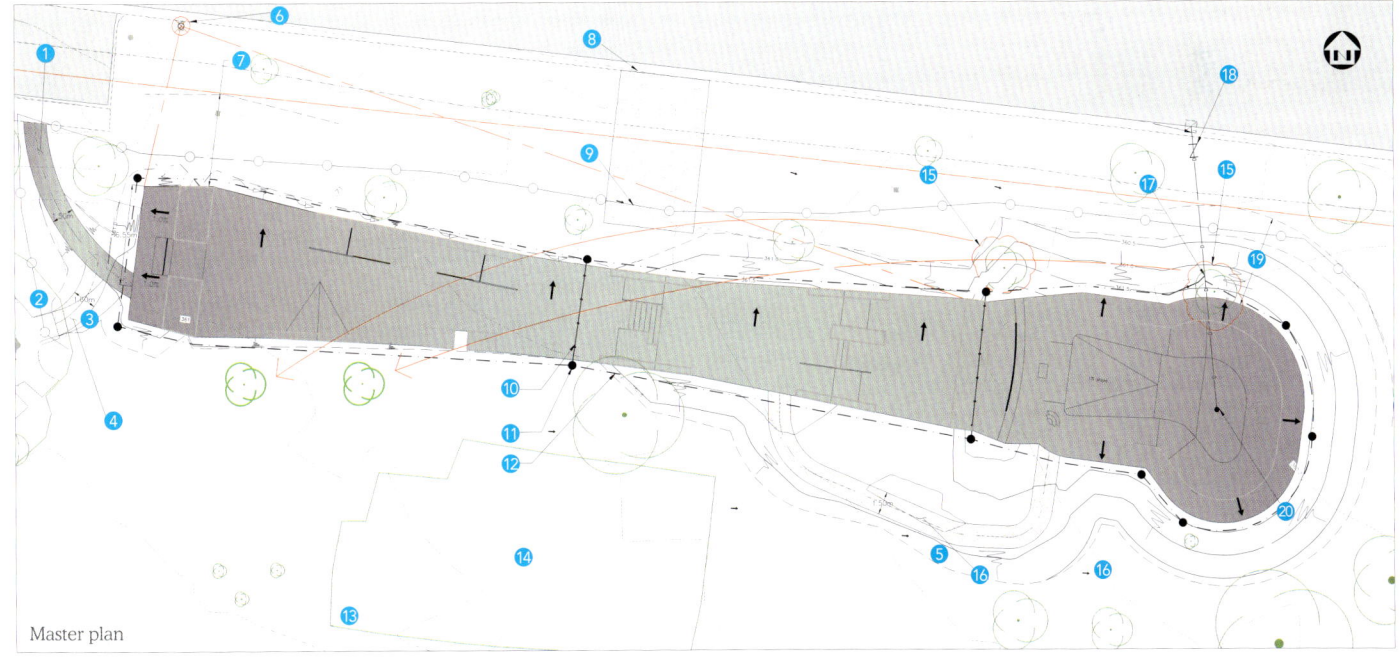

Master plan

1. Proposed 4.9-inch-wide (1.5-meter-wide) donor concrete pathway
2. Wall
3. Pergola
4. Proposed 4.9-inch-wide (1.5-meter-wide) asphalt path
5. Grass
6. Water valve
7. 19.7-foot (6-meter) offset from skate park to property line
8. Vehicle tracking pad
9. Erosion and sediment control fence
10. Solid storm pipe to connect clean outs
11. 3.9-inch (10-centimeter) clean outs
12. Exterior perimeter: 3.9-inch (10-centimeter) perforated pipe
13. Flower bed
14. Vegetable garden
15. Tree to be relocated
16. Proposed 4.9-inch-wide (1.5-meter-wide) wide asphalt path
17. Connect perimeter drain to storm line
18. Canplas back water valve or approved equivalent
19. 19.7-foot (6-meter) offset from skate park to property line
20. Area drain

- Storm pipe
- Perforated pipe
- Asphalt path
- Ex. coutour (1 m vertical separation)
- Proposed coutour (0.2 m vertical separation)
- General slope direction

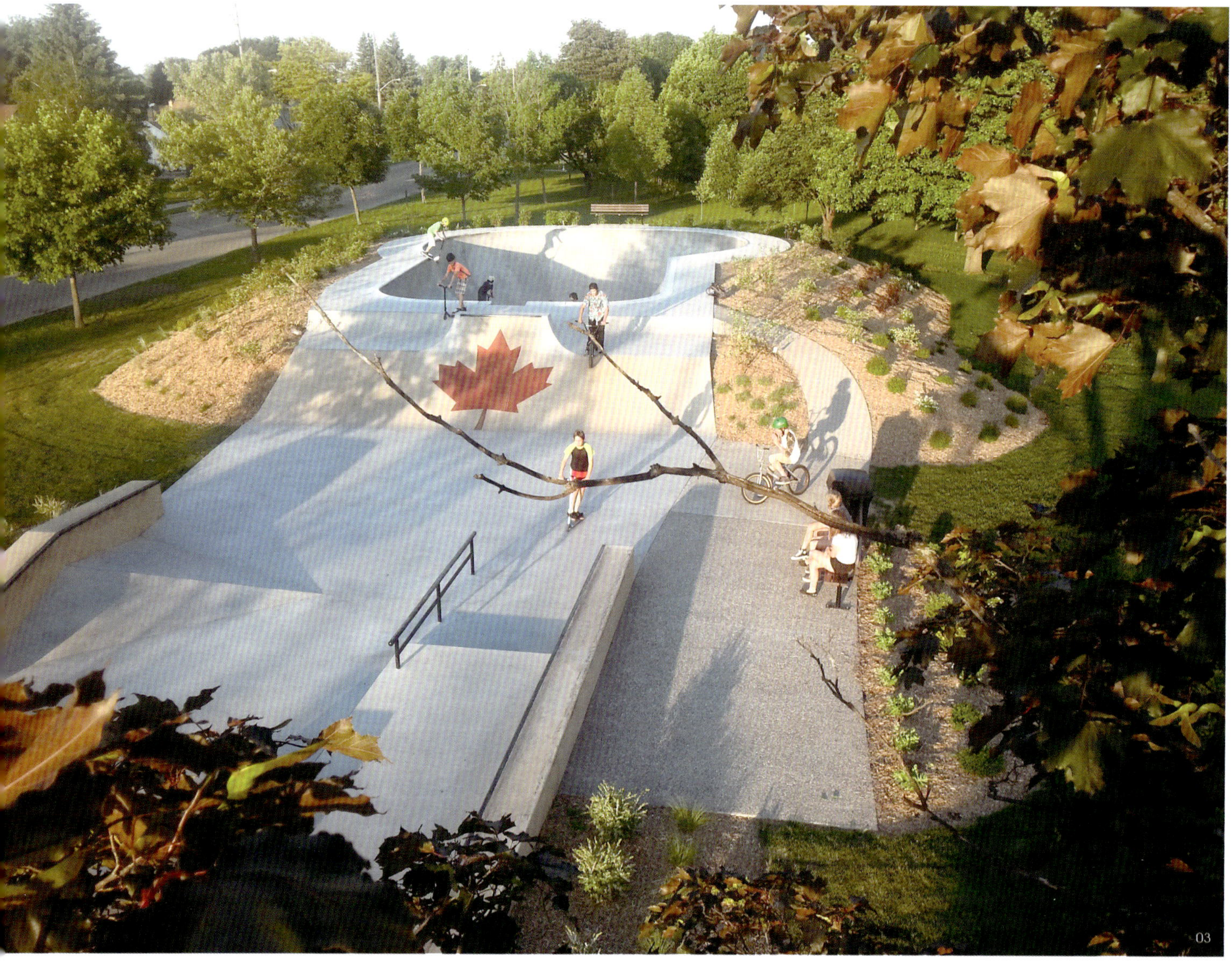

03
/ Looking east at the maple leaf bank-to-barrier and the replica pool
04
/ Entry pathway with donor recognition stones
05
/ Tech flat ground area
06
/ Detail of tech flat ground area, specifically the stacked manual pad/ledge/rail combo
07
/ Floating wedge-to-wedge gap with stacked manual pad combo in background

161

Sportpark Meerpark

Location /
Amsterdam, The Netherlands

Area /
5.9 acres (2.4 hectares)

Completion date /
2010

Landscape design /
Carve

Photography /
Carve

Inner-ring green areas

Cities are still growing physically, expanding on the outer borders and increasing density from within. This urban development changes the use of large existing green areas, like sports parks, within the periphery of these cities. For economical reasons, these green areas are often being built with dwellings or offices, and the former functions are relocated at the outskirts of the built conglomeration. At the same time, parks are used more intensively (partly due to the changing demographics) and green areas play an increasingly important role in daytime recreation. This results in a new challenge, which is to be answered in urban areas worldwide lest parks are left at the periphery, even though there is a growing need for green areas in the urban environment. How can we maintain these green areas, adjust and adapt them to the current need for community parks? Sport park Middenmeer-Voorland can be seen as an example for transformation of green spaces within a changing urban environment.

Transformation

The former sport park is a green area in the eastern district of Amsterdam, located between the city districts Watergraafsmeer, Diemen, and the circular highway. A corridor of the city's ecological main structure runs through this plot. The splendid green areas in between the sports park are hardly used. Considering the changing demographic situation, the question was raised of whether this space could be transformed to be used by the community. Could it be transformed into a public park? The city council took the challenge to reinvent this sports park into a community park.

The sport park consists of 10 fields, an athletics track, a basketball court and a skate park, all spread around a central, green, elongated strip of land. This strip is part of and connects to the adjacent building blocks and is an important axis in this 1930s layout of Amsterdam. It's primarily used as a main biking route connection from Amsterdam to Diemen. The strip of land was divided into several smaller parts by bike and pedestrian lanes. In the proposal for the new park, the pathways were restructured, and pedestrian and bike lanes were merged, and transferred to one side. An open green area emerged, big enough to accommodate the proposed mixed features, fitting new leisure trends and the desired additions for an urban community park.

① Parking zone
② Central zone
③ Play zone

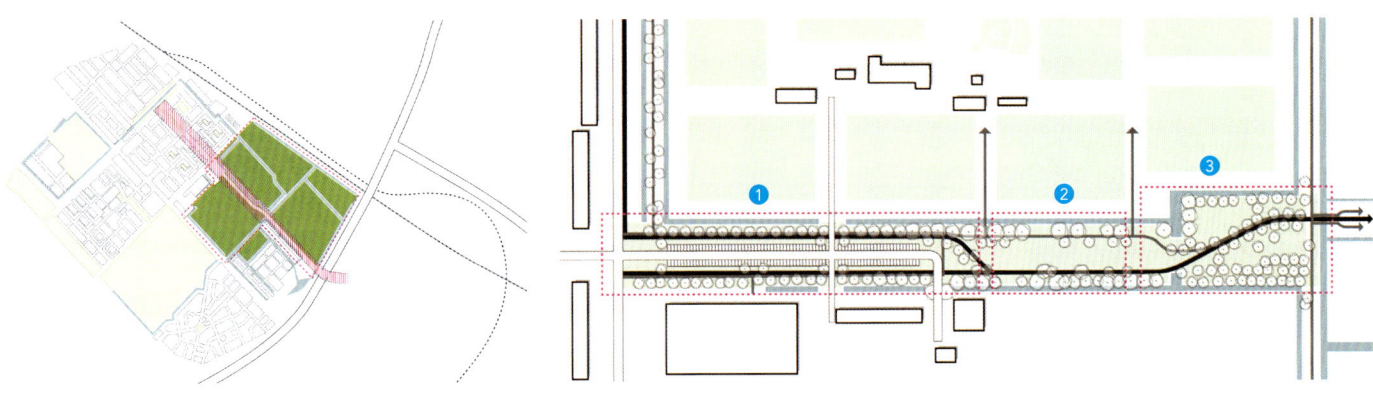

Context   New situation

01
/ Central zone with new bike path
02
/ Central zone with picnic and barbecue facilities

03

04

03–04
/ Play zone with natural character, and hill

05–06
/ The play zone contains a professional boulder wall

Site plan

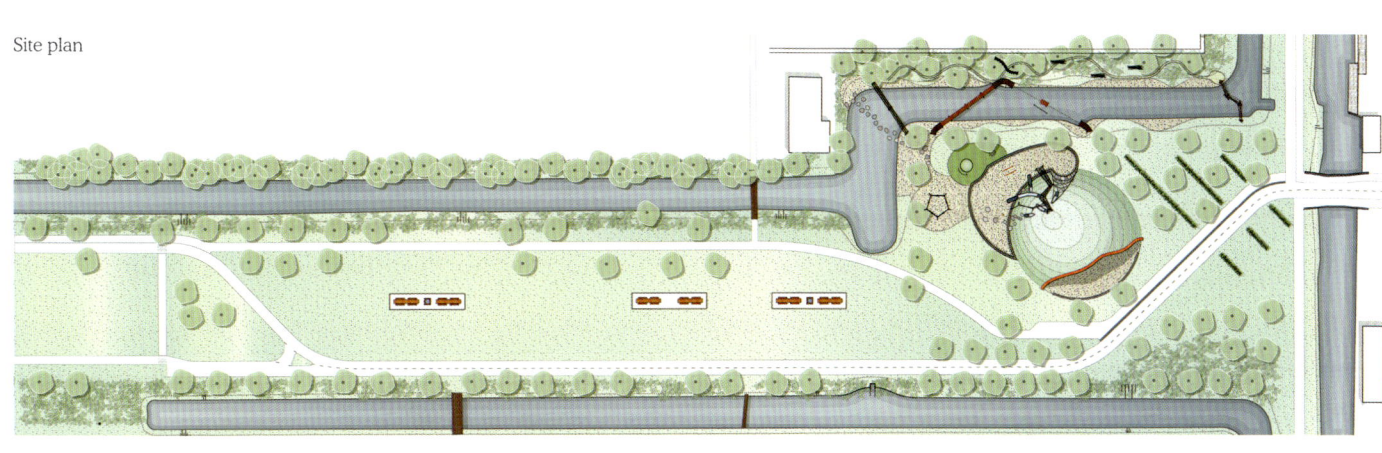

Lippepark Schacht Franz

Location /
Hamm, Germany

Area /
33 acres (13.4 hectares)

Completion date /
2013

Landscape design /
Scape Landschaftsarchitekten GmbH

Photography /
Matthias Funk, Thorsten Hübner, Hans Blossey

Client /
City of Hamm

The former site of the mining shaft 'Schacht Franz' was developed through intensive public participation to become the largest sport and leisure park in the district of Herringen, western Hamm. Comprehensive public participation was established through a competition and an advisory board that received more than 100 project ideas to review and select from. These project ideas, such as the 'square of the five world religions', have been taken up by the planners and developed with the participation of artists into recognizable places of the city park.

The park has a clear basic structure, in which all the paths and attractions are organized around the central lawn. In the north of the complex is a fun sport park with a professional skate park including a pool, jump hill, street plaza, all-weather sports field, climbing wall, parkour facility, and a lounge and a foyer with a pavilion. In the western forest park there is a playground and the 'square of five world religions'. The eastern noise barrier has been transformed into a spacious embankment park with a promenade, and terraced sitting places that face onto the central event place. Furthermore, a path goes through on the top of the embankment with its viewpoints to the surrounding landscape. The southern entrance plaza, defined by the viewpoint on top of the rampart and birch grove, is the highly visible emblem of the park. In the center of the park, at the spot of former shaft, is an information point for mining and social history in Herringen.

The design language combines all the elements into a park image, while creating an exciting contrast of different spaces. The eastern edge of the park is defined by the straight promenade, the pasted slim gardens, and the linear rampart, and the rows of trees have a very clear and straightforward design. The western edge of the park, developed from an overlapping structure of curved grass bands, with a backdrop of individual tree groves and games, barbecue and meeting places, creates a smooth transition from the wood to the open park meadow.

Master plan

01
/ Aerial view
02
/ Park promenade

03
/ Park promenade
04
/ Terraced sitting place
05
/ Skate park
06
/ Square of five world religions
07
/ Skate park aerial view

170

Plan

① Sport park
② Foyer
③ Memorial place of former mining industry,
④ Play round
⑤ Terraced sitting places
⑥ Forest park
⑦ Central lawn
⑧ Square of the five world religions
⑨ Promenade
⑩ Embankment
⑪ Entrance

08
/ Playground
09
/ Park view
10
/ Central lawn
11
/ Swing by the central lawn

171

Moabiter Stadtgarten—Park on the former freight station Moabit

Location /
Berlin, Germany

Area /
3.2 acres (1.3 hectares)

Completion date /
2012

Landscape design /
glasser und dagenbach, landscape architects

Photography /
Udo Dagenbach

The basic concept was to design an urban garden in which the residents had a useful platform as large as possible to develop their activities, using a clear, easily understandable outline. The parks provides services for families as well as for senior citizens. The free space in front of the former freight depot Moabit offered the possibility for various uses, such as a space for art and culture, a location for events, a playground or a meeting point in the cozy beer garden. It now has a curved path, with seats, leading to the building and to the rear areas of the park. On either side of the forecourt are created lawns under a bright canopy of 100 Japanese pagoda trees (Sophora japonica). Their crowns are cut flat, like a roof.

The area east of the building shall be provided to the public for individual use. In a collaborative development process, the split area could develop, for example, into a mosaic of kitchen garden, school-based 'laboratory garden', and comfortable meeting place. The citizen garden receives raised planting beds and structuring rank elements. On the west side of the building is the playground with various play and activity opportunities for children and adults.

For the design of the playground, children and young people between four and about 10 to 12 years were surveyed. Many wishes were considered, such as a wave path for bicycles, crates, towers of wooden boxes that point to the former use of the freight depot, partner swings, nest swings, and a bobby-car race track. At the north side of the park, the terrain is banked, slightly rising so that a 'balcony' is created. Sloping to the south, a generous lawn/wildflower meadow arises as an orchard with fruit trees and shrubs, whose proceeds are used by the residents. The noise-protection wall is designed as a concave concrete wall with a structure like 'egg-coal', a reference to the use of the site as a freight depot.

Master plan

01
/ Lawn with fruit trees and benches for picnicking

02
/ Access to the northern entrance is built out of red concrete walls

Perspective of design plan

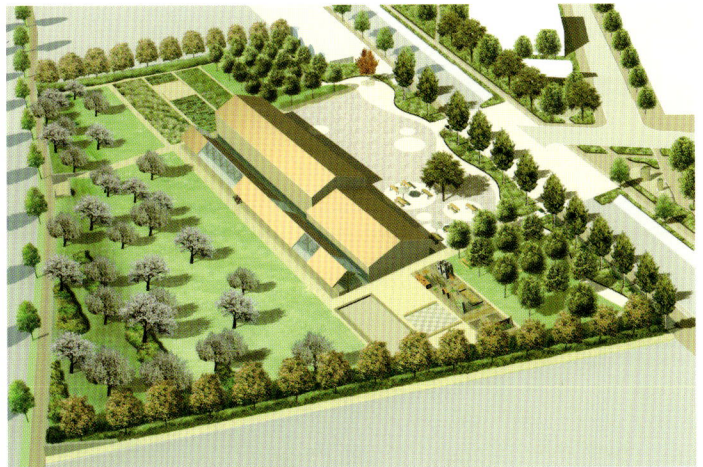

Perspective of lawns under a roof of Japanese pagoda trees (Sophora japonica)

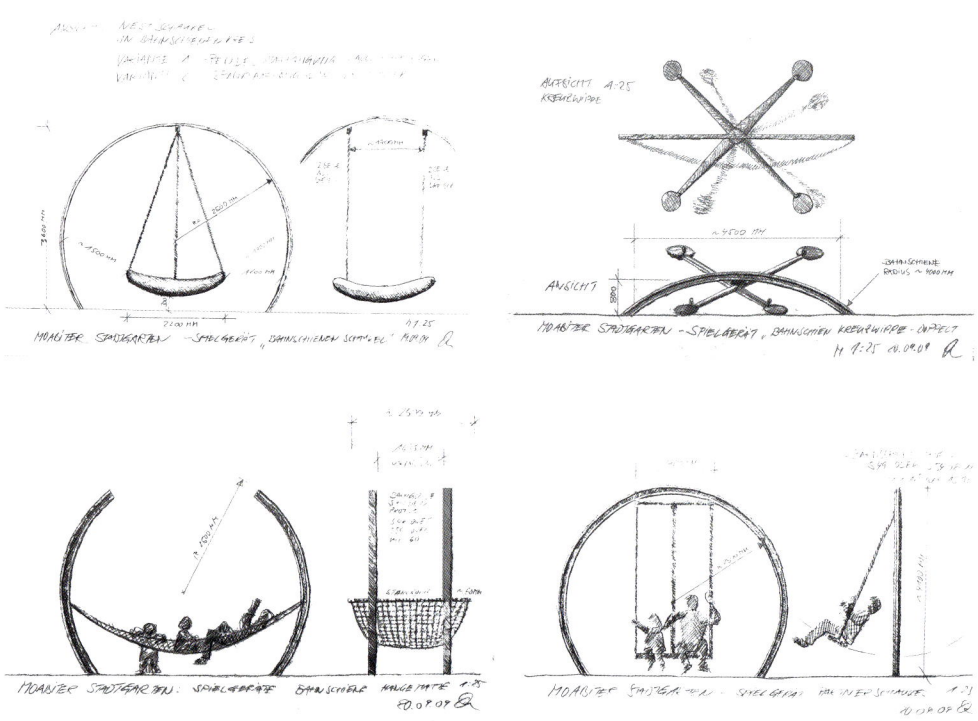

Design sketch for different types of swings suggesting used railway tracks

03
/ An overturned suitcase out of wooden boxes and railway ties for balancing, a reference to the old freight station
04
/ Partner swing on a rack of bent rails
05
/ Hammock on a rack of bent rails

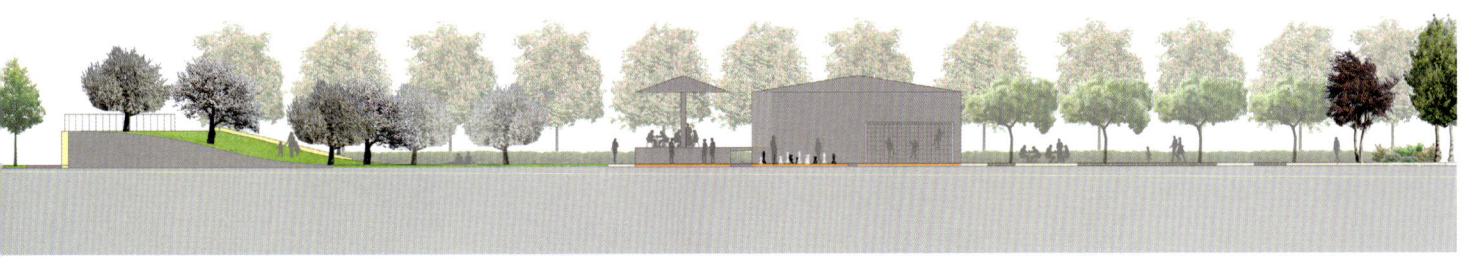

Cross-section through the entire grounds

06

07

06
/ A trampoline, a wooden train and a tower of boxes to play on are references to the old freight station
07
/ The playground on the west side of the building
08
/ Playground with a tower of wooden boxes and climbing wall made to look like leftovers of the freight station

Schmul Park

Location /
New York, USA

Landscape design /
James Corner Field Operations

Photography /
Jeffery Totaro

In other areas of Schmul Park, flowering meadow plantings are also structured around color gradients. A variety of notable natives that primarily flower in yellow and purple—black-eyed susan, clasping coneflower, Stiff goldenrod, grass-leaved goldenrod, purple coneflower, Ohio spiderwort, pale purple coneflower, purple joe-pye weed, common milkweed and White wood aster—are planted in masses to create a mid-summer attraction. The large-scale massing echoes the great meadows to be found in the interior of the surrounding larger area of Freshkills Park. The introduction of native meadow in Schmul Park draws a primary landscape feature of Freshkills' interior outward.

The design proposal for Schmul Park recast existing site programs—that were set amid a uniform asphalt surface—in softer, more colorful, more playful and topographically dynamic settings. The play area, for example, uses yellow, blue and orange poured rubber to create a mound-scape reminiscent of the striking topographies elsewhere in Freshkills Park. A soft rubber surface hosts two bays of new swings, one for toddlers and another for primary school children; a new custom tot-fort built into a medium-sized mound; a new custom 7 feet (2 meters) high slide integrated with the largest of all the play mounds; an updated spray shower that boasts two shower towers and four fan jets; a custom cast-in-place concrete ellipse sand box; and a variety of Gametime X-Scape multi-use equipment: an X-linear climber, a net climber, and a track ride. Further into the park, the basketball courts and the handball courts are transformed by their elliptical fence enclosures. These custom-designed fences create unique spatial volumes with varied pole-spacing rhythms to dramatize the fences' elliptical shapes.

01
/ Blue rubber playing area
02
/ Full view of children's playing area
03
/ The play area uses colorful poured rubber

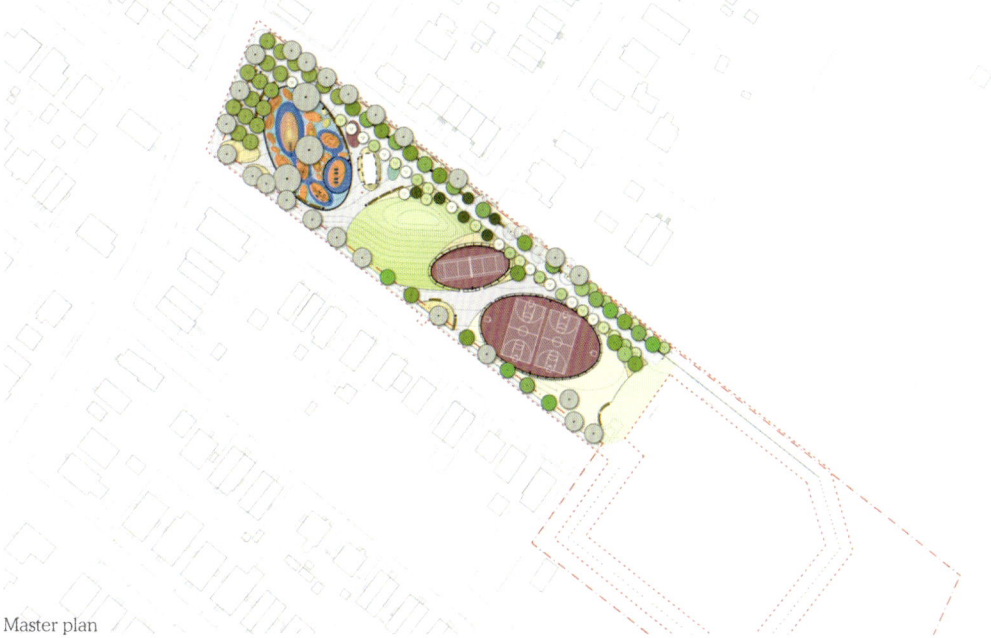

Master plan

Perhaps the most significant part of Schmul Park's sustainability strategy is its stormwater management approach. The old park was completely impermeable as it was paved with asphalt in most areas. From the proposed poured rubber with a stone screening base, to the concrete pavers, porous concrete sidewalk, flexi-pave court surfaces, (both the flexi-pave and the poured rubber use recycled tires) and the lawn and meadows, all the new surfaces allow water to infiltrate in situ. Several stormwater features work hand in hand with these porous surfaces. A rain garden is sized to capture and infiltrate water. A bio swale along the northeastern edge of the park provides overflow for the rain garden. The porous surface of the courts is actually a significant element of an infiltration system, with large gravel retention cells located beneath court surfaces.

Concept rendering

04–06
/ Permeable pave

Basketball concept rendering

181

Lemvig Skatepark

Location /
Lemvig, Denmark

Area /
**23,680 square feet
(2200 square meters)**

Completion date /
2013

Landscape design /
EFFEKT

Photography /
EFFEKT

Client /
Lemvig Municipality, Realdania, Lokale og Anlægsfonden

In the spring of 2013, Lemvig Municipality faced a group of citizens eager to transform an empty industrial lot on the city's harbor front into an area of leisure and recreation. In order to meet the demands of the local population, EFFEKT worked closely with representatives from different user groups to develop a new type of urban space. The result of this collaboration was an integrated skate park and urban park that offered a range of programmatic features and recreational opportunities. Set in beautiful surroundings, the park has created a new social space in Lemvig, attracting skaters and families from the entire region.

'The harbor, having displaced most of its activity along the coast, had become a residual wastescape of maritime activity. By envisioning the skate and park as a social gathering space that would attract people of all ages and interests, we believed it could become a catalyst for revitalization that would rebrand the harbor front as a recreational hub and reintroduce the harbor as an important asset to the city,' says MikkelBøgh of EFFEKT.

From the start, the design team knew that the project would need an array of ingredients to differentiate itself from the grey, black, and rust-tinted surfaces of the immediate surroundings, the consequence of a downturn in the local fishing industry. By challenging the typology of the skate park—an otherwise mono-functional greyscape—alongside a thorough investigation of surfaces in public space, they were able to design a hybrid platform that would accommodate a multitude of social and recreational activities. Skateboarding originated in streets, existing with a multitude of other urban activities. As it grew in popularity and became commercialized, the sport and culture was moved into these grey parks were it became isolated from the same city that originally fueled, challenged and inspired the skaters. By merging skateboarding with a multitude of other recreational activities and reintroducing the skate culture back into the city center, the skateboarders and other groups of the population will benefit greatly from this new co-existence on the harbor, and potentially breath new life into an otherwise abandoned area that has great potential.

Site plan

01
/ Bird's-eye view of whole skate park
02
/ Basketball field

Function zoning map

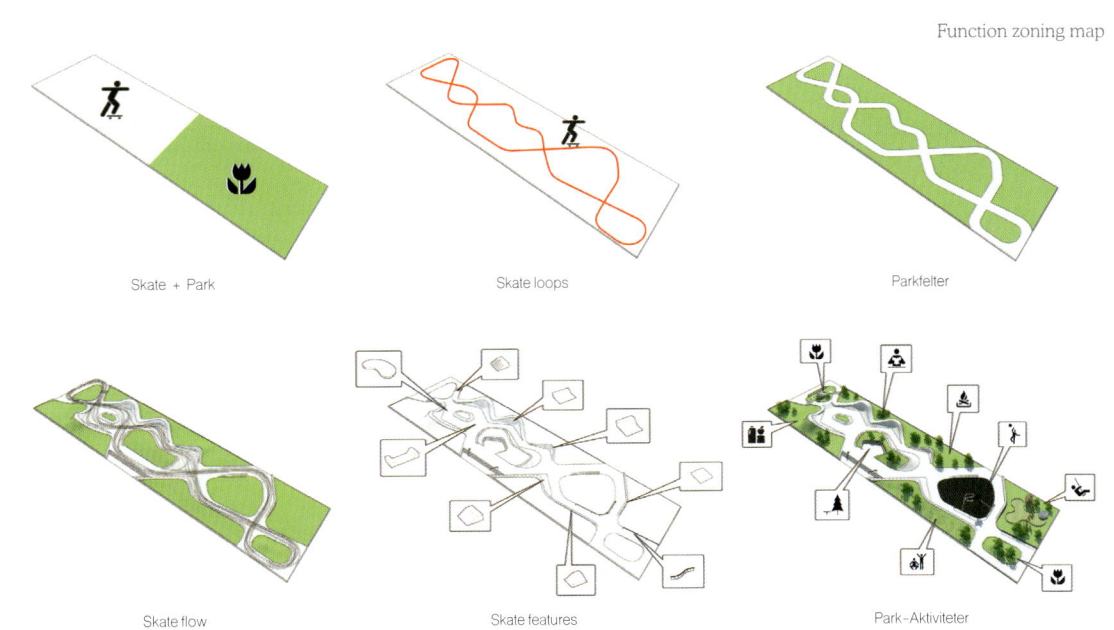

Skate + Park

Skate loops

Parkfelter

Skate flow

Skate features

Park-Aktiviteter

184

03
/ Sandpit beside basketball field
04
/ People using skate facility
05–06
/ Grass area

05

06

3D modeling

① 3.9 to 4.7 inches (10 to 12 centimeters) of beton
② 3.9 to 4.7 inches (10 to 12 centimeters) of asphalt
③ Mulch
④ Grasses
⑤ Boundary
⑥ Soil
⑦ Sand

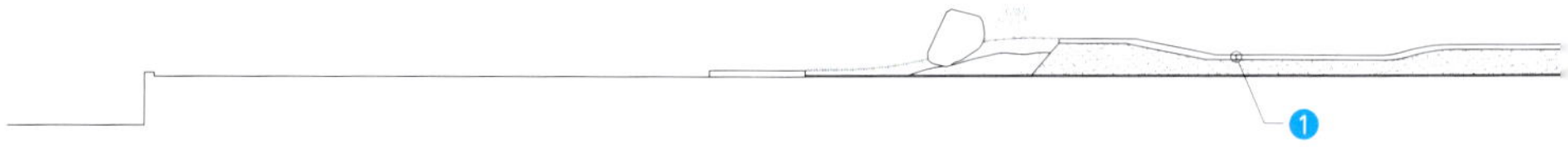

Section

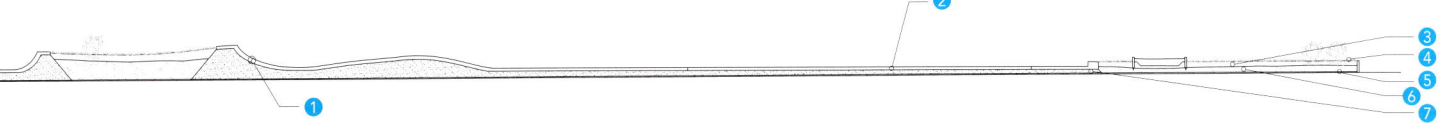

07
/ Basketball field overlapping with skating area
08
/ The main skating area
09–10
/ Kids enjoying game time in the park

Zhangmiao Exercise Park

Location /
Shanghai, China

Area /
43,056 square feet (4000 square meters)

Completion date /
2013

Landscape design /
Archi-Union Architects

This is a typical example of a public space in the Workers New Village Area, a symbol of time. Designers at Archi-Union Architects planned to reverse the original urban matrix structure through new mini-landscape research and designs of the street corner to provide more public space for the aging society. The design process is under the guidance of Landscape Urbanism, to consolidate urban pedestrian and green systems. The final purpose is to increase sport opportunities and to enhance life for communities through urban renewal. They utilized the circular runway to provide more possibilities for morning runs and walking, more space in the square for dancing, and the long corridor with prefabricated steel structures for young couples. With these kind of micro renewal projects, they explored the possibility of democratic, civic, and public property of the modern city space. This street corner is also our small practice in urban renewal.

The design of Zhangmiao Exercise Park shows Chinese designers' attitude towards the city. Through the self-generating energy, it shapes the urban space. With the combination of runway, square, and landscape, an ecological system is built at the corner space of the city. The street corner was only filled and leveled up to meet the basic requirements of the citizens, but did not provide many choices or public activities. The designers considered the functional requirement, and integrated the urban dynamic element into it. Wind and solar energy provide the nighttime lighting. The vertical grass vegetation creates different spatial possibilities. The corridor space becomes a sheltering space for citizens. The jogging path, which is paved with plastic cement, becomes the liveliest space in the whole area for people hanging out at night. The civic and public property of the modern city space is fully represented in this street corner.

01
/ Aerial view of whole exercise park
02
/ Conceptual plan

Site plan

Combined elevation

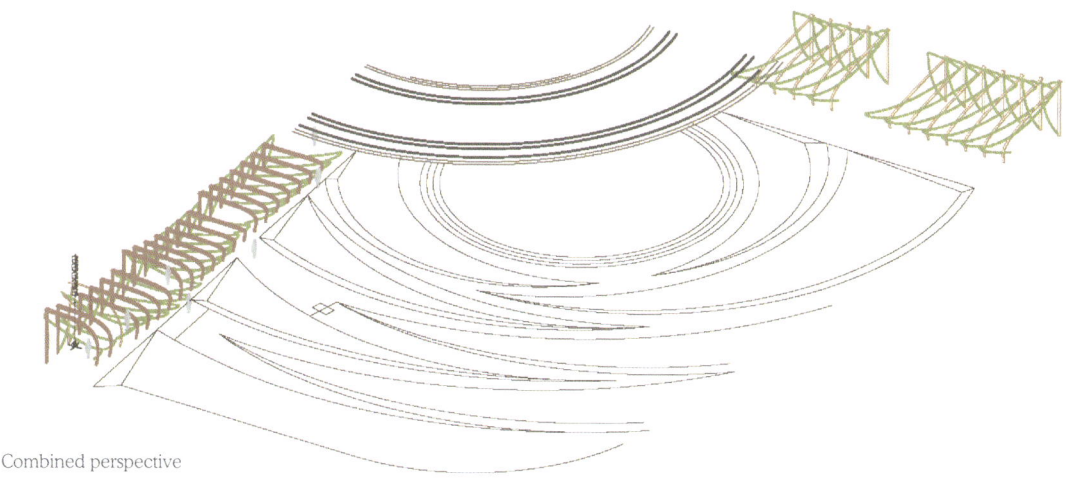
Combined perspective

03
/ Plants during early spring
04
/ Local people exercise in the park

04

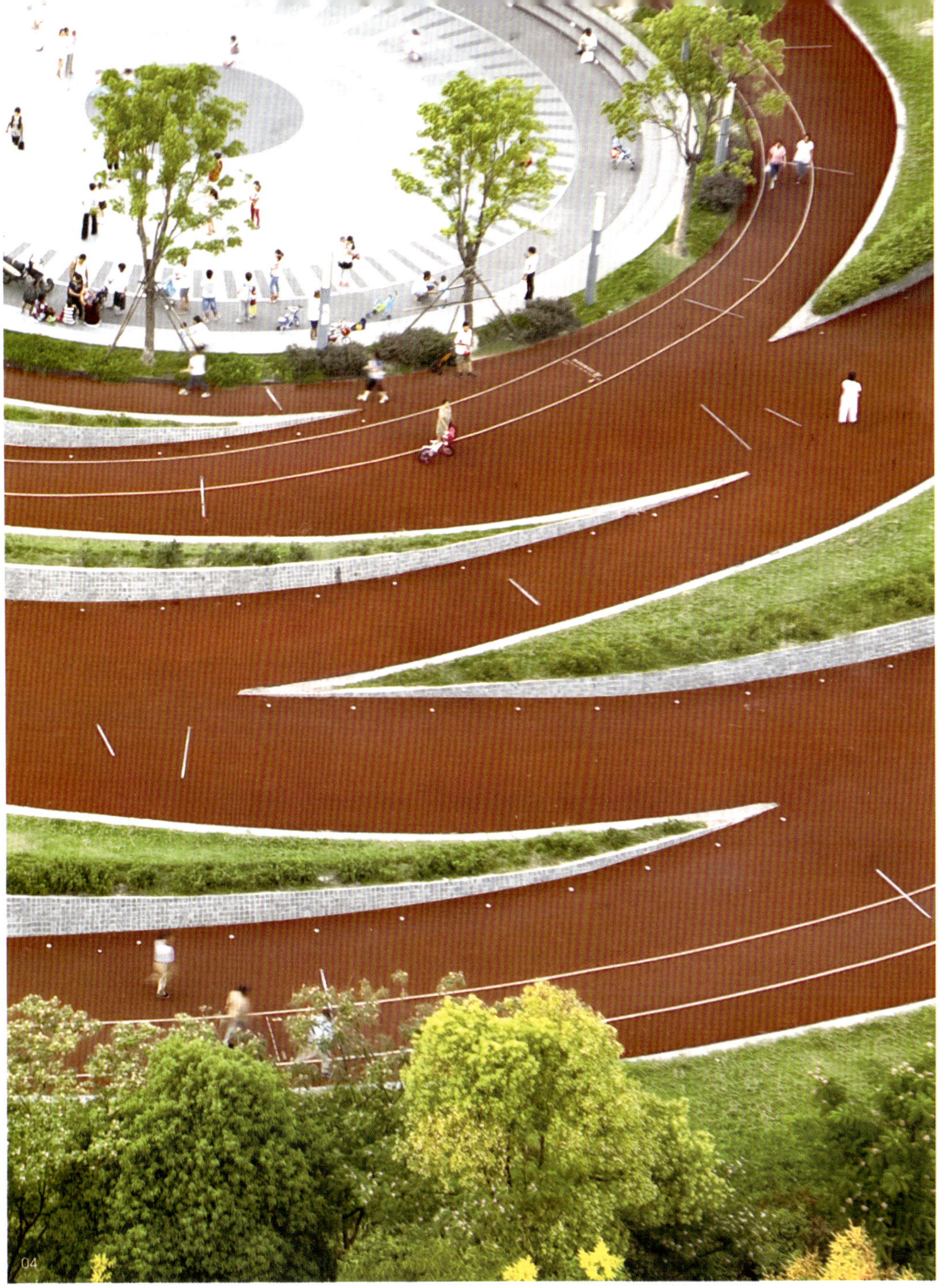

① Entrance
② Reserved square
③ Event square
④ Park
1
2
3
4

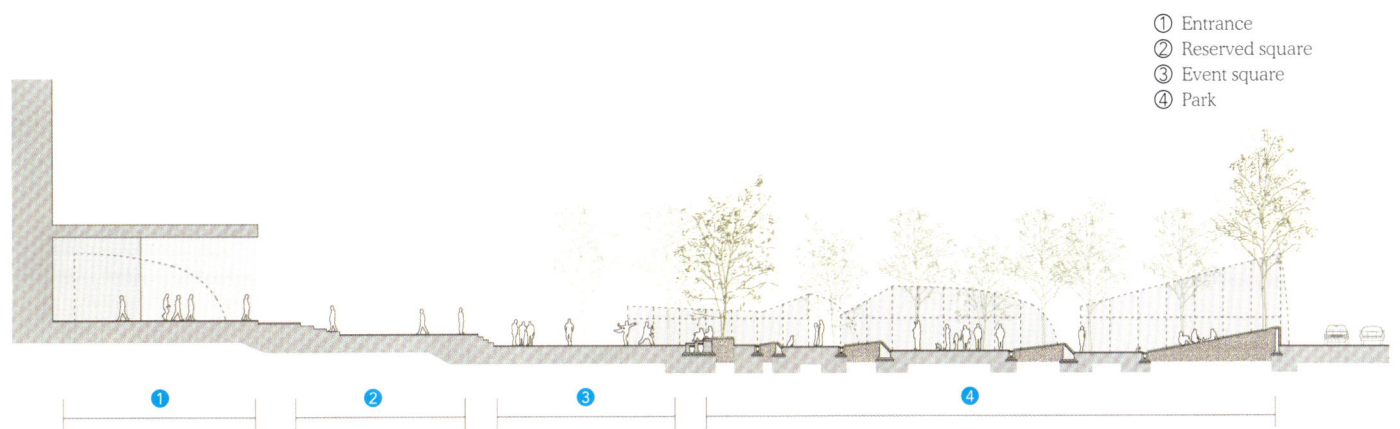

Elevation

05–06
/ Horizontal bars
07
/ Aerial view
08
/ Running tracks

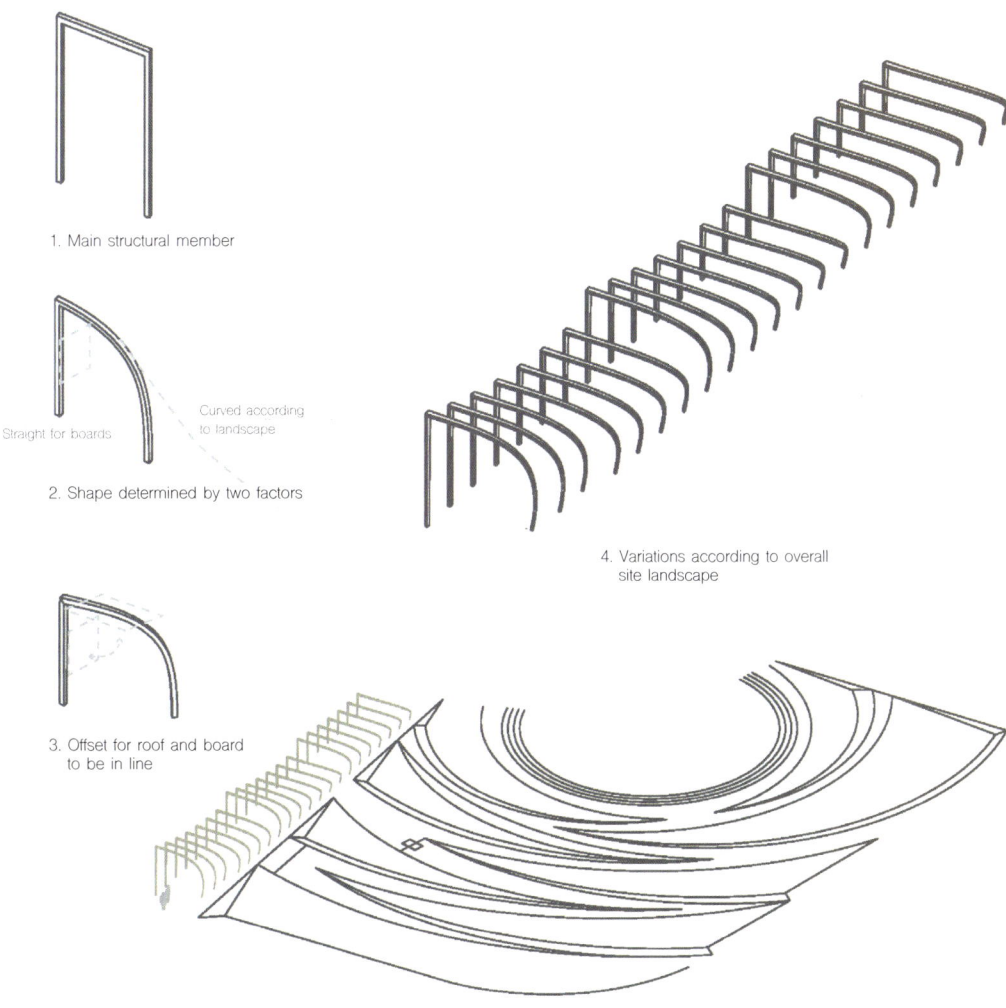

1. Main structural member

Straight for boards — Curved according to landscape

2. Shape determined by two factors

3. Offset for roof and board to be in line

4. Variations according to overall site landscape

Part A: Main structural member

Belconnen Skate Park

Location /
Canberra, ACT, Australia

Area /
**30,139 square feet
(2800 square meters)**

Completion date /
2012

Skate park design /
Oxigen, CONVIC

Budget /
AU$1.8 million

Photography /
Oxigen, CONVIC, Julia Coddington, Manteena

Client /
ACT Government

Given its historical significance in Australia's skating landscape and critical place in designers' maturing interest in skateboarding and BMX, the Belconnen Skate Park reflects both its past and represents the future. It remains an iconic and relevant skate park in the history of skating in Australia. It represents a connected landscape that integrates the skate park into the broader Canberra open space system.

Extensive consultation and background investigation were undertaken in collaboration with the Canberra Skateboard Association and business owners, local schools, youth centers, local skaters, and the University of Canberra. This has ensured great community acceptance and ownership and care of the space by the young people who frequent it. Consultation found that the preference was for street plaza-style obstacles. This is linked to the progression of riders wanting to hit obstacles as laid out in urban streets, such as ledges and stairs with hand rails. Rather than being an eyesore, these objects were developed and integrated into the landscape as sculptural forms. These contemporary obstacles are unique and distinguish Belconnen Skate Park from other parks around the world.

① New bridge and weir
② John Knight Memorial Park
③ Terraces
④ Future kiosk
⑤ Future welands with boardwalks
⑥ Ginniinderra college
⑦ Belconnen Skate Park
⑧ Existing bowl refurbished
⑨ Belconnen Skate Park
⑩ Emu bank

Master plan

01
/ Aerial view
02
/ Blue concrete skate terrain

195

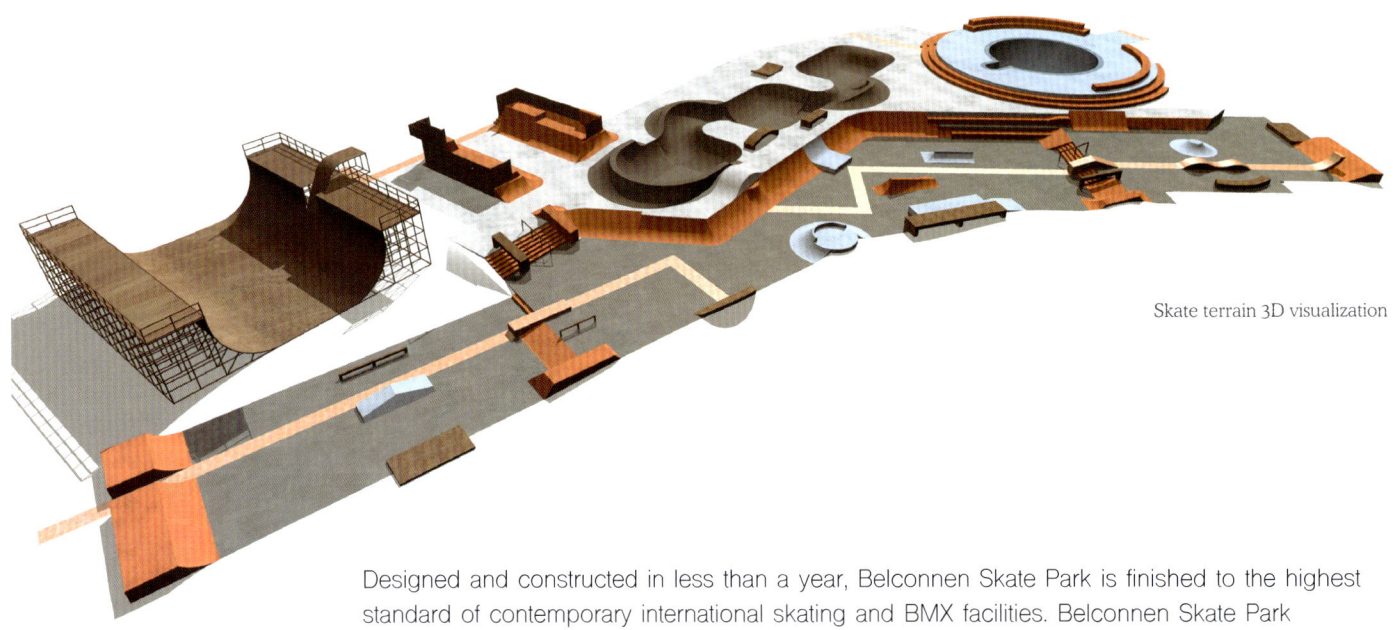

Skate terrain 3D visualization

Designed and constructed in less than a year, Belconnen Skate Park is finished to the highest standard of contemporary international skating and BMX facilities. Belconnen Skate Park integrates forms, colors, and materials found within the urban framework, and incorporates them into a highly technical skate park. This typology of artistic skate-park design is an Australian first. The design responds to the challenging levels of the banks of the adjacent lake. A 9.8-foot (3-meter) level change is incorporated in the design, with the colorful concrete forms stepping down to the lake and forming a skate-able 'terrain' that challenges all skating abilities. A new street skate plaza has a mix of highly sculptural skate-able obstacles, a flow area/snake run, a mini ramp, and terraced seating with views over the skate park to the lake. A variety of colors and textured concrete finishes are utilized so that the skate park reads as an exciting terrain to explore, yet melds into the public realm as one. This combination of form and color provides an exciting, dynamic, and fresh skating experience.

03
/ Mini ramp looking north over Eastern Valley Way Inlet
04
/ The shelter and terraces are located to provide views across the skate park and lake
05
/ A variety of skate-able forms along the southern side of the park.
06
/ Corten-edged obstacle tree pits

Wylde Mountain Bike Trail

Location /
Cecil Hills, NSW, Australia

Area /
3.95 acres (1.6 hectares)

Completion date /
2014

Landscape design /
Group GSA

Budget /
AU$2 million

Photography /
Simon Wood

Client /
Western Sydney Parklands Trust

Awards /
AILA NSW Awards 2015—Design in Landscape Architecture Award
AILA NSW Awards 2015—Premier's People's Choice Award

The Wylde Mountain Bike Trail is located in the heart of Western Sydney within the Cumberland Plain Woodland of the Western Sydney Parklands. The project provides a new active precinct and destination within the Parklands focusing on mountain bikes and BMX. Designed in conjunction with DirtzTrax'n'Trailz, Wylde provides parking, shelters, and informal lookouts with a wide range of trails to cater for beginners to more experienced riders. The bike facilities include pump tracks, jump runs and a 7.45-mile (12-kilometer) mountain-bike course. The park and trails provide for daily use as well as cater for intensive visitation and camping during major bike events.

Special factors in this project were:
- meeting the growing demand as requested by the community for mountain bike facilities within the Sydney Basin and adjacent to a residential growth area;
- responding to the demand for regional recreation facilities for Sydney;
- providing a place for social interaction and activity for these communities;
- catering to a range of abilities for both children and adults while the entry precinct provides facilities for bike riders as well as park visitors;

01
/ Entry precinct with bike wash bays and viewing mound behind
02
/ Viewing mound and start of the 'jump runs'
03
/ Large group shelter
04
/ Entry precinct with the 'jump runs' and 'pump track' and connection to trail

- allowing people to enjoy recreation in and among protected Cumberland Plain Woodland, which is a unique experience;
- integrating trailhead and car-park facilities with the natural landscape;
- simple and robust design elements and structures responding to mountain bike culture and aesthetic;
- developing a strong identity and focal point for visitors at the entry precinct through the provision of seating, shelters, and trail-viewing points;
- providing diverse trail options for a range of riding abilities including challenging jumps and a pump track; the length and topography of the Cecil Hills site allows for an MTB trail that provides fitness for riders for all levels;
- adaptable design, able to function as a daily recreation facility for a regional catchment and to cater for larger crowds during race events; and
- providing trails and a welcoming facility for the mountain-biking community with the opportunity for riders and visitors to escape, explore, be challenged, and connect with nature.

05–06
/ Viewing mound and starting
  point for the 'jump runs'
07
/ Connecting path to trail head
08
  Small group shelter
09
/ Event mode plan

Venecia Recreational Park

Location /
Temuco, Chile

Area /
**90,416 square feet
(8400 square meters)**

Completion date /
2014

Landscape design /
Jaime Alarcón Fuentes

Photography /
Treile films

Client /
Municipality of Temuco and Ministry of Housing and Urbanism

Venecia Recreational Park has been developed by a government program that will revitalize neighborhoods in critical areas of the city, through an integrated plan of social and urban interventions.

This park fills the consolidated lack of public urban space of recreation, relaxation, and sports, including it in a surrounding river plan of Temuco city. This park, due to its high intensity of use and scale within the area, allowed the development of a highly participatory project where a citizen concept was developed at an intermediate level, embracing the community and individual neighborhood interest, for example, the integration of typical Chilean games such as greasy pole, troy as and hopscotch, as well as the staging of massive performances, and urban picnics. In conjunction with the community, this park was called the Urban Lounge.

The main idea was to develop an intermediate-level project, which could answer to the lack of space in housing where a living room—usually the gathering place of the family, and center of the development of childhood—was not a priority at home. The housing density was dominating; the use of land in building overtook the area, and this emptiness in the city was transformed into an opportunity to increase and consolidate the quality of public spaces.

As a consequence, several spaces for regular use were designed. They were connected with an access ring at the inner part of the park, where the dead spaces were transformed into temporary spaces and their use was defined depending on the weather, season, and festivity periods.

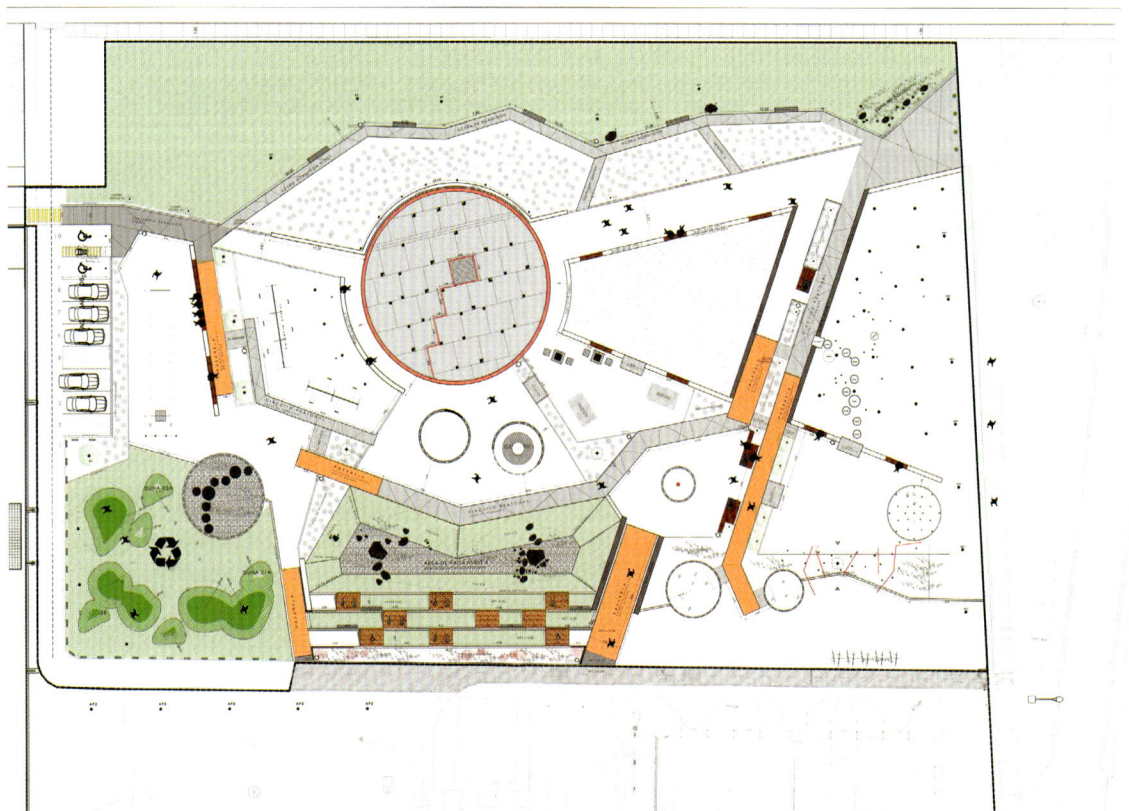

Site plan

01
/ Aerial image of the park
02
/ Natural drainage of urban park and picnic terraces
03
/ Tubes balanced on draining area

Process analysis and design—the transformation from a place of rejection in a room of neighborhood ties

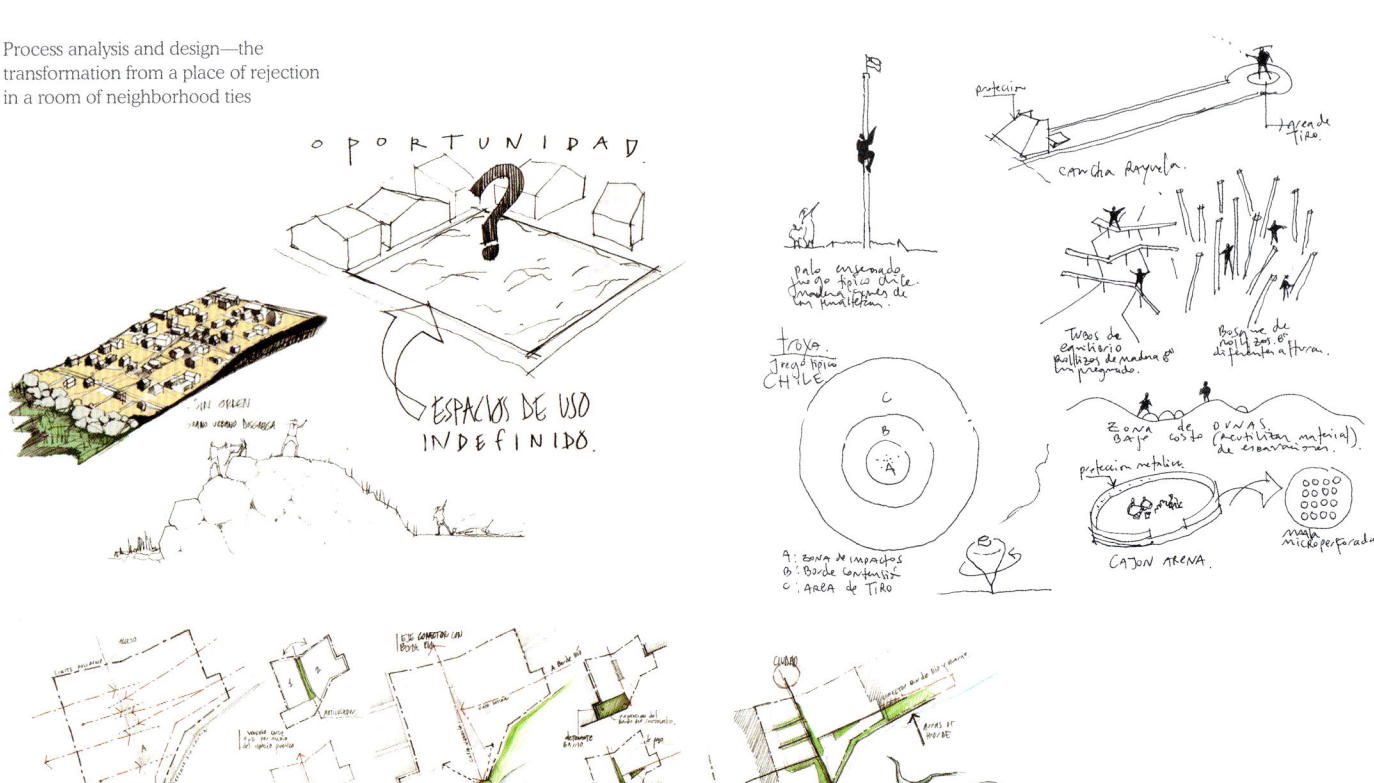

04
/ Dispersion elements in children's play area
05
/ Hopscotch area accompanied by a bench of native wood and stones from the river Cautin
06
/ Youth groups' multipurpose area
07–08
/ Children's playground
09
/ Sandbox with perimeter ring

Culture and activity space in Hedehusene

Location /
Hedehusene, Denmark
Area /
**69,965 square feet
(6500 square meters)**
Completion date /
2013
Landscape design /
LIW planning
Budget /
5.8 million Danish krone
Photography /
Alexandra Quaade del Campo
Client /
Hedehusene Council for City Renewal, City of Høje-Taastrup

The culture and activity space is located on what used to be just an ordinary parking lot in a public housing area on the edge of Hedehusene, a suburban town in the greater capitol area around Copenhagen, characterized by large residential developments from the late 1970s to 1980s.

In a greater context, the space is an important link between the city park, the general residential area, and the path to the station, sports center, tennis hall, FDF scout house and a new cultural center with a mosque for the Danish Immigrant Culture Association. As such, the space has enormous potential as a local square offering a wide range of activities for different uses.

However, because of the location and the functions of the surrounding buildings, the space should accommodate cars as well as being a safe and vibrant urban space. Taking up this challenge, the existing parking lot was designed with a focus on optimizing the possibilities for positive interactions between physical activity and parking in an open, freely available space without barriers. Graphics on the asphalt and the location of play and training facilities tell drivers where to park, while inviting the citizens of Hedehusene to meet, play, and interact.

The site is designed with great flexibility in relation to recreational activities and with a zoned parking area, which ensures that visitors can park without getting into conflict with the people undertaking activities.

Site plan

01–02
/ Swings and horizontal bars for kids in multifunctional playing zones

The project development was carried out in a close dialogue with stakeholders and users about their wishes for activities at the site and about the best design for optimal performance for accommodating all, from parked cars and motorcycles to flea markets, crossing cyclists, and pedestrians, children, and adolescents playing ball, climbing, and hanging out.

The project was described as 'the country's best example of how to use a parking space for physical activities and a meeting point, for those who'd rather watch' in a press release from The Danish Foundation for Culture and Sports Facilities, who co-financed the project.

05

03
/ Soccer field
04
/ Running track
05
/ Parking area

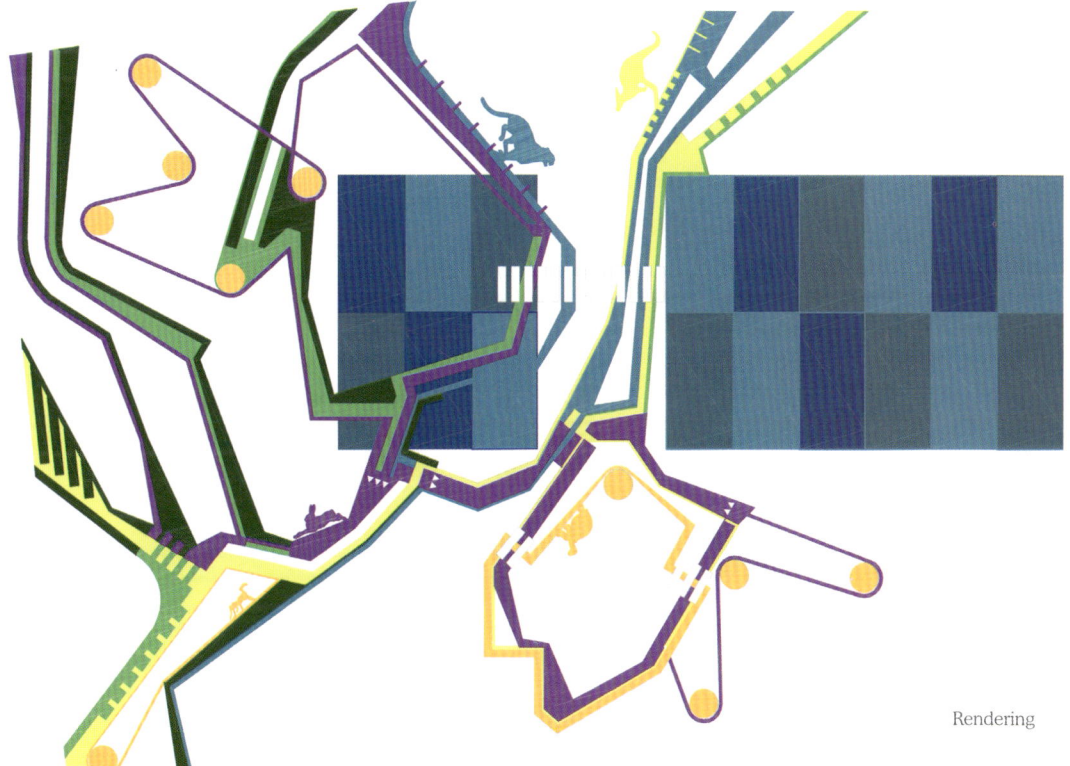

Rendering

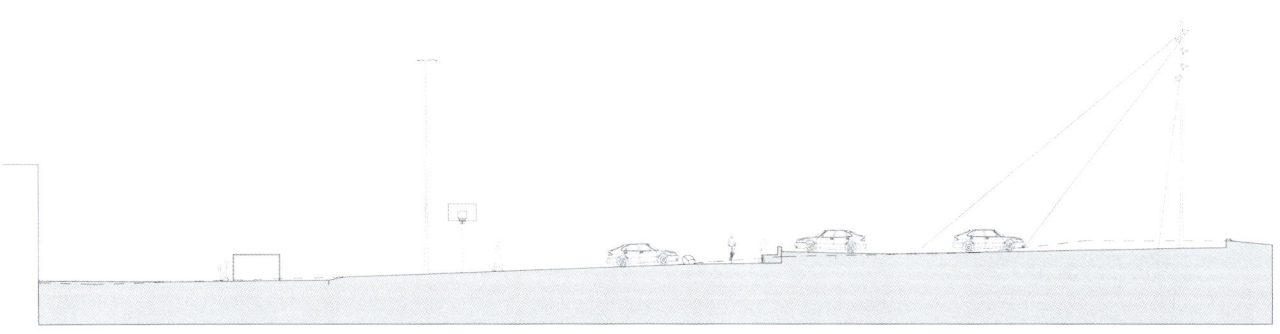
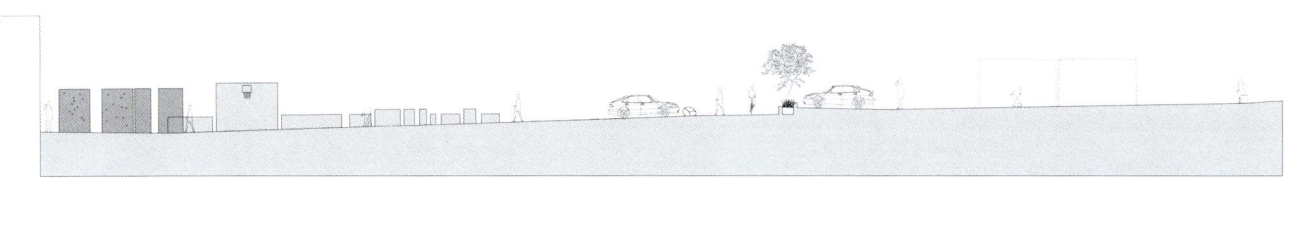
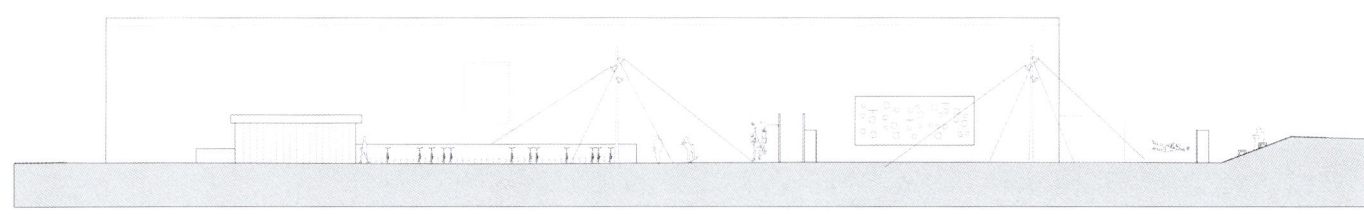

Sections

06–07
/ Colorful pavement attracts children
08
/ Child playing soccer
09
/ Safe climbing wall
10
/ Walls for basketball and soccer training

Rocket Park Mini-Golf Course

Location /
New York, USA

Area /
9245 square feet (860 square meters)

Landscape design /
Mark K. Morrison Associates

Architecture design /
Lee H. Skolnick Architecture + Design Partnership

Budget /
US$1.3 million

Photography /
New York Hall of Science

Client /
New York Hall of Science

Rocket Park Mini-Golf at the New York Hall of Science is an outdoor miniature golf course with nine themed holes that introduce visitors to elemental rocket science. Each hole represents a particular aspect of a space mission, from blastoff to splash-down, the trajectory forming the basis for a narrative structure. The behavior of the golf ball in each explains principles of astrophysics in an Earth-bound simulation.

The client envisioned this unique educational environment as a vehicle to demonstrate classic Newtonian physics—a key component in science education. Lee H. Skolnick Architecture + Design Partnership worked with a miniature-golf-course designer to establish the overall planning and layout. Tying the course together is a central plaza area representing a lunar surface, complete with a replica Mercury space capsule that serves as a practice putting 'green'. The seamless, poured-in-place EPDM surfacing comprises 100 percent recycled tires, and adds a subtle 'moonwalk' bounce to visitors' steps. Bench seats and attractive landscaping help control crowding on busy days and offer sightlines from which caregivers can watch their children.

The look and feel of the project is inspired by the popular culture and space age iconography of the late 1950s and early 1960s. The structures comprising each hole feature streamlined boomerang shapes, Sputnik-like starbursts, and atomic orbits in their design. These motifs recur on large sign discs at each hole, which carry educational information and instructions for completing each activity. Custom illustrations explain the various physics concepts being engaged at each hole. Structures at each hole are fabricated of painted steel with automotive coatings, stainless steel, aluminum and fiberglass—for maximum outdoor durability—with some incorporating motorized elements to create 'hazards' or signal a successful putt. The colorful hardscape design, varied challenges, retro-style graphics, and landscaping come together to form an out-of-this-world rocketship journey through space.

LHSA+DP's architects worked with a commercial miniature golf course contractor to establish the overall planning and layout, studying recommended relationships between holes, traffic flow and pacing of visitors

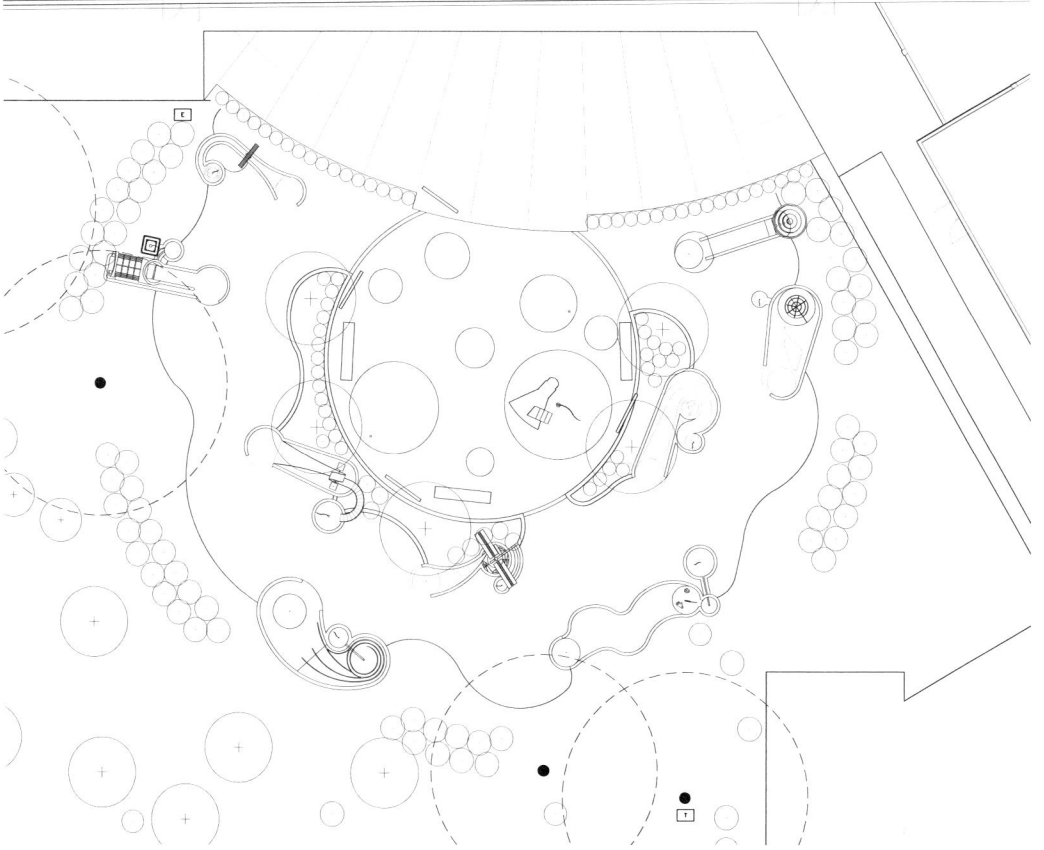

01
/ Two rockets—a Titan II and an Atlas, each more than 100 feet (30.5 meters) tall—serve as the visual backdrop for Rocket Park

02
/ LHSA+DP's designers created nine distinctly themed holes that introduce visitors to the elemental physics principles of rocket science

03–05
/ Located near the main entrance to the facility, this bright and fancifully colored mini-golf course sends an immediate message to museum-goers that this place is going to be interactive, hands-on and fun

06
/ The course takes participants on a journey to Jupiter, around an Earth orbit, on a supply-run to the International Space Station, and other adventures

LHSA+DP designed each hole so that the actual behavior of the golf ball would explain real examples of astrophysics principles, in an Earth-bound simulation

① Embankment
② Gravity return gutter
③ Scenic Mars hemisphere
④ Scenic Jupiter sphere
⑤ Scenic painted planet Earth flagpole cap
⑥ Flag design by exhibit designer
⑦ Golf ball retrieval area
⑧ Flag
⑨ 5-foot (1.5-meter) turning radius

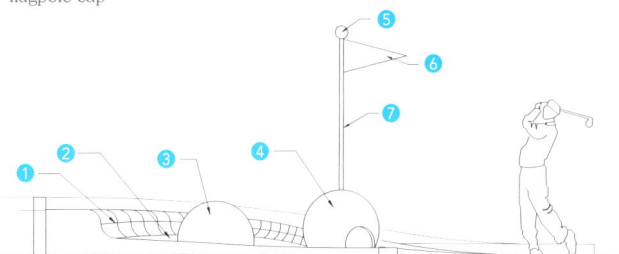
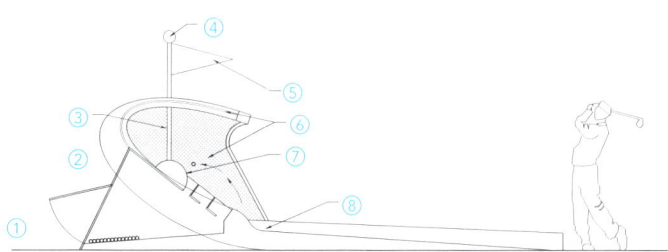

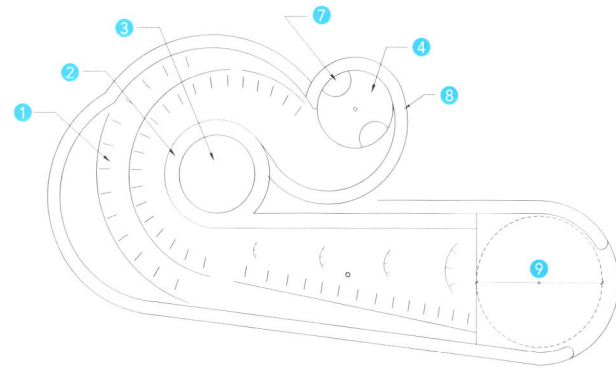
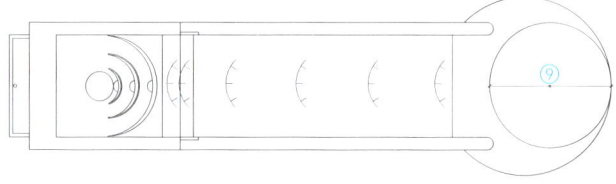

① Locked golf ball compartment
② Access door w/cam lock
③ Flagpole
④ Scenic painted planet Earth flagpole cap
⑤ Flag design by exhibit designer
⑥ Mesh barrier
⑦ Target Earth model
⑧ Golf 'skee-ball' ramp
⑨ 5-foot (1.5-meter) turning radius

Original drawings by the LHSA+DP design team for Rocket Park mini-golf holes

07–08
/ A mini-golf course provided the New York Hall of Science with an engaging way to approach the subject matter of astrophysics in a familiar, family-friendly way

09–10
/ The look and feel of the project is inspired by the popular culture of the 1963–64 World's Fair, which occurred on the very the same site, with original graphic design by LHSA+DP

Nordic Ski Centre Planica

Location /
Planica, Slovenia

Area /
54.4 acres (22 hectares)

Completion date /
2015

Landscape design /
Studio AKKA

Ski jumps, towers and bridges /
Studio abiro architects

Central building and service and warm-up units /
Stvar architects

Budget /
€40 million

Photography /
Miran Kambič

Client /
Institute of Sport of Republic of Slovenia Planica

The main aspect of design is based on a profound relation between construction, the constructed site, and its natural setting. The precise design of topography, the systematic selection and reduction of material, bold shapes, and clear geometrical forms, all line up with the exciting silhouette of the mountains and the calmness of the spruce and beech forest. The project works on many levels and seems to combine solid versus soft, resistant versus ephemeral, cold versus warm, monumental versus intimate. The seasonal changes span from the cold and sharp image of the mountains referring to the simple geometry of the topography and the concrete structures, to the colorful abundance of the late summer, when the perception of the wooden details and green slopes is exposed.

As Planica is set at the forefoot of the largest protected area in Slovenia and forms one of the most exciting entryways to the Triglav National Park, large sport facilities take their own, restrained, stand. Planica is already symbolically charged, which renders all excessive design redundant. The alpine setting of this precise sport facility is unique and recognizable. The refinement of the image is thus added on other levels, mainly on those of use and orientation. Design follows technical and organizational requirements of a large sport facility by which it clearly reveals the new character of the space. It stands in contrast to the natural dynamics of the surrounding mountainous landscape and creates an organized, functional and technically flawless counterpart to the magnificent alpine frame, perfected by the logic of engineering. The ski jumps that fan across the landscape introduce a spatial order that unites all elements into a non-hierarchical whole.

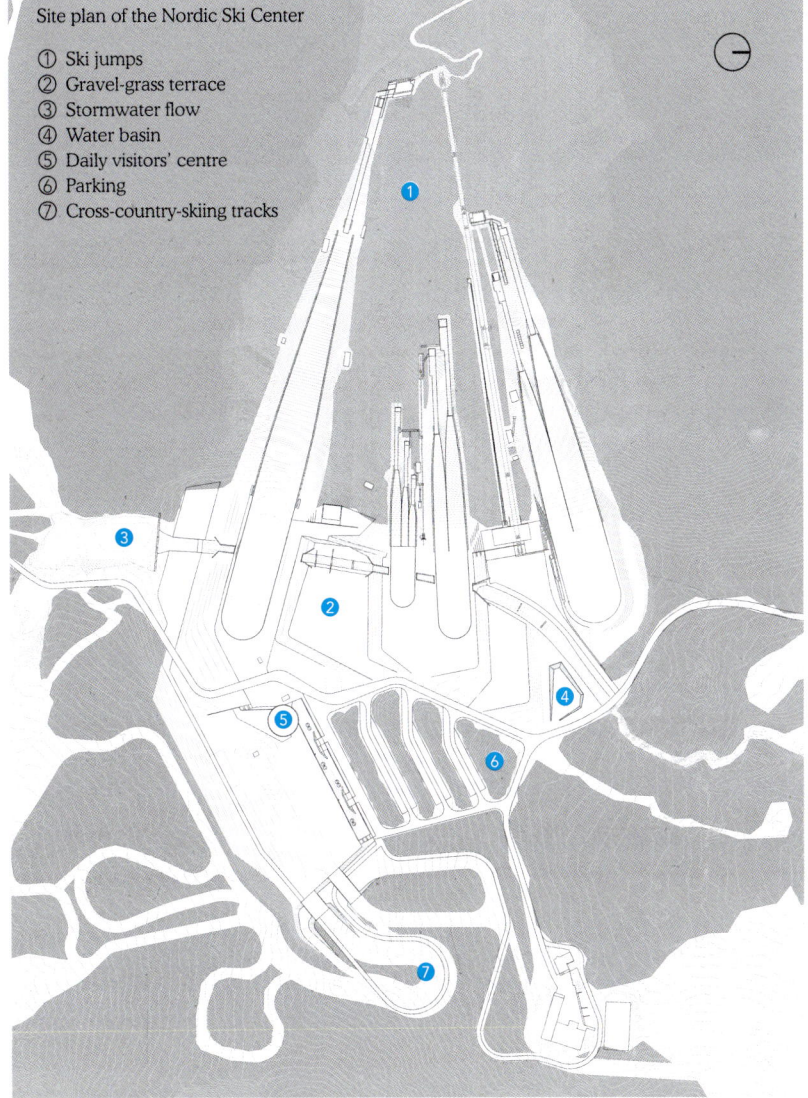

01
/ The design of the Nordic Ski Center acknowledges its setting in the magnificent alpine valley
02
/ Bird's-eye view of the outruns and the cross-country center

Site plan of the Nordic Ski Center
① Ski jumps
② Gravel-grass terrace
③ Stormwater flow
④ Water basin
⑤ Daily visitors' centre
⑥ Parking
⑦ Cross-country-skiing tracks

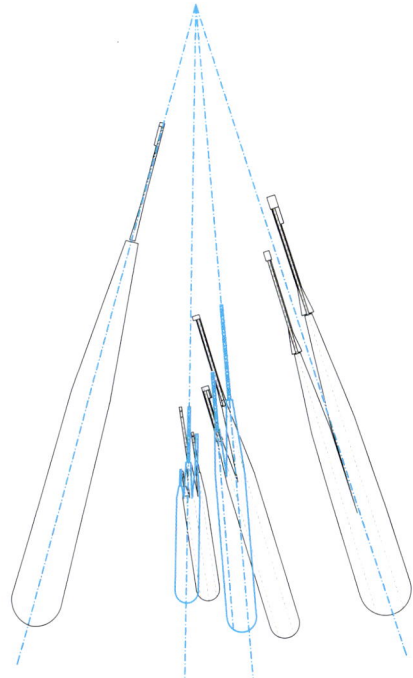

The fanlike arrangements of the ski jumps introduces spatial order

Ski jumps are usually designed to facilitate large-scale events with extensive infrastructure and demanding logistics. When more than 30,000 people come to this fragile valley, the form of the architecture gives way to its operational function, while on the everyday level, when a handful of young ski jumpers would come to train in solitude, its simplicity and robustness re-awaken and monumentally yet respectfully stand at the entrance into the valley. All service buildings, including the daily visitors' center, were pushed to the edges to free the bottom of the valley for long vistas.

04

03
/ The training ski jumps for children

04
/ Flying hill and the seven ski jumps of the Nordic Ski Center fan across the slope

03

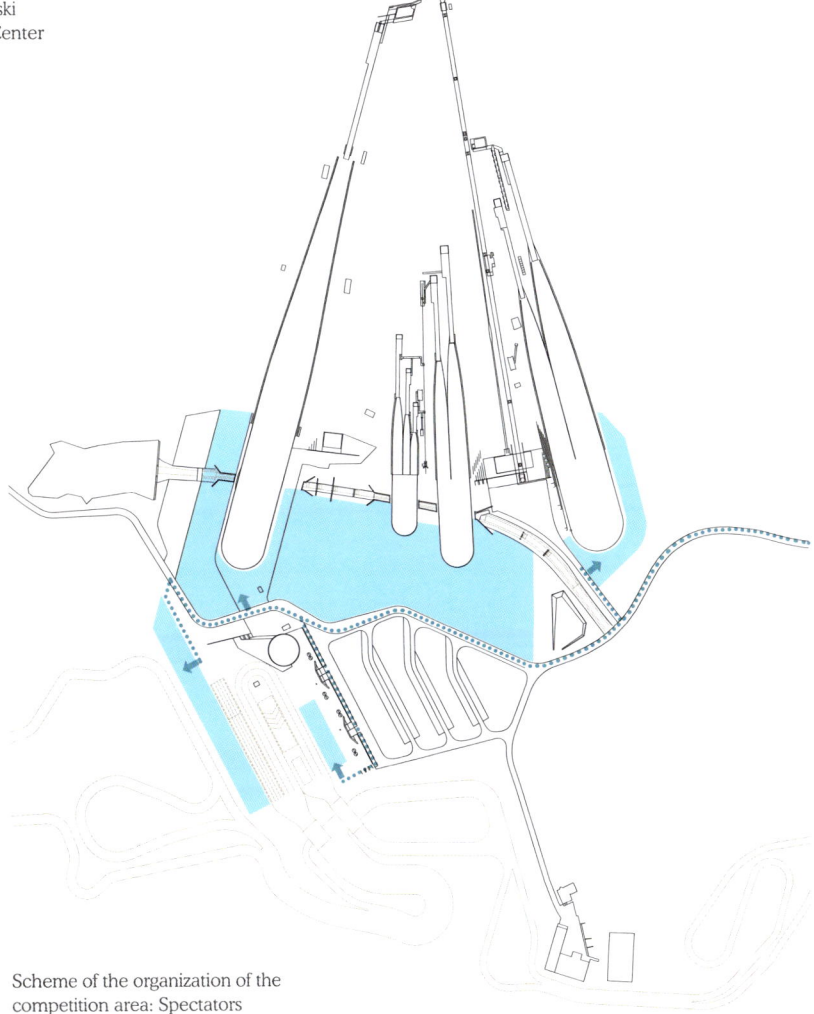

Scheme of the organization of the competition area: Spectators

05
/ Cross-country stadium with ski jumps as background
06
/ HS 139 judging and TV tower
07
/ The terraces for spectators along the flying hill outrun

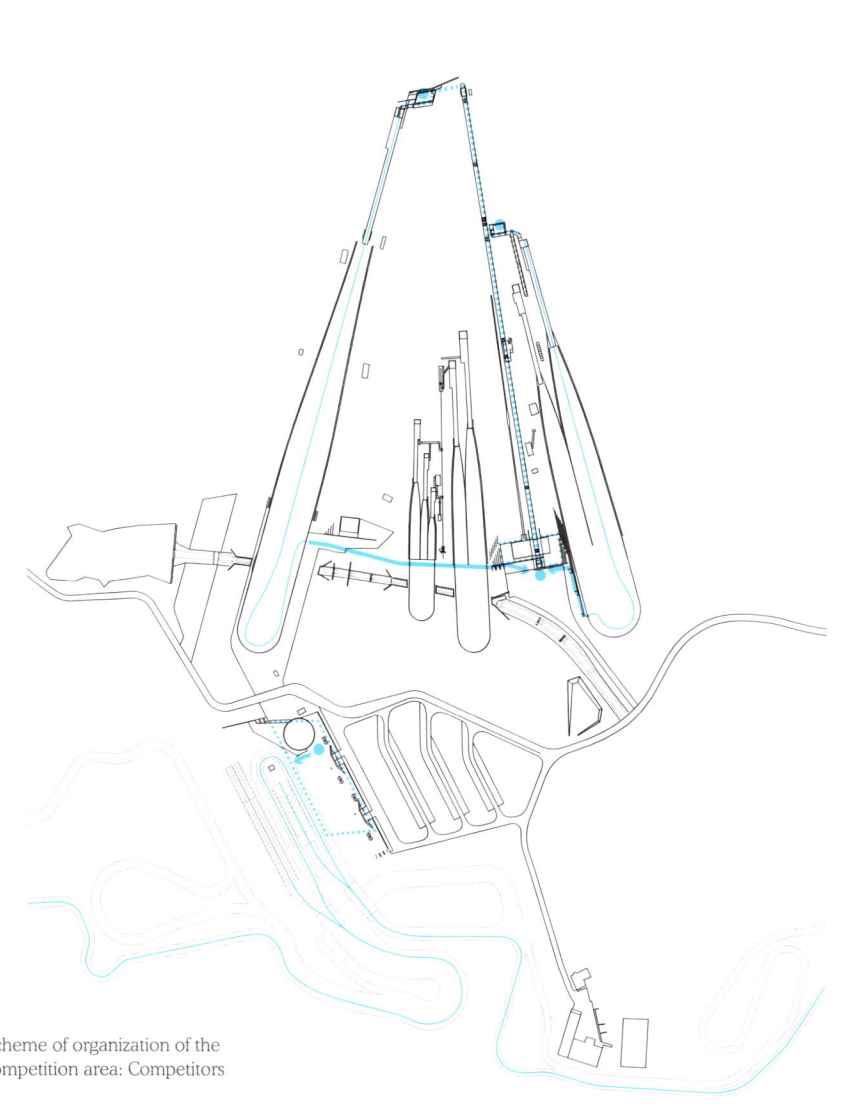

Scheme of organization of the competition area: Competitors

10

09
/ HS 84 ski jump carefully set into the existing forest

10
/ Cross-country skiing lanes set into the existing forest are used for competitions as well as recreation

11
/ Stormwater-flow control protection fence design responds to the architectural language of the ski jumps

Sportpark Gaarden

Location /
Kiel, Germany

Area /
86 acres (35 hectares)

Completion date /
2013

Landscape design /
kessler.krämer Landschaftsarchitekten

In parallel to the basic design of the first construction stage, a design manual has been compiled and agreed to by all involved parties. This manual provides the park with a homogenous design and serves as a quality assurance tool for further constructions. Furnishing objects such as benches, litter bins, signs, railings, and lamps are standardized, as the structure and quality of flooring, track surfaces and ramps are defined.

The intention is to give the Sportpark a unique appearance to gain attention beyond the district and to stimulate the population to identify with the park. When compiling the design manual, the previously (through a participatory process) developed communication elements such as the logo and the color 'cyan blue' were incorporated—even the 9.8 to 16 feet (3 to 5 meter) vertical athlete sculptures at the entrances and the blue floor coverings.

The design elements of the park are not only characterized by a unique appearance, but also by the highest possible durability and resistance to vandalism, at low maintenance costs. Tables and benches are made of solid steel, with seating and table surfaces of robust plastic. Metal instead of wood it is used for the sport and play equipment. Another very important criterion was the widest possible range of uses for all elements. An example is the benches that can be used from a wheelchair and even utilized by skaters.

Master plan

01
/ The sports park is a popular meeting point
02
/ The 'roll and hop' playline in blue rubber
03
/ The carousel is also suitable for wheelchairs

While creating an overall concept for this open space and the design manual, the Institute for Sports and Sport Sciences (University of Kiel) developed a model for a 'community of interests'. Therein the local sports clubs, partners of welfare work, and municipal co-operators are represented. This community meets regularly, supports the operation as the further development of the park, and is open to new partners.

The sports park is public and available at no cost to everyone. It is open for individual athletes and teams, so sport clubs and self-organized sports can take place side by side. People with different cultural backgrounds, of different ages, and with various physical abilities can use the sports park equally for sports and socializing. The paths to the facilities are barrier-free to welcome people with physical handicaps as well.

Renderings

04
/ The modeled hillside with play and picnic areas

05–06
/ One of the play areas is designed for climbing and balancing

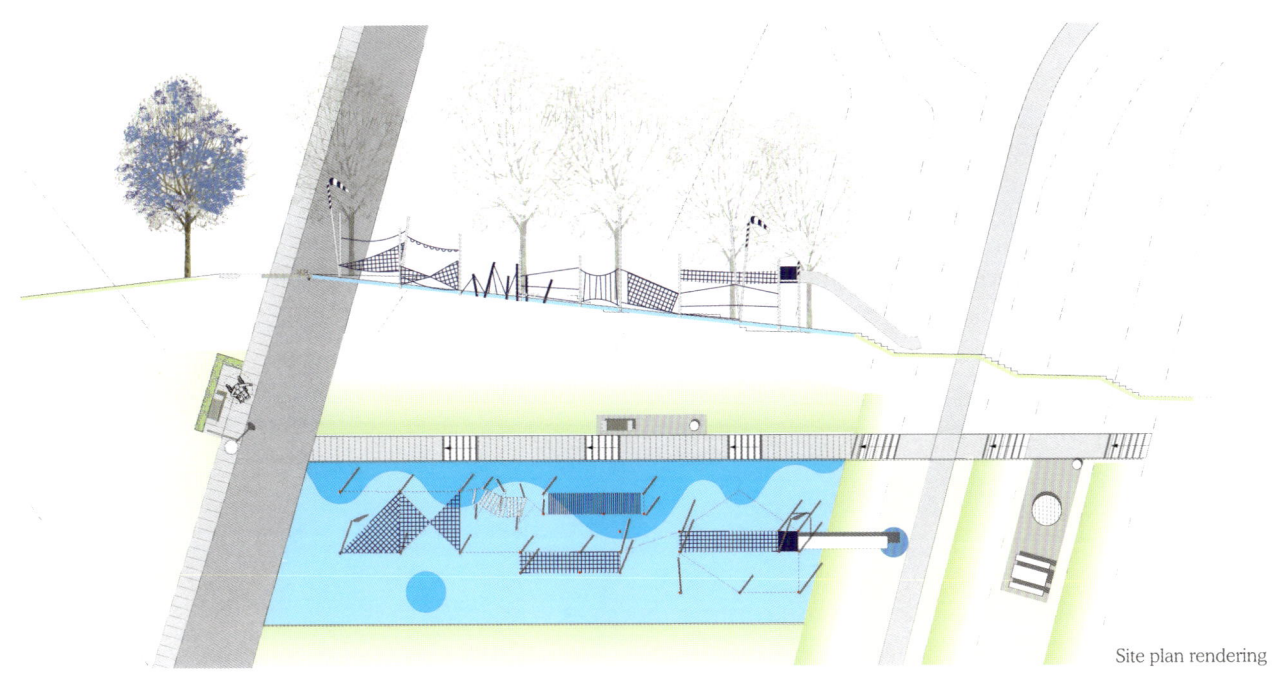

Site plan rendering

07
/ 19.7-foot-high (6-meter-high) steel poles mark the entrances to the sports park
08
/ Streetball
09
/ The fitness area for seniors is placed beside the ball game area
10
/ All play and sport areas are made in blue rubber

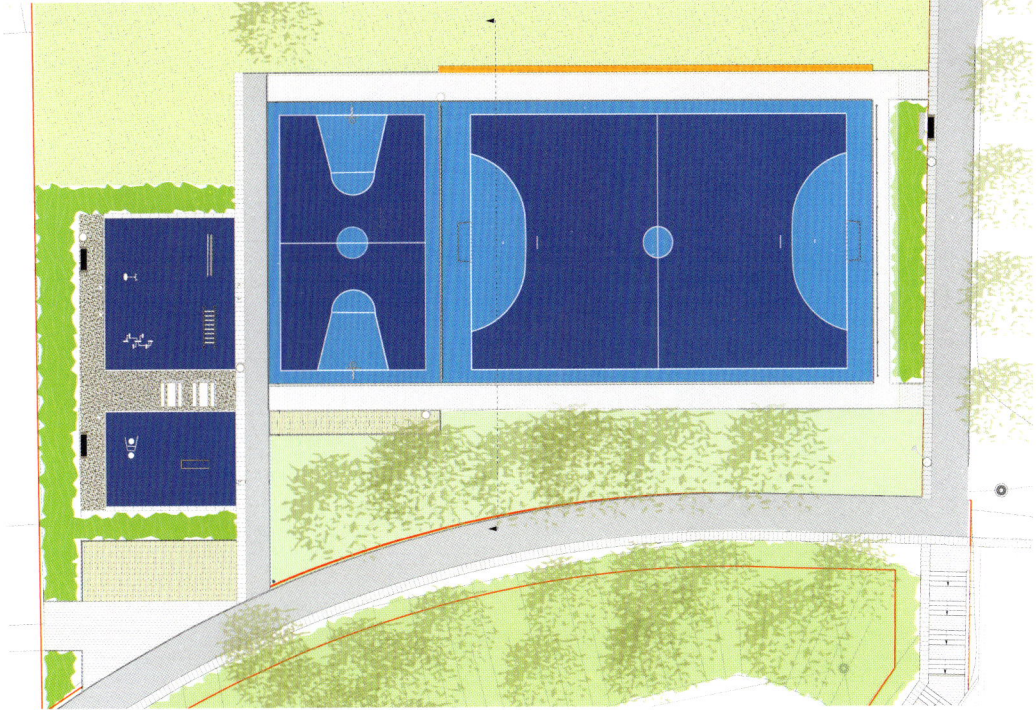

Plan for the ball game area

Basketball plan drawings

Multifunctional sports facility in Ratingen

Location /
Ratingen, Germany
Area /
3 acres (1.2 hectares)
Completion date /
2012
Landscape design /
Betonlandschaften/ Maierlandschaftsarchitektur
Budget /
€340,000
Photography /
Ralf Maier, Sandra Stein
Client /
City of Ratingen

After the heavy rain in June 2005, the city of Ratingen decided to build a rainwater retention basin in the western district. At that time, there were millions of dollars in damages by floods. At the site of an existing park near the ice stadium, an underground rainwater retention basin was planned; it can hold up 600,350 cubic feet (17,000 cubic meters) of water.

Due to the dimensions and position of the ceiling of the retention pond, it was not possible to intervene deeper than 37 inches (94 centimeters) in the ground. Moreover, southeast of the park runs a gas line. The multifunctional sports stadium and the playground equipment could not be built above the rainwater retention basin. In addition, no trees but only small shrubs could be planted in the area. Northeast in the park, there was an area that could meet all the requirements of a skate park. For inline hockey, an area could be found in the west area.

The skate park was planned in cooperation with the local skate club. The skate park is divided into two main areas: a street area and a skate bowl. The street area is characterized by the use of concrete slabs without bevel, whereby a space character is generated. A bank-hip, the curb and rail offer many possibilities for tricks. In addition, you can play the game 'Skate' in this area and ride BMX Flatland. Near the street area, benches were set up for relaxation and for spectators.

- Concrete flat/table
- Bank
- Transition
- Curb
- Cooping
- Asphalt
- Concrete slabs
- Waterbound gravel

① Ice sports hall
② Industrial building
③ Skate street area
④ Inline hockey field
⑤ Multifunctional sports stadium
⑥ Playground
⑦ Underground rain storage reservoir
⑧ Fence
⑨ Gas pipeline corridor
⑩ Ball fence
⑪ Inspection manhole
⑫ Pedestrian bridge approach
⑬ Existing foot path
⑭ Balancing log
⑮ Waterbound gravel
⑯ Bird's nest swing

Master plan

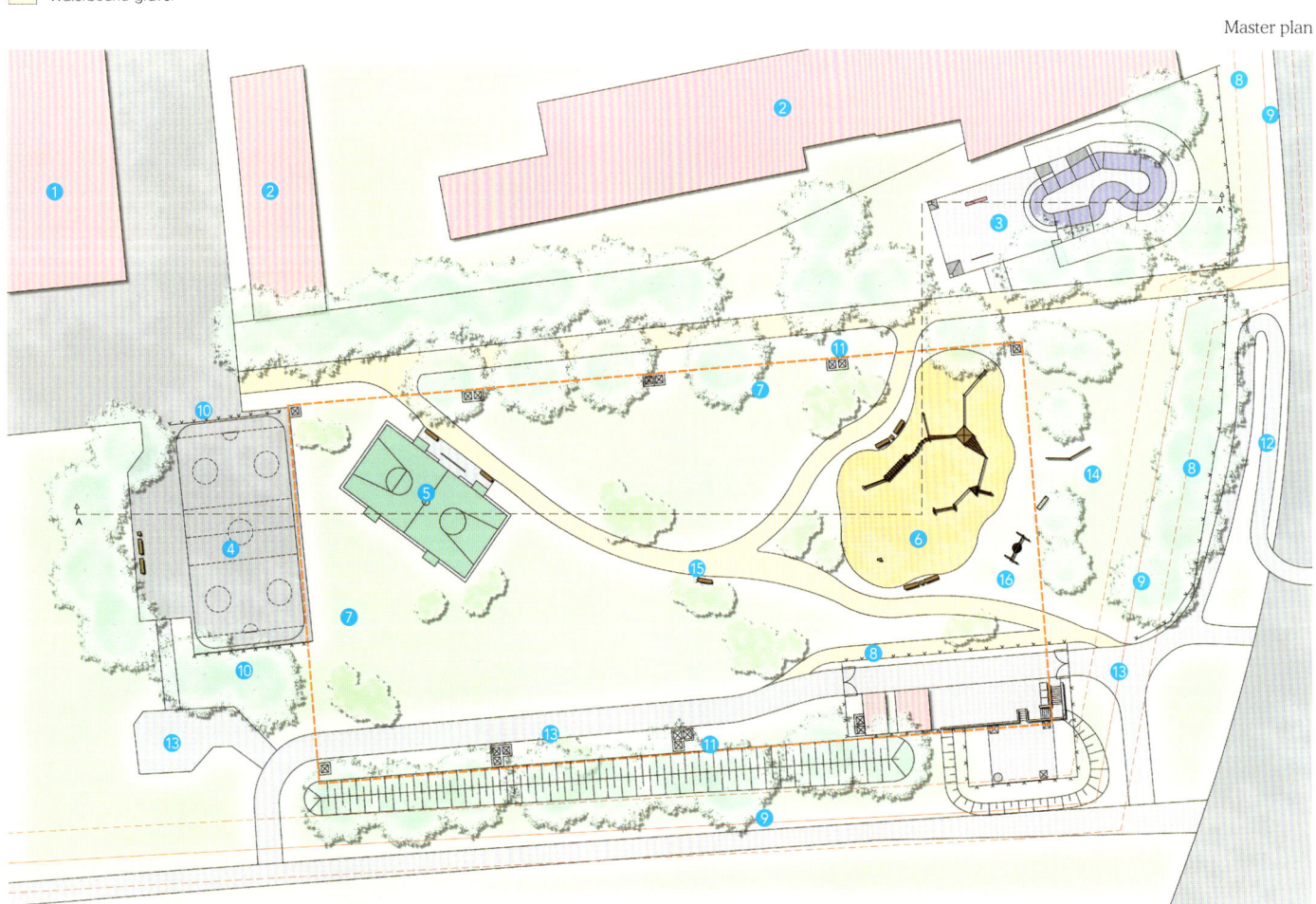

01
/ Street hockey players in Ratingen
02–03
/ Kids playing football in the multifunctional sports stadium

04

05

234

04
/ No-hander by a BMX rider in the skate pool
05
/ Teenagers watching bikers and skaters
06
/ A skater jumps at the bank-hip

The skate bowl is a 'bowl' constructed in situ in concrete. A unique and custom form was created according to the wishes of the users by shaping and smoothing the concrete completely by hand. So already the subsequent identification of the skaters with the skate park was strengthened, through letting them participate in the planning process.

① Chill area
② Inline hockey field
③ Multifunctional sports stadium
④ Play-sports-and chill-lawn
⑤ Playground
⑥ Footpath
⑦ Street skate area
⑧ Skate bowl
⑨ Underground rain storage reservoir

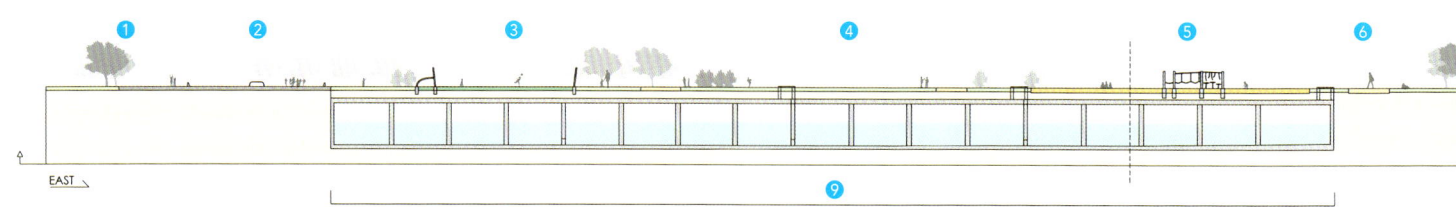

Section

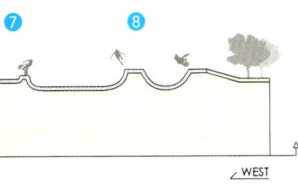

07
/ Father playing with his son at the playground
08
/ Kids playing and relaxing at the playground
09
/ The playground invites kids to play and relax

Children's Bicentennial Park

Location /
Santiago, Chile

Area /
9.9 acres (4 hectares)

Completion date /
2012

Landscape design /
ELEMENTAL

Budget /
US$4 million

Photography /
Cristóbal Palma

Client /
Parque Metropolitano / Junta Nacional de Jardines Infantiles

Chile has had incredible economic growth in the last decade, but the urban standards have not increased proportionally. Santiago, for example, has no single place to go for a long walk. Spaces such as rivers, strands, and hills tend to be associated to the geographical features of cities, but in Santiago, the river has already been used for a highway. The only place left is an old agricultural canal running at the base of the Metropolitan Park, the San Cristobal Hill. It is a 6.2-mile (10-kilometer) horizontal, continuous path that could be transformed into a pedestrian promenade. A 9.9-acre (4-hectare) Children's Park on the hillside, besides being constructed to celebrate the bicentennial of Chile, can be considered as the initial phase of a promenade that will be completed in the coming years.

The designers of the park were looking for two things: they wanted to use the difficulty of the terrain, being on a hillside, to solve a classic dilemma of children's games: make them safe or make them fun. The steep slope allowed for the necessary height to make them fun without threatening safety. A slide of 19.7 feet (6 meters) (fun) on level ground implies that a child has to be about 13.1 feet (4 meters) from the ground (dangerous). In this case, the slope allowed a child to climb to a very long slide and still always be 11.8 inches (30 centimeters) from the ground. The same happens with a tree house: instead of vertically climbing the tree trunk to the foliage, the slope allows for a child to walk horizontally to the top of the tree.

① Entrance
② Administration
③ Services
④ Storeroom and warehouse
⑤ Coffee shop
⑥ Flower shop
⑦ Kiosk
⑧ Rustic trail
⑨ Amphitheater
⑩ Service entrance
⑪ Inferior funicular station
⑫ Superior funicular station
⑬ Water fountain
⑭ Terrace
⑮ Water games
⑯ Stairs and slides
⑰ Swings
⑱ Fence playground
⑲ Tree houses

Site plan

01
/ 9.9-acre (4-hectare) Children's Park on the hillside of Santiago

02
/ The slope allows a child to climb to a very long slide and still be 11.8 inches (30 centimeters) from the ground, without danger

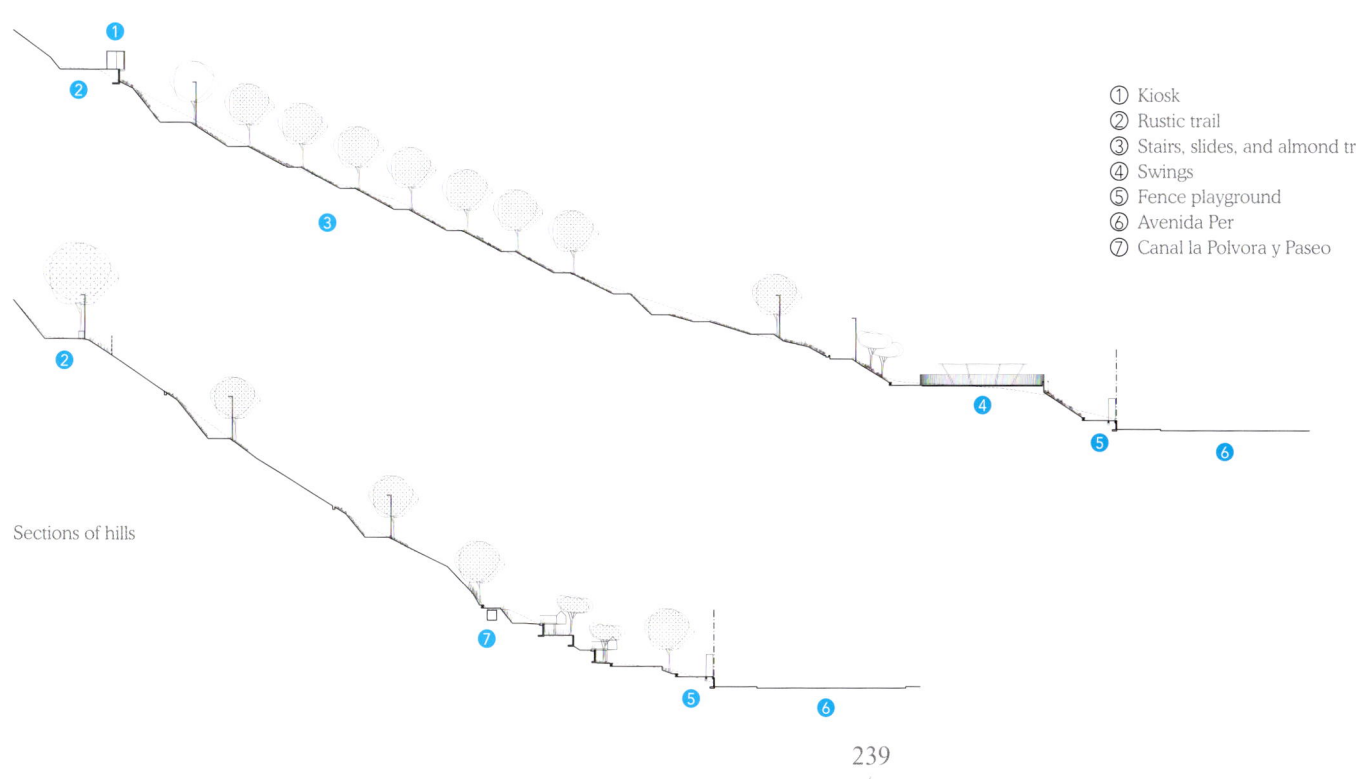

① Kiosk
② Rustic trail
③ Stairs, slides, and almond trees
④ Swings
⑤ Fence playground
⑥ Avenida Per
⑦ Canal la Polvora y Paseo

Sections of hills

240

03
/ Children's Bicentennial Park view from the top of the hill
04
/ Slides in the Children's Bicentennial Park
05
/ Swings in the Children's Bicentennial Park

① Wood cladding
② Tubular profile 4 by 0.1 inches (101 by 3 millimeters)
③ Plastic cylinder
④ Existing wall
⑤ Existing concrete floor
⑥ Projected concrete floor 3% pending
⑦ Polyurethane seat
⑧ Tubular profile 5 by 0.2 inches (127 by 5 millimeters)

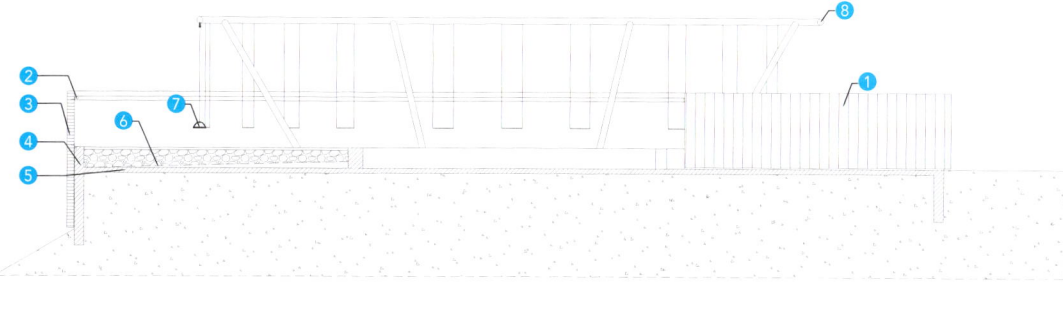

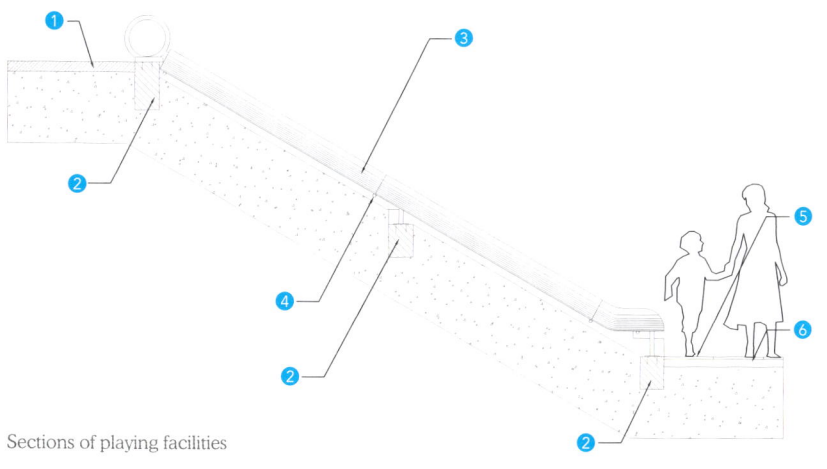

① Chemical stabilized pavement
② Concrete foundation
③ Plastic slide
④ Plastic slide union
⑤ Security rubber floor
⑥ Concrete

Sections of playing facilities

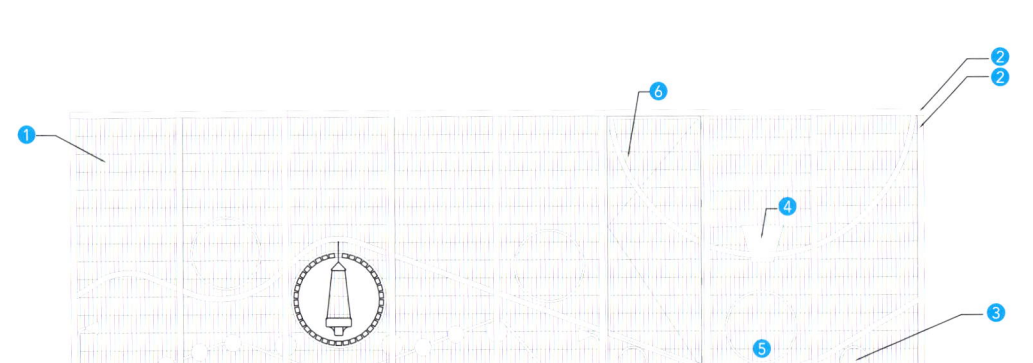

① Chemical stabilized pavement
② Full concrete sphere
③ 2/3 concrete sphere
④ 1/2 concrete sphere
⑤ 1/3 concrete sphere

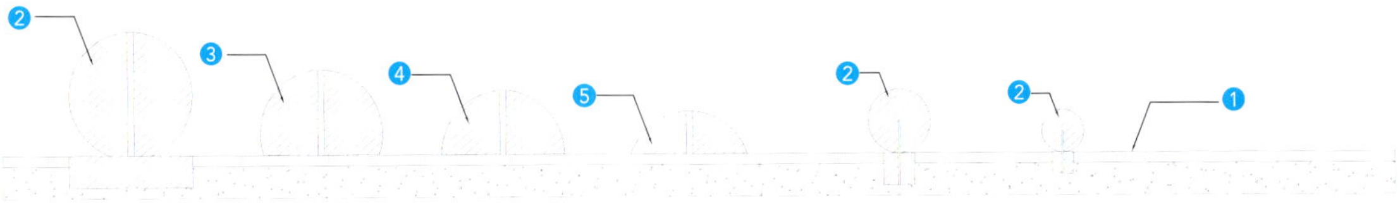

Sections of playing facilities

① Acma net type Acmafor
② Metal perimeter 3 by 3 by 0.8 inches (75 x 75 x 2 millimeters)
③ Plastic cylinder
④ Plastic drum
⑤ Entrance
⑥ Registration desk

06–08
/ Fence playground

Philadelphia Navy Yard Corporate Center

Location /
Philadelphia Navy Yard, Philadelphia, USA

Area /
5 acres (2 hectares)

Completion date /
2015

Landscape design /
James Corner Field Operations

Budget /
US$7.4 million

Photography /
Ralf Maier, Sandra Stein

Client /
Liberty Property Trust

Field Operations has designed the 5-acre (2-hectare) Central Green at the heart of the Philadelphia Navy Yard Corporate Center. The site was historically marked by wetlands, meadows, and bird habitat and is growing into Philadelphia's most innovative and progressive corporate neighborhood. The zones are an outdoor space for creative expression. The uses include a fitness station, an amphitheater/'sun lawn', a hammock grove, bocce courts, ping-pong tables, a communal table, and a 'bio-basin' for stormwater.

The design unites the cutting-edge urban potential of the site with its native habitat, resulting in a new type of environment that is sustainable, green, and natural as well as social, active, and urban. A 20-foot-wide (6.1-foot-wide) social track organizes the site's circulation and frames a unique, immersive interior park featuring flowering meadows, a hammock grove, an outdoor amphitheater, bocce courts, and fitness stations.

Areas for active recreational play and areas that create opportunities for quiet gatherings are nicely balanced. For example, the site's language is enhanced by the use of a long X-shaped table for picnics and meetings. Nearby, a cluster of yellow hammocks are threaded between a grove of conifers that allow for a restful refuge. Lawns also offer space to relax.

Another recognizable feature is the use of yellow, which pops out with an energizing effect. Every opportunity is taken to use this cheerful yellow: from the clusters of Adirondack chairs on the lawns to the ping-pong tables, moveable bistro tables and fitness zone equipment.

① Intrepid Avenue
② Rouse Boulevard
③ 12th Street
④ Normandy Place
⑤ Sun lawn
⑥ Social track
⑦ Food truck parking
⑧ Flowering meadows
⑨ Bocce court
⑩ Wet meadow
⑪ Hammock grove
⑫ Table tennis
⑬ Trx Fitness area
⑭ Conference table
⑮ Lounge lawn
⑯ Clock tower
⑰ Birch lawn

Site plan

01
/ Aerial photo of whole park
02
/ Aerial photo of amphitheater/
 'sun lawn'

03
/ Running track
04
/ Sun lounges
05–06
/ People enjoying activities in the central green park

248

07–08
/ Bocce courts
09–10
/ Table tennis

11
/ Fitness area provide free and casual exercising equipment for individuals

12–14
/ People enjoy relaxing and socializing in the public space

Index

P144

a2arquitectos

San Andrés 16 2A
28004 Madrid, Spain
Telephone: +34 699 93 96 97
Website: www.a2arquitectos.com

Under the direction of the architects Juan Manzanares Suárez and Cristian Santandreu Utermark, this studio is dedicated to the creation, adaptation, modification, and management of architectural and urban planning projects of all kinds. The studio undertakes building, urban planning, interior design, furniture design, and both renovation and new building projects. It specializes in projects related to the tourist sector and has carried out numerous projects in different hotels in Spain and France.

P188

Archi-Union Architects

Building 36–38, Wuwei Creative Industrial Park
1436 Jungong Road, Yangpu District
Shanghai, China (200433)
Telephone: 86 21 5596 7071
Website: www.archi-union.com

Founded in 2003 by Dr Philip F. Yuan (Associate Professor, CAUP, Tongji University), Archi-Union Architects is a Shanghai-based architectural design firm, which is a Grade A design qualification certified by the Ministry of Housing and Urban-Rural Development. It provides solutions to architectural problems through a combination of academic research and practice, specializing in architecture, urban planning, and interior design. Archi-Union employs more than 60 people in design and construction disciplines, and has successfully completed more than 20 projects in the past decade.

Archi-Union has managed to introduce a design style that is an amalgam of the global trends and the local traditional architectural approach. From this stems the low-tech digital fabrication method 'Digital tectonics', which merges the concepts of tectonic construction and ecology that are catalyzed through a parametric design process, in essence combining digital technology and craftsmanship.

Archi-Union's projects have been reported by many international and national architectural design media, including T+A, UED, UA, Arquitectura Viva, Abitare China, AD China, Dezeen and Archdaily.

P40

BASE

Paris Office
208, rue Saint-Maur
F-75010 Paris, France
Telephone: 00 33 1 4277 8181
Website: www.baseland.fr

BASE (Bien Aménager Son Environnement/Build A Super Environment) is a team of associates founded by three government-approved (dplg) landscape architects from the Versailles National School of Landscape Architecture: Franck Poirier, Bertrand Vignal and Clément Willemin. BASE founds its reflection on a cross-analysis between urban (architecture/landscape) and aesthetic (garden art/contemporary art) approaches.

The projects' implementation is based on the status and nature of spaces, all the while taking into account the evolving and unreachable character of the city and the territory. Since 2000, BASE has carried out the design and supervision of landscape (public parks, city parks, tourist parks, outdoor public areas, linear developments) and urban (urban planning and road works) projects.

PP54, 56, 80, 140, 148

Carve

Kortenaerplein 34
1057 ne Amsterdam, The Netherlands
Telephone: +31 (0)20 427 5711
Website: www.carve.nl

Carve is a design and engineering bureau that focuses on the planning and development of public spaces, particularly for use by children and young people. Their clients include local governments, developers, manufacturers of playground equipment, architects, and landscape architects. The bureau was set up in 1997 by Elger Blitz and Mark van der Eng. Over the past 18 years, Carve has grown into a company within which several design disciplines meet, from industrial design to landscape architecture. They consider playgrounds an integral part of public space, and strive for playgrounds to be inviting places to be discovered; providing room for different groups and ages, and several forms of use. Their playgrounds are challenging and safe at the same time. Faced today with too many restricted areas for kids only, facilities strictly focus on certain age groups. They are filled in with prefabricated furniture and are directive as well as limited in terms of use.

PP36, 96, 118, 194

CONVIC

Unit 13, 46–50 Regent Street
Richmond, Victoria
Australia 3121
Telephone: +61 3 9486 9899
Website: www.convic.com

Successfully partnering with governments around the world, CONVIC has developed a global reputation for innovation and quality, building a wealth of national and international knowledge and experience in the process.

Because CONVIC specializes in the development of action sports facilities, the team manages everything from start to finish: concept, planning, design, construction, and maintenance for the life of the space. CONVIC delivers certainty and control over concepts, budgets, and scheduling. Expert planning and ongoing customer support deliver facilities that enhance communities for years into the future.

CONVIC's multi-award-winning portfolio of safe, social youth spaces has enriched communities globally. With a team of in-house landscape architects, skate-park designers, and civil and structural engineers, CONVIC can offer a selection of proven skate-park plans or create a unique, custom solution.

P182

EFFEKT

Blågårdsgade 8, 2nd Floor
2200 Copenhagen N, Denmark
Telephone: +45 3535 3631

EFFEKT is an architectural collaborative based in Copenhagen, Denmark, operating in the fields of architecture, planning, urban space, landscape design, and research.

The company was established in 2007 and currently employs 30 full-time staff under the creative direction of the two partners: Tue Hesselberg Foged and Sinus Lynge.

As part of the new generation of Danish architects revitalizing the nordic tradition, EFFEKT in recent years distinguished itself on both the national and international scene through high-profile projects, exhibitions, and publications.

P238

ELEMENTAL

Av. Los Conquistadores 1700, Piso 25 A
7520282 Providencia, Santiago, Chile
Telephone: +56 2 2963 7500
Website: www.elementalchile.cl

ELEMENTAL (Alejandro Aravena, Gonzalo Arteaga, Juan Cerda, Victor Oddó, Diego Torres) is a Do Tank founded in 2001, focusing on projects of public interest and social impact, including housing, public space, infrastructure and transportation. A hallmark of the firm is a participatory design process in which the architects work closely with the public and end users. ELEMENTAL has built work in Chile, the United States, Mexico, China and Switzerland. After the 2010 earthquake and tsunami that hit Chile, ELEMENTAL was called to work on the reconstruction of the city of Constitución, where they had to draw on all the previous experiences. The approach developed proved to be useful for other cases where city design was used to solve social and political conflicts.

P172

glaßer und dagenbach, landscape architects bdla, IFLA

Breitenbachplatz 17, 14195
Berlin, Germany
Telephone: +49 (0)30/ 6181080
Website: www.glada-berlin.de

Colleagues Silvia Glasser and Udo Dagenbach have been creating innovative parks and landscapes since founding their partnership in 1988. They are dedicated to producing the highest quality landscape and garden architecture, especially focusing on public parks and gardens. Silvia Glasser earned her Diploma in Landscape Architecture in 1985, and is also a state-approved gardener specializing in perennials.

Udo Dagenbach earned a Diploma in Landscape Architecture in 1986, and is also a state-approved landscape gardener, as well as a sculptor of stone. He studied stone sculpture at the University of Art in Berlin and worked under Professor Makoto Fujiwara, especially as the principle project sculptor for the Bundesanstaltfür Geowissenschaften in Hannover—a land art project. The small office is primarily engaged in new construction of public parks and private resort projects as well as the reconstruction of listed gardens and parks.

P198

Group GSA

Level 7, 80 William Street, East Sydney
NSW 2011, Australia
Telephone: +61 2 9361 4144
Website: www.groupgsa.com

Group GSA is an award-winning, integrated design practice offering architecture, landscape architecture, urban design, and interior design.

Established in 1979, the practice currently ranges from 190 to 200 professional staff with offices in Sydney, Melbourne, Brisbane, Gold Coast, Shanghai, Ho Chi Minh City, and Toronto, and an alliance office network both nationally and globally.

Group GSA is recognized as one of Australia's top 10 design firms, and has completed many landmark and innovative projects across its varied sectors.

The landscape studio offers particular experience in landscape architecture and urban design. Focus is on the delivery of responsive and innovative design solutions, embracing client expectations, community values, and environmental sustainability.

They manage the project process from feasibility to delivery as a highly collaborative process between all team members, from the client to the operator, to the consultant team and other stakeholders.That is their 'designing ideas to life journey'.

P226

kessler.krämer Landschaftsarchitekten

Neustadt 16
24939 Flensburg
Telephone: 046 1318 0110
Website: www.kesslerkraemer.de

P132

Kinnear Landscape Architects

3rd Floor West
1-3 Coate Street
London E2 9AG
Telephone: +44 (0) 20 7729 7781
Website: www.kland.co.uk

Kinnear Landscape Architects (KLA) was founded in 1991 by Lynn Kinnear and has become a practice recognized throughout Europe as one of a small number of UK practices pushing a new agenda in UK landscape design. The practice has a track record of innovative projects that combine a conceptual approach to the Art of Landscape Architecture with an enthusiasm for new ideas and an open approach to working with others. They continue to win awards for their work and their unique approach to collaborative working and the positive contribution this gives to regeneration.

KLA has experience of working in the public and private sectors, both as lead consultants coordinating large groups of consultants and as consultants working with architecture-led teams. Their projects often have complex client and stakeholder groups and rely on a variety of different funding streams. This experience has allowed them to successfully guide, facilitate, and implement the curation of urban space.

P212

Lee H. Skolnick Architecture + Design Partnership

75 Broad Street Suite 2700
New York, NY 10004, USA
Telephone: 212 989 2624
Website: www.skolnick.com

Based in New York City, Lee H. Skolnick Architecture + Design Partnership (LHSA+DP) is an award-winning, multi-disciplinary design firm specializing in education, museum and corporate facilities, exhibits, interactive experiences, and graphic identity. LHSA+DP believes that the ideal architectural experience tells a story, taking a person on a journey, expressing ideas, eliciting emotions, and revealing knowledge. The firm was founded by Lee H. Skolnick, FAIA, a renowned conceptual thinker, author of *What is Exhibition Design?* and an accomplished architect dedicated to exploring the use of design as an interpretive tool that connects people and ideas. Recent projects include Sony Wonder Technology Lab in New York City, the Summit Elementary School in Casper, Wyoming, the Children's Library Discovery Center for Queens Library, and Muzeiko, Bulgaria's first children's science center.

P206

LIW planning

LIW ApS, Vesterbrogade 95 C, 3 sal, 1620 København V
// Hvide Hus Vej 3. 401 8400 Ebeltoft
Telephone: +45 28106460
Website: www.liwplanning.dk

LIW planning is an award-winning firm with a pronounced professional standard at the intersection between architecture, planning, landscape, and urban environments.

Their professional approach is characterized by a thorough reading of the site and its context combined with an undogmatic method of problem solving. They don't work from predesigned repetitive principles, but create rational interpretations of the site of each project.

They meet complex challenges with pragmatic and aesthetic solutions, which are both architecturally strong and locally embedded. They believe that the architectonic power and complexity at the large planning scale of a physical environment can translate into sensuous experiences. Physical as well as social and cultural contexts are the point of departure, whether it is in the open landscape or the urban realm.

P48

Maclennan Jaunkalns Miller Architects

19 Duncan Street, Suite 202
Toronto, Ontario M5H 3H1 Canada
Telephone: 416 593 6796
Website: www.mjmarchitects.com

MacLennan Jaunkalns Miller Architects (MJMA) is a group of passionate designers and architects who are invested in the ideals of place making that amplify the quality of life, and give value to social and cultural aspirations, whether they are centered on education, wellness and recreation, or the workplace.

MJMA has evolved from a 20-year legacy of making community buildings, to building communities—in towns and cities, on campuses, within organizations, and across playing fields.

While they have historically excelled in the sports and recreation sector, their design skills have led to work across different building typologies and at various scales. An increasingly diverse portfolio speaks to an innovation culture at MJMA that drives all designs. This spirit of innovation, cultivated with clients who are enthusiastic about creating meaningful architecture that positively contributes to the built environment, has resulted in more than 40 national awards, including the Governor General's Medal in Architecture.

Maierlandschaftsarchitektur

Telephone: +49 22 1139 5906
Website: www.maierlandschaftsarchitektur.de

Today there are many people who spend a large part of their time skateboarding and biking.

When planning, the participation of the local skate and BMX scene is very important. Participation in the development process with suggestions, ideas, discussion, etc. not only increases the interest in the new skate park, but results in the best possible acceptance by the future users.

The company encourages skaters and cyclists to participate during the planning phase in order to bring understanding and appreciation of the decisions taken. They communicate with representatives of cities and towns, and especially with the users. Thus the best results in planning and implementation of such recreational facilities can be obtained.

They create a space that attracts skaters and bikers from all over the world and gives the locals the attractive opportunity to live their chosen lifestyle.

Mark K. Morrison Associates

242 West 30th Street
New York, NY 10001, USA
Telephone: 212 629 9710
Website: www.markkmorrison.com

For more than 30 years, Mark K. Morrison Landscape Architecture (MKM) has been committed to excellence in public, campus, and private design. The firm has conceived and implemented projects on a variety of scales in the Northeast, as well as in Asia and Africa. MKM has offices in New York and Boston. The team of designers, authors, educators, and builders share a culture of service, quality, and hands-on construction administration services.

Each project requires a high level of craftsmanship and innovation, and individualized solutions that emphasize restorative practices in site development, stormwater management, and environmental sustainability. The firm has worked on a variety of complex urban sites, and staff are knowledgeable in landscape technologies that allow them to enhance living architecture from city streets to major infrastructure to rooftops.

Open communication with clients has been a key to success; they seek community and stakeholder involvement with design input, and transform site knowledge and client needs into sustainable and enduring site structure.

Mecanoo

Oude Delft 203
2611 HD Delft, The Netherlands
Telephone: +31 15 2798100
Website: www.mecanoo.nl

Mecanoo, officially founded in Delft in 1984, is made up of a highly multi-disciplinary staff of more than 160 creative professionals from 25 countries. The team includes architects, engineers, interior designers, urban planners, landscape architects, and architectural technicians.

The company is led by its original founding architect and creative director, Francine Houben, technical director Aart Fransen and financial director Peter Haasbroek, who are joined by partners Francesco Veenstra, Ellen van der Wal, Paul Ketelaars and Dick van Gameren.

The extensive collective experience, gained over three decades, results in designs that are realized with technical expertise and great attention to detail. Mecanoo's projects range from single houses to complete neighborhoods and skyscrapers, cities and polders, schools, theatres and libraries, hotels, museums, and even a chapel.

Oxigen

98–100 Halifax Street
Adelaide, South Australia 5000
Telephone: +61 8 7324 9600
Website: www.oxigen.net.au

Oxigen is an integrated design practice that feeds off the multi-disciplinary skills of its staff working within a collaborative studio environment. Skills come from formal qualifications in landscape architecture, urban design, architecture, urban and regional planning, industrial design and urban horticulture, meshed with the experience of realized projects that span strategic master plans and policy development to built form. A portfolio of completed environmental and cultural projects defines the practice and gives it a strong reputation within the field.

Oxigen's approach is always specific to the site, drawing the principles for design from the site context, climate, ecology, and usage. No two design outcomes can be the same if they are derived from a fundamental understanding of the place and its uniqueness. As a practice, Oxigen is not constrained by formulas that can work against site-specific design.

Sasaki

600 North Shaanxi Road
Building 10, Suite 402–408, Jing'an District
Shanghai, 200040, China
Telephone: +86 21 5109 0906
Website: www.sasaki.com

Collaboration is one of today's biggest buzzwords—but at Sasaki, it's at the core of what they do. They see it not just as a working style, but as one of the fundamentals of innovation. They think and work beyond boundaries to make new discoveries. They are diverse, curious, strategic, and inspired. Their practice comprises architecture, interior design, planning, urban design, landscape architecture, graphic design, and civil engineering, as well as financial planning and software development.

Among these disciplines, they collaborate equally. No one practice area is dominant over the others—and each is recognized nationally and internationally for professional excellence. On their project teams, practitioners from diverse backgrounds come together to create unique, contextual, enduring solutions. Their integrated approach yields rich ideas, surprising insights, unique partnerships, and a broad range of resources for their clients. This approach enables them to work seamlessly and successfully from planning to implementation.

While their disciplines offer depth of expertise, their studio structure engenders breadth, innovation, and interdisciplinary collaboration. The Campus Studio focuses on institutional work and the Urban Studio focuses on civic and commercial work. From their headquarters in Watertown, Massachusetts, They work in a variety of settings—locally, nationally, and globally. Their Shanghai office offers focused support and business development for their work in China. Their offices are vibrant and dynamic, featuring open workspaces that reflect their dedication to collaboration and facilitate a synergistic process.

Scape Landschaftsarchitekten GmbH

Friedrichstrasse 115a, 40217
Duesseldorf, Germany
Telephone: +49 211 3020 37 0
Website: www.scape-net.de

Spectrum Skateparks Inc.

PO Box 37016 RPO Lonsdale
N. Vancouver, BC V7N 4M4 Canada
Telephone: 6049865683
Website: ww.spectrum-sk8.com

Fifteen years of Spectrum has produced more than 321 acres (130 hectares) of skate parks in North America, Europe and Asia, cementing them as one of the world leaders in creating insane terrain. More than 160 built projects demonstrate the firms ability to deliver world-class, eye-catching, ripping skate parks at the best value.

An elite team of skate park designers, engineers, landscape architects, fantastic human beings, rabid skaters, artists, and master builders are inspired by the knowledge that skate parks improve communities, extending a hand to a segment of youth that can be hard to reach and underserved, providing them with their place in the community to get rad.

The firm accepts only a select number of projects each year so that they can deliver the highest level of service and responsiveness to all of their valued clients, ensuring that the process is professional, efficient, fun, and rewarding for all parties. Their passion and dedication is inspiring, and all clients receive the highest level of service, regardless of whether the project is large or small.

P62

Streiff Architekten GmbH

Streiff Architekten
Pfingstweidstrasse 6
8005 Zurich, Switzerland
Telephone: 044 271 6470
Website: www.streiff-architekten.ch

The office for design, architecture, and landscape design was founded in 1989 by Vital Streiff, a graduate from the Swiss Federal Institute of Technology in Zurich (ETHZ). The main topics of the architectural work are unusual, including challenging tasks such as a firefighter training camp or a freestyle park. Those assignments require a deep understanding from a team of experts.

P218

Studio AKKA

Igriška 3
1000 Ljubljana, Slovenia
Telephone: +386 (0) 599 61012
Website: akka.si

The AKKA team has been driven by the quest for quality, which, they believe, is achieved by socially and environmentally responsible development. Over the past six years, their work has focused on landscape and urban design, mostly for public clients. In these fields, they have been pursuing design solutions without pre-conceived ideas, with a conviction that problems always differ according to space, program and expectations. Each design creates a new story, a result of its contextual grounding. Sensitive response to this variety of tasks can help broaden the imagination and increase the well-being of people. Recently AKKA extended its designs to private gardens, aspiring to respond to very personal tastes and desires. Their projects now range from town planning to parks and gardens, from playgrounds to town squares and historic renovations, regardless of scale and type of interventions.

P108

Subarquitectura

Av Estacion 87 A 03005 Alicante
Mediterranean west coast
Telephone: +34 965 135 914
Website: www.subarquitectura.com

Subarquitectura is made up of Andrés Silanes, Fernando Valderrama and Carlos Bañón.

They are architects from the University of Alicante and have Masters of Complex Architectures from the University of Alicante.

They have built the tram stop and plaza on the traffic roundabout of Sergio Cardell (2006), which was awarded at the IX Spanish Bienal of Architecture. They have been nominated for the Mies Van Der Rohe Awards (2009), and finalists at the Valencian Community Awards (2008), won second prize at Lamp Lighting Solutions (2008), received an honorable mention at the Balthasar Neumann Prize in Germany, and selected for the 10 Best Designs in the World by the London Design Museum (2008).

Also they have constructed various sports facilities, including the Sports Pavilion in Pedreguer, the Hercules C.F. remodelling and the 3D Athletics Track in Alicante (2010), which has been recently awarded the Silver Medal and the Accessibility Distinction by the International Olympic and Paralympic Committees. In 2010, Subarquitectura was nominated by Yosihiaru Tsukamoto (from Atelier Bow-Wow) for the Iakov Chernikhov International Prize.

P126

Sweco Architects

Sweco AB (publ)
Box 34044
S-100 26 Stockholm, Sweden
Telephone: +46 8 695 60 00
Website: www.swecogroup.com

Sweco is a client-driven organization with offices at more than 100 locations. The group's decentralized and result-oriented business model means that all energy can be focused on the business and work of the client projects. Operations are conducted in seven business areas: Sweco Sweden, Sweco Norway, Sweco Finland and Estonia, Sweco Denmark, Sweco Netherlands, Sweco Central Europe and Sweco Western Europe. Sweco also has subsidiaries in Lithuania, the Czech Republic, Bulgaria, Poland, Germany, the Netherlands, Belgium, UK and Turkey.

PP72, 76, 102

TOPOTEK 1

Gesellschaft von LandschaftsarchitectenmbH
Sophienstrasse 18, Berlin, Germany
Telephone: +49 (0)3 0246 2580
Website: www.topotek1.de

TOPOTEK 1 was founded in Berlin in 1996 by Martin Rein-Cano. It works around the field of landscape architecture and understands itself as a traveler within the fringe areas of typologies and scales, jaunting into architecture, urban design, music, and art. The hybridization of topics and disciplines, the removal, transmission and re-contexualization of various design features and objects, and the staging and design of scenographic sequences are just some of their key strategies.

The alertness and receptiveness to the general contemporary discussion is maintained through this working method. The global movement of society and culture continually redefines the broad spectrum of possibilities in relation to the constitution of public space.

TOPOTEK 1 develops concepts through a critical understatement of the given realities and a deep historical knowledge. This provides solutions and designs that fulfill the modern requirements of variability, communication and sensuousness.

P92

Zukclub

Telephone: +79032578871
Website: www.zukclub.com
Email: zukclub@mail.ru

Zukclub is a respected group of street artists from Moscow, established in 2002. Today, Zukclub is one of the best of the Russian crews who started their career with graffiti.

Zukclub has created a lot of personal works, collaborated with many different brands, and taken active part in graffiti and street art festivals and shows both in Russia and abroad.

Zukclub's art has gone through several stages: first they mainly worked with characters and recently have moved to muralism.

Zukclub art is defined by bright, vibrant colors, and dynamic and rather chaotic compositions. The style is universal and can be successfully applied to large-scale murals, canvases, and commercial projects.

Published in Australia in 2016 by
The Images Publishing Group Pty Ltd
Shanghai Office
ABN 89 059 734 431
6 Bastow Place, Mulgrave, Victoria 3170, Australia
Tel: +61 3 9561 5544 Fax: +61 3 9561 4860
books@imagespublishing.com
www.imagespublishing.com

Copyright © The Images Publishing Group Pty Ltd 2016
The Images Publishing Group Reference Number: 1196

All rights reserved. Apart from any fair dealing for the purposes of private study, research, criticism or review as permitted under the Copyright Act, no part of this publication may be reproduced, stored in a retrieval system or transmitted in any form by any means, electronic, mechanical, photocopying, recording or otherwise, without the written permission of the publisher.

Title:	Sports Parks: Directions in Design for Recreational Zones
Author:	Jim Barnum (ed.)
ISBN:	9781864706475

For Catalogue-in-Publication data, please see the National Library of Australia entry

Printed by Everbest Printing Investment Limited., Hong Kong/China

IMAGES has included on its website a page for special notices in relation to this and our other publications. Please visit www.imagespublishing.com.

Every effort has been made to trace the original source of copyright material contained in this book. The publishers would be pleased to hear from copyright holders to rectify any errors or omissions.
The information and illustrations in this publication have been prepared and supplied by the Jim Barnum and the individual contributors. While all reasonable efforts have been made to ensure accuracy, the publishers do not, under any circumstances, accept responsibility for errors, omissions and representations, express or implied.